THE SMALLEST PAWNS IN THE GAME

By the same author

Earth My Friend
Duel of Eagles
The Last Emperor
Time and Chance

Peter Townsend

THE SMALLEST PAWNS IN THE GAME

Little, Brown and Company

Boston Toronto

COPYRIGHT © 1980 BY PETER TOWNSEND

ALL RIGHTS RESERVED. NO PART OF THIS BOOK MAY BE REPRODUCED IN ANY FORM OR BY ANY ELECTRONIC OR MECHANICAL MEANS INCLUDING INFORMATION STORAGE AND RETRIEVAL SYSTEMS WITHOUT PERMISSION IN WRITING FROM THE PUBLISHER, EXCEPT BY A REVIEWER WHO MAY QUOTE BRIEF PASSAGES IN A REVIEW

LIBRARY OF CONGRESS CATALOG CARD NO. 80-82518

FIRST AMERICAN EDITION

PRINTED IN THE UNITED STATES OF AMERICA

Contents

Introduction		ix

PART I

1	The Story Begins	3
2	Famine Takes Its Toll in Russia	9
3	The Young Victims of Guernica	14

PART II

4	The Martyrdom of Polish Children	27
5	To Hell by Train	38
6	Raïa, the Girl with the Yellow Star	43
7	The Children of Jastrebarsko	50
8	Aharon in the Underworld	59
9	Bombs Cannot Discriminate	65
10	At Hiroshima and Nagasaki	67

PART III

11	Post-war 'Peace'	77
12	Hong Pae and the Will to Survive	84
13	'The Winds of Change'	93
14	Nkusi in Exile	99
15	Mumbamba from Kolwezi	108
16	Biafra – 'the Children's War'	112
17	Prison or Exile: Equatorial Guinea	119
18	The Flight from Idi Amin	127
19	The Cost of Freedom: Bangladesh	135
20	Cypriot Messengers of Death	145
21	Children at Arms: Bissau	151

22	Bloodshed at Soweto	163
23	Good Zimbabweans	173
24	The Zimbabwean Coin Reversed	182
25	Ethiopian Refugees	186
26	With the Sahraouis	195
27	The Torture of Children: South America	199
28	Children of the Boat People	206
29	The Agony of Cambodia/Kampuchea	217
30	The Muslim Orphans from Burma	224
31	Children at Arms: Belfast	228
32	In the Palestinian Camps	236
33	Revenge or Forgiveness?	241

Epilogue: Nothing Has Changed — 251

Acknowledgements — 254

Bibliography — 263

THE SMALLEST PAWNS IN THE GAME

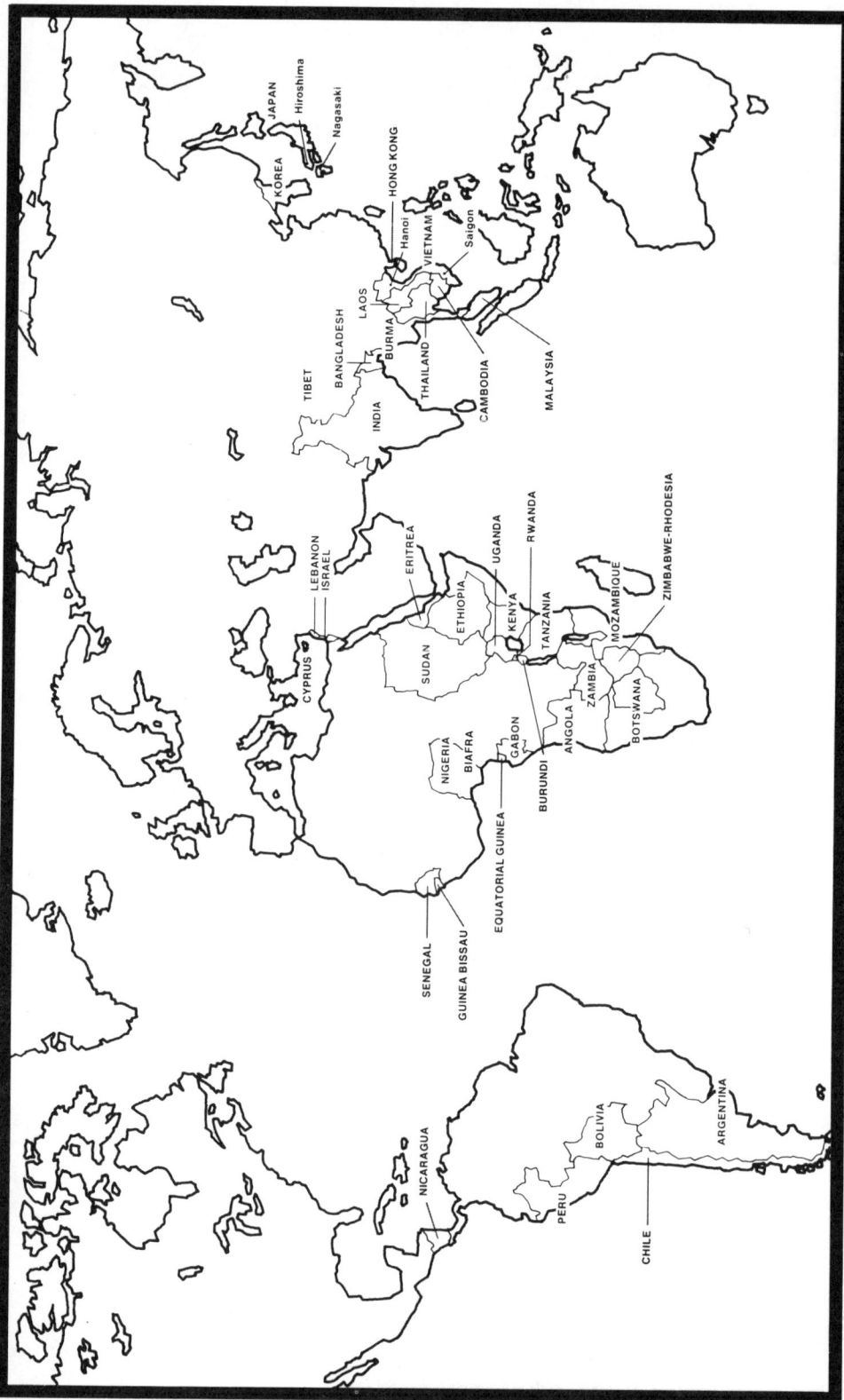

Introduction

The original idea behind this book is not mine. It belongs entirely to my friend Georges Belmont, who has edited and translated three of my previous books for Robert Laffont, my French publisher.

The theme that Georges had in mind was a protest against the continuing murder, both physical and moral, of children – those innocent, defenceless beings in whom every man worthy of the name must see not only his own descendants and, as such, the perpetuators of the human race, but the future parents of a better humanity.

When, at the suggestion of Robert Laffont, Georges asked me to write this book I accepted without a moment's hesitation because my own feelings coincide exactly with his. World War II, which claimed millions of young lives, was fought, we understood, to put an end to tyranny, including the tyranny of racial and religious persecution. But since then new tyrants have arisen and between them driven millions of people to flee their homes and their countries. Ten million – that is the number of refugees in the world today. More than half of them are children; meeting and writing about some then have made me realize only too clearly what it would mean to me if my own teenage children were numbered among them.

Victims of disaster, man-made and natural, are devotedly aided by countless official and voluntary organizations whose never-ending appeals for funds are, to be sure, most generously answered. But although, thanks to the media, the world has never been more aware of the refugees in its midst there is never enough help to go round. Unfortunately, the media have so accustomed us to the afflictions of others that we tend to regard what we see (or hear, or read) as a legitimate form of paid entertainment, almost like a play or a movie. The sight of a child, bombed out or abandoned on the battle scene, terror and incomprehension written on its face – that pitiful impression, when brought to you (in your armchair) on TV, or over the radio, while driving the car or doing the household chores, or reading the morning paper on the way to work, seldom inspires more emotion than a gun battle in a western. Perhaps less.

Many war correspondents and photographers have all the same published books which leave us with a dramatic and lasting record of their personal encounters with children in the midst of tragedy. I admire them for their deeds and am thankful to them for taking me (in safety) right into the heart of the human disaster, whereas my own encounters took place after the worst was over. The advantage that a book has is that its printed word remains between its two covers instead of, like the facts recorded by the media, disappearing next day into the dustbin or up the chimney, or simply fading into oblivion.

For this book, I have used information from three kinds of sources: documents naturally. Next, testimonies written by people now dead and others still living, including the many letters I have received. The third type of information comes direct from the mouths of children and adolescents I have met all over the world. Generally, they were between eight and eighteen years old, but occasionally victims of an on-going conflict were older.

To obtain these eye-witness accounts from children and 'ex-children', victims of war and persecution, I contacted the International Union for Child Welfare in Geneva. They most kindly agreed to co-operate. They sent out an urgent and moving appeal to their representatives and members throughout the world asking for such accounts.

The result of the appeal was shattering. Very few replies of any use were received. Which suggests that even the very victims of tragedy, as much as we who look on day by day through the media, are resigned to their sufferings, or afraid of appearing as witnesses, or just desirous to forget the horror of it. And so – to paraphrase the Bible story – I went out into the highways and byways of the world, into the bush, the jungle and the desert and down to the seashore in search of children and 'ex-children' with stories to tell.

The venture was fraught with problems. First, there was the desperate shortage of time – ten months in which to research and write about a vast subject and finish the manuscript in 1979, the United Nations' Year of the Child. The logistic problem, too, was formidable so I turned to Air France, old and unfailing friends, who responded immediately to the humanitarian aspect of my task and promised me both material and moral support. Together we very soon worked out a three months' non-stop itinerary to destinations as far apart as Belfast, Beirut and

Bujumbura, Nairobi and Nagasaki, Dacca and Dar-es-Salaam, Libreville, Lusaka and Kuala Lumpur.

An awkward problem arose: visas. For example, I wanted very much to talk to people who, as children, had lived through the great famine of the twenties in Russia as well as the siege of Leningrad and the battle of Stalingrad. I applied for a visa, but after the Russians (in Paris) had sat on my passport for a month I had to snatch it back from them. I longed to visit Hanoi and talk to the children who had so cruelly suffered in the war in Vietnam. My request for a visa was refused without explanation. There were other countries, notably Latin America, where the political situation made it impossible to go and gather information on the spot from the child victims of the conflicts which have convulsed those countries. Generally, however, but not always, I was able to find child refugees who were free to speak, though not in the most flattering terms, of the regime they had fled.

For this reason, I have often had to change names and camouflage details. One thing, however, there is no need to conceal: the constantly expressed yearning of the young ones to return to their mother-country – given only the guarantee of safety and the respect of human rights.

While on the subject, I must say that I am concerned only with humanitarian, and not with political issues. I have tried, despite my feelings, to avoid taking sides, believing that we all, who are adult and articulate, are to some extent responsible for every man-made disaster. Children, on the other hand, rarely have any clear idea why they are being shot at or bombed, why their parents are arrested, tortured or killed. So as this book is essentially about the sufferings of children through war and persecution I do not – any more than they – go deeply into the reasons. Dates, historical and political data are indicative but not of fundamental importance. It is the children who count. So, before a decor which may seem all too scanty, the children walk on and say their bit. And if I have given the book a basic, if somewhat irregular, chronological structure and not, for example, a geographical one, it is because time, better than space, serves my theme – which is that since the beginning of recorded history down to the present day the harm that men do to children has not changed, unless it be for the worse (though, fortunately, the good they do is infinitely greater).

To resume, I have made no attempt at a study based on facts and figures, nor at a comprehensive history. This must be obvious from the omissions – regrettable, but inevitable owing to lack of time and forbidding political circumstances. I have simply tried, with all my heart, to depict from real life the bewilderment, terror and sorrow of children who are caught up in the conflicts of their elders.

Once at my destination, it still remained to find the children. The International Union for Child Welfare, as I have said, were first on the scene with their representatives and members in various countries. Then UNICEF came quite spontaneously to my assistance and put their great world-wide organization at my disposal. Through their office in Geneva and in various outlandish places I received from them the most precious help. Finally, I asked the headquarters in Geneva of the United Nations' High Commissioner for Refugees to bless my undertaking – which they did, quite unofficially, but in such a willing and efficacious manner both in Geneva and the world over that their help was one of the most rewarding and inspiring aspects of my research. From the International Committee of the Red Cross and from the League of Red Cross Societies I also received, when the occasion arose, the warmest co-operation. I must emphasize that the action of all these organizations was strictly and scrupulously limited to bringing me in contact with children. From then on it was entirely between the child and me; we alone, and no one else, are responsible for the facts, sentiments and opinions expressed in this book.

There was yet another problem, a sentimental one. The research and writing of the book caused me an enforced and prolonged separation from my wife and my young children. But we all agree that it has been a small sacrifice made in sympathy for those numberless children who have been forcibly separated – for ever – from their fathers and often from their mothers, too.

So for three months I travelled the world in search of children and 'ex-children'. I spoke to scores of them and from them coaxed, not always without difficulty, the story of their sufferings. Not infrequently during my talk with a boy or a girl tears were shed; it was really heartrending having to lead the child right up to breaking point. But those who broke down were wonderfully brave; they quickly regained possession of themselves and went along with me when I told them that I had only followed their story to its tragic climax in order to feel myself the measure of their sorrow. Which moves me, as I think of them so far away from my own comfortable stronghold in the consumer, the 'affluent' society, to plead: please help them. They speak so modestly of their terrible sufferings and bear them with such perfect dignity, even to the point of forbearance towards their persecutors. After all they have endured they long for a better world. There is no limit to their needs – until, perhaps, that which they lack can be recompensed by what we possess.

The first part of this book, based as it is on documents and written testimonies, gives an idea of the evil done to children in the past, through war and persecution. The record is limited to *man-made* disasters, which have brought more lasting suffering to mankind than the sum of all natural disasters.

The voices of living children telling the truth about the atrocities still being perpetrated against them at this very time form the second part of the book, which is modelled from the very clay of life itself, with its mingling of conflicting passions, of fears, hopes, despair, the will to live and the triumph, the miracle of survival. This part is drawn clean from what children have told me, in their own simple words; it is a live, *viva voce* and up-to-date testimony. Our talks took place in mid-1978, since when I have had no further news from them. I finished writing the book in mid-1979. Where situations, e.g. Uganda and the Vietnamese Boat People, etc., have since changed I have, when possible, added a last-minute note to bring the reader up to date. Of new situations, like the Nicaraguan civil war and the massacre of children in Bokassa's Central African 'Empire', I can only say that, while it has not been possible to write about them, they only go to prove that there is no end yet to the massacre of the innocents.

Children are not a pressure group; they seldom get a chance to speak out for themselves and when they do they are not often heard. Those who have spoken to me are but a tiny handful of a numberless, suffering multitude. But they have told me enough to show how, in this very age which, we smugly congratulate ourselves, is one of progress and enlightenment, children are still being orphaned, murdered or left wounded in body and mind because of the ambitions, the blind folly and the collective bestiality of men, many of whom pass for the leaders and law-keepers of the land, or for benefactors of our civilization.

The sufferings of these children are a warning to us whom, with our own children, war and persecution have for one generation – so far – not touched. But who can tell when they may? So let us close ranks with the children who have suffered already before us, while praying that our own may be spared. What we owe to those children and what they need is love – in whatever form possible. To know they are cared for, from however far away, makes them feel safer than can a bomb shelter or a host of protecting bayonets. Children need to know before anything else that they are loved.

However much we may be lured into believing that life has never been so good the truth is that we live in times which have never been more dangerous. Secretly, fearfully we wonder what the future, our children's and that of all mankind, may hold. As we do so we would do well to reflect on one inescapable fact: children are the future.

But war's a game, which, were their subjects wise,
Kings would not play at.

William Cowper, 1731–1800

Part One

CHAPTER ONE

The Story Begins

About thirty centuries ago a three-month-old baby was found floating in a kind of basket beside the banks of a river in Egypt. It was not that its mother wanted to rid herself of an unwanted child. On the contrary, she had kept her baby hidden for three months in defiance of a royal decree: 'And Pharaoh charged all his people, saying, every son that is born ye shall cast into the river.' At least this one little victim survived. And the charming irony of the story is that the person who found him was the king's own daughter, who later adopted him, calling him Moses, 'because I drew him out of the water'. So in a sense the princess was the first known initiator of the Save the Children movement which in our times has become world-wide, inspiring tens of thousands of generous and devoted people.

Many centuries after Moses, hardly had the news of the birth of the child Jesus spread with the message 'on earth peace, good will toward men', than Herod, fearful of the prophecies, ordered the organized killing of infant children, 'from two years old and under', in and around Bethlehem in his kingdom of Judaea.

Whether or not the Massacre of the Innocents ever took place (some doubt it) the story remains a symbol of the martyrdom of children at the hands of men. To this day, despite the handshakes and smiling effusions of peace and good will exchanged, before our very eyes, between the rulers of this world, these men behind the scenes are trading for all they are worth the weapons which will massacre, indeed are massacring, more innocents. It is to these men alone that belong the blame and the shame of the continued sufferings of children through war and persecution. It is they who incite and command, it is their policies, wicked or simply misguided, but in every case backed by the free-for-all traffic in weaponry, which are responsible for bringing terror, destitution and death to countless multitudes of children. 'Why do they want to kill us?' is the question for ever on the lips of those helpless, uncomprehending young. Why, they wonder, were they – despite themselves – brought into the world, so soon to be killed, maimed and orphaned?

Alas, from Herod to Hiroshima, from Pharaoh to Biafra, Vietnam and the phalangists of Lebanon, the martyrdom of children goes on unchanged, unless it be for the worse. One thing, though, has changed: if men are doing more harm than ever to children they are also doing more good. Inestimably more. The aid brought to the world's suffering children, together with the children's own fortitude, are the only features which relieve the shameful, desolate scene.

Of all the iniquities that can befall a child (or anyone for that matter) none is worse than to make it suffer and die without knowing the reason. Men know – more or less – why they go to war. Children do not, unless they have been brainwashed. Even then they are no less pitiable victims of the violence which is none of their making. No doubt the children of the Jewish citadel of Massada were told they were about to be murdered in a worthy cause, of which, if it was eventually theirs, they were still its totally innocent victims. It was in the year A.D. 73 and they just happened to be there with their parents. In a last, heroic but vain stand against the Romans, the Jewish garrison, rather than surrender, decided to die taking their women and children with them. Ten executioners, who were in turn to be their own executioners, were chosen to dispatch the garrison, families and all. It is difficult to imagine that the children really wanted to die, however noble the cause of their fathers. Their only small comfort was to feel the arms of their father and mother around them as they bared their young necks to the sword.

History is misleading – or rather misleads. Most young English schoolboys regard the Black Prince as the spirit of chivalry. But he was responsible, in 1370, for a massacre horrible enough to disillusion his most fervent admirer. At his sack of Limoges, 'It was a great pity,' wrote an eye-witness, 'to see the men, women and children that kneeled down on their knees before the Prince for mercy.' Notwithstanding, the Prince had three thousand men, women and children slain and beheaded that day. Henry V, on the other hand, forbade his men to capture children.

When, about thirty years after Henry V's death, Sultan Mohammed II laid siege to Constantinople, the Christian city resisted. So, instead of sparing it, Mohammed granted the three days of pillage to which his soldiers were entitled. They slew everyone they met, children not excepted. Babies, considered valueless, were slaughtered. The pillage over, the Sultan inspected the loot and the captives. He kept the fairest of the boys and girls for his own seraglio. It was said that Mohammed sent four hundred Greek children as a gift to each of the Sultan of Egypt, the King of Tunis and the King of Grenada. He demanded the fourteen-year-old son of the Megadux Notavas, a boy of exceptional beauty, for his own pleasure. When the father refused both were decapitated. Even two of the Emperor Constantine's young godchildren were taken into the Sultan's seraglio. The girl, Thamar, died there; the boy, refusing to yield to the Sultan's lusts, was slain.

Today, five centuries later, such hideous scenes seem remote, unimaginable. But many of the children I have met in recent months have told me of bestialities which rival those of the lascivious Sultan.

Though the suffering of children is usually attributable to the lusts and ambitions of men, women are no exception. It was on the initiative of a woman, Catherine de' Medici, that there occurred one of the most ferocious massacres in history in which children were not spared. It began in Paris as the tocsin sounded, earlier than usual, on the morning of 24 August 1572, St Bartholomew's Day. Amidst the scenes of carnage witnessed that day was that of the young Marquis de Conti begging mercy for his tutor, Brion, who was killed before his eyes; of a little girl, naked, dipped in the blood of her dead father and mother; of ten-year-old children, incensed by the killers' blood lust, dragging a new-born child across the cobbles; of other babies emptied by the basketful into the Seine; of children who, having cut off the genitals from the body of Admiral Coligny, dragged the headless corpse through the gutters of Paris.

After the massacre Catherine de' Medici received the congratulations of the Catholic powers and the Pope had a medal struck. At a Thanksgiving Mass held in Rome the prayer went up: 'Almighty God ... taking heed of Thy servants' faith, Thou hast granted them a splendid triumph; and we humbly beg Thee to continue what Thou has begun ... in the name of Christ.' Christ, who said, 'Suffer the little children to come unto Me' without any definition of creed or colour.

In 1857, British children, simply because, through no design of their own, they happened to be the sons and daughters of their parents living in India, were the pathetic, fortuitous and undeserving victims of another blood-crazy fanatic: Nana Sahib. On 6 June sepoys of the Indian Army mutinied at Cawnpore and for several days the small garrison, almost entirely whites with a few loyal sepoys, endured a heavy bombardment of round shot and grape. During those frightful days of bombardment children were killed and babies were born – one, to the wife of Dr Derby, under the shelter of a gun-carriage – only to be massacred with their mothers later. For, after twenty days of bombardment, the garrison surrendered; the Nana promised the women and children a safe passage by boat down the Ganges to Allahabad. Such was the joy, wrote an eighteen-year-old girl, Amelia Horne, that 'the soldiers were singing and dancing and they tried to get up a little fun for the children. One man whistled a jig while the other started to dance.' Their joy was short-lived. No sooner were the wounded, the women and children aboard the boats than the mutineers opened fire and the massacre began. Then, Amelia Horne goes on, 'the cavalry waded into the river with drawn swords and cut down those who were still alive . . . the air resounded with the shrieks of the women and children and agonized prayers to God for mercy . . . my poor little sister . . . moaned most piteously "O Amy, don't leave me".'

Lieutenant Mowbray Thomson, who was in the one remaining boat afloat, saw Mrs Swinton hit by round shot and collapse overboard. Her six-year-old boy begged him to explain: 'O, why are they firing on us? Did they not promise to leave off?'

'Why are they firing on us?' He spoke for millions of children, before him and since, who do not understand why men want to kill them.

A hundred or more women and children survived. They were locked up in a tiny house, Bibighar – the house of The Ladies – under the supervision of the most terrible lady of all, Hussani Khanum – 'the Begum', a prostitute's maid. It was under the direction of the Begum, in that miserable hovel, after another two weeks of torture from hunger and thirst, that all the women and children, some two hundred in number, were butchered.

General Neill, who arrived shortly afterwards with General Havelock's relieving force was 'at a loss to describe the horrors of that human slaughter-house' still strewn with women's and children's clothes – petticoats, skirts, slippers, stays, straw hats and bonnets, 'all of them covered with blood'. It was Neill who swore that 'every stain of that innocent blood shall be cleared up and wiped out . . .' Indeed, the British Army in turn revenged the 'cursed women-slayers' with the utmost cruelty.

In North America, the massacre of the Red Indians continued until the end of the nineteenth century. 'There was no hope on earth and God seemed to have forgotten us,' said Red Cloud, the last of the great Chiefs. In 1890, in the Moon when the Deer shed their Horns (17 December) a hundred refugee Indians reached Big Foot's camp near Cherry Creek. Big Foot, himself under orders of arrest, started off on 28 December with his people to Red Cloud's camp at Pine Ridge. Intercepted on the way by the Seventh U.S. Cavalry, the band of 350 Indians, of which 230 were women and children, were escorted to camp at Wounded Knee Creek. Next day, while the Indians were being searched for arms, a shot was fired. Then, said Turning Hawk, 'immediately the soldiers returned fire and indiscriminate killing followed'. When the 'madness', as Turning Hawk called it, at last ended nearly three hundred Indians, men, women and children, lay dead. The wagon-loads of wounded Sioux (four men and forty-seven women and children) reached Pine Ridge that night. The Episcopal Mission was thrown open to shelter them from the freezing cold. As they were carried into the candle-lit church those who were still conscious could read on a banner strung across the pulpit: Peace on earth, good will toward men.

At the start of the twentieth century an effort was made to segregate non-combatants from the battle scene. During the last phase of the South African war, from 1901 to 1902, the British General Kitchener, his armies harried everywhere by the Boer commandos, retaliated by confining the Boer families within barbed wire camps. This has earned for the British (who were preceded in the matter by a few years by the Spanish in Cuba) the unenviable reputation of being the inventors of concentration camps – the name they themselves gave to those camps in which the Boer families were herded. Yet these camps were never intended as places of torture. The inmates, like the British soldiers, lived in bell tents; they ate soldiers' rations and slept under army blankets. The camp commanders were not wicked men, but they were often quite unable to cope in the face of shortages of essential supplies, including drinkable water, milk for babies and nursing mothers, medicines, clothes and even shade from the scorching sun – but above all the crushing numbers of internees, crowded into forty-seven camps where the average child death-rate rose higher than at any time since the Great Plague of London in 1665. From June to August 1901, 3,245 children died from disease.

Into the midst of this dreadful scene where war, in the words of Sir Henry Campbell-Bannerman, then leader of the Liberal Party, was being conducted by 'methods of barbarism', there entered a frail-looking, forty-year-old English lady, Emily Hobhouse, daughter of a village parson and well connected. Having helped to organize the South African Women and Children's Distress Fund she sailed (second class) to South Africa. The first camp she visited, near Bloemfontein, contained 2,000 people, including 900 children; they were dying one after another from typhoid. 'Boil all water,' she ordered, and somehow procured an old locomotive boiler for the purpose. There was no milk so she collected some skinny cows which had survived Kitchener's scorched earth policy, gathered food for them and boiled the four buckets full of milk they gave every day. The journal Emily kept and the letters she wrote to her aunt, Lady Hobhouse, were printed in the newspapers, circulated to members of Parliament. They caused a political crisis. Though the camps continued to exist they were removed from the hands of the military; the death-rate which, among children, had averaged as much as 629 per thousand per year, was brought down to twenty. Even so, according to a Boer estimate, 26,000 women and children died in the concentration camps.

CHAPTER TWO

Famine Takes Its Toll in Russia

It has been fatuously remarked that the Boer War was the last gentlemen's war. The truth is that it was the sinister harbinger of total war.

The World War I non-combatants, children of course included, were the deliberate targets of the enemy's guns, bombs and – an ever more effective weapon – blockade. After three years of bloody, muddy slaughter on the Western front the Allied and German armies remained locked in static, indecisive combat. But at sea they held and steadily tightened the stranglehold upon each other. Mutually, the British and German naval blockades were reducing the two countries to starvation. In February 1917 Germany, in retaliation to the British blockade, declared unrestricted submarine warfare. The German Navy promised victory by the end of April. That was Britain's worst month in shipping losses; only six weeks' supply of food remained.

But, in Germany, despite the Navy's promise of victory, children were on the verge of starvation and had been for months. While commissions of well-dressed and amply-fed gentlemen visited the homes of the miserable and emaciated, bent solemnly over half-starving children and promised to help, the aid they may have inspired did little good. According to Lina Richter, in her book *Family Life in Germany under the Blockade*, children born during the blockade averaged between four and five pounds in weight; it was almost impossible to find baby linen, and cotton goods had almost entirely disappeared. Countless mothers, instead of wrapping their newborn babies in swaddling clothes, had to wrap them in newspapers. No sooner born, babies went short of food. Milk was very scarce and its price beyond the reach of many. On the fighting front the blockade – on each side – tightened and the military men and politicians congratulated themselves. But behind the lines it was the young and their mothers who were paying the price.

Ruth von der Leyen, Chief Woman Missionary at the Berlin

Children's Courts, blamed the starvation blockade for the huge increase in juvenile crime. 'The reformatories and the prisons are completely full ... in Stuttgart in three months 273 children were convicted.' The most frequent crime was theft from the fields. Mothers sent their children to forage because they could not endure to see them starving. And the little ones were conscious of their mothers' suffering. Often, when sentenced, a child would reply 'but I only took a cabbage to give mother a pleasant surprise.'

Starvation weakened a child's resistance to temptation. Boys stole from their fathers, sold clothes – anything that the family possessed – to obtain food. Girls simply sold themselves 'because they are taken by their lovers to restaurants where they can get plenty to eat'. 'Were all these young ones born thieves, criminals and good-for-nothings?' asks Ruth von der Leyen. 'No! the war has made them what they have become.'

But World War I saw the development of other forms of frightfulness against non-combatants. One was the transfer *en masse* of whole populations with a view to their eventual extermination. Such was the fate of the Armenians whom the Turks decided to deport to Mesopotamia in 1915.

Subsequently, the Turkish armies surrendered; it was then that Sergeant Gledhill, of the Norfolk Regiment, was posted to Mesopotamia. There, among the thousands of Armenian refugees, he had, despite his 'harassed feelings' to 'combine the functions of nurse and doctor and exercise control'. There were children of all ages, including babies in arms, some only just born. Among them was a ten-year-old boy, Sarkis Toumadian. Now an old man of seventy-three his eyes filled with tears as he remembered: 'I lived in Zeitoun, a little village in the Taurus. My ancestors had lived there for centuries. Then the frightful exodus to Mesopotamia began. Many of us never got there.' The Turkish soldiers 'like hideous monsters' savaged the women and children. Some were beaten to death. Others died of hunger, exhaustion or disease. 'The stronger ones,' Sarkis went on, 'gave us scraps to eat and I remember feeling like a dog which follows anyone who shows it the slightest kindness.' The boys and girls were eventually taken on by artisans who taught them weaving and pottery and basketwork. But it was difficult, for most of them were mutilated. Some had only one leg, others had lost an arm or a hand, and others their sight. The girls had been raped, after which the soldiers had cut off a foot or a hand or both ears. 'One evening,' related Sarkis, 'when they were laying into me – for the fun of it, as they said – one of them shouted "We shall do the same to every Armenian so that your race will disappear for ever".'

Another, and novel, method of direct assault against non-combatants was aerial bombardment. In 1917, Mrs Florence Colepeper was eleven and lived in a street in Poplar, in London's East End. Near her home was a church and next to it a school with infants on the ground floor, girls on the first and boys on the second. On 13 June, after an air-raid warning, Florence was sent home from her school nearby. She will never forget what followed. 'When I reached my street a terrible sight was revealed. The school had been bombed. Pupils were coming out covered in yellow powder ... screaming, crying, some injured, all distressed. Parents were frantically searching for their children ... there were heart-rending scenes'.

Florence believes this was the first daylight raid on London. The dead at the school included a boy of twelve, a girl of ten and fifteen infants under five.

Children like Florence were being conditioned to endure worse. In a P.S. to her letter to me she adds: 'the whole of the area, schools, church and street, was destroyed in the 1940 "Blitz".'

Though total war was still in its infancy it was set on a course which would lead to Auschwitz and Buchenwald, to Dresden, Hiroshima and Nagasaki. And to the end of the human race if the human race does not outlaw war for ever and seize and extinguish the torch of violence that it passes on to its children, who pass it on in turn from one generation to another.

World War I killed ten million soldiers and ten million civilians. In the wake of this immense and mournful harvest of death came the gleaners, disease and famine, which between them gathered in twenty million more dead. The vanquished nations were destitute. The shadow of famine lay over Vienna, Prague and Budapest, over the whole of Germany and Poland. For want of clothes and shoes children went barefoot and in rags; many missed the free food handouts because they had not even rags to wear. In September 1919 Herbert Hoover, Director of the American Relief Administration (and later President of the United States), estimated that, in Eastern Europe, there were between four and five million children dying of hunger.

No area was more disastrously hit by famine than the Ukraine, Russia's rich granary. Five armies had crossed and recrossed its territory, feeding off the land. After the 1917 October Revolution and the ensuing counter-revolution, civil war raged there. The 'Reds' were ruthless in requisitioning food from the peasants. To this 'war communism' the peasants reacted by reducing sowing and hiding their harvested grain. The drought of early summer 1921 did the rest. The crop failure that year affected an area inhabited by twenty million people. By July a million peasants were fleeing their parched and empty fields in the hope of escaping the famine. By August eight million children were starving. 'Bread' was made out of anything that could be ground into 'flour': chaff, straw, sawdust, grass, roots and leaves; it caused worms in the intestine and in turn disease and death. By September hundreds of thousands of children were dying of hunger. Mothers, rather than see their babies die of hunger, threw them into the river. Dr Nansen, the famous explorer, now acting for the International Red Cross, reported in November 1921 that in Kazan 'hundreds ofthousands must inevitably die of hunger and disease if sufficient help is not sent'. At a cemetery were 'eighty dead stacked one upon another, mostly children, stripped of their clothing which was needed by the survivors.' The population, he went on, 'was resigned, suffering and dying as they wait for help, and unable to believe that the other peoples of Europe will refuse to come to their assistance.'

Indeed there was not a nation in Europe — and beyond — which failed to help, including even those who were themselves sorely hit by famine. Yet there were among the leaders of the victorious nations some who argued: 'It would be better to let these children die. If they grow up they will only turn against us.'

Notwithstanding, huge quantities of food and supplies were distributed to the suffering Russians by foreign charitable organizations. Scores of doctors and nurses headed for Russia; many died there, victims of typhus and cholera. Still the aid, generous as it was, could not arrest the famine's terrible ravages. By February the famine revealed its most ghastly aspect: cannibalism. It was unsafe for children to go into the streets. A Russian girl living at Saratov, in a letter to her English pen-friend, explains why: 'Children cannot go out into the suburbs even by day because there are people who kidnap them and kill them to eat.' As late as June 1922 Dr Nansen's technical expert, Jean de Lubersac, was reporting, at Odessa, the case of a child bartered for four kilos of bread, of a mother and father who had sold some of their children to be slaughtered as food.

It was not until 1924 that the Ukraine began to recover from the famine. Looking back on it and the revolutionary years, these are some of the things that children remembered. 'I have seen eighteen revolutions,' a schoolboy writes. 'Oh if only one could keep what is good! It would be best to wipe out these years and never remember them again. We were so used to shooting that we got frightened when it was still.' Another boy writes: 'For six months we lived on nettles and roots. When I was eleven years old I saw people shot, hanged, drowned and even tortured. I saw piles of wounded lying on the ice for three days.'

With their young eyes and open minds children only see the essential. 'I saw a list of people who had been shot and read Daddy's name there. Mother came to us and said: "You are orphans now. Your Daddy is dead". They came and fetched our uncle away and later we found him in a big hole with lots of others. When Daddy was shot I realized what a revolution means. He was shot because he was a doctor.'

And from a very small child the perennial question: 'I don't understand why everybody wanted to kill us.'

CHAPTER THREE

The Young Victims of Guernica

The carnage and misery caused by World War I kindled the hope in men's hearts that it was the war which would end all wars. It drove many sincere, high-principled leaders to seek a form of international society which would ensure a world in which the young would at last be safe from violence. The League of Nations was founded. But the noble-minded men – especially those of the United States, Britain and France – though intent on outlawing war, were, when it came to the point, weak, undecided and divided among themselves. Before long, their hesitations and disagreements were regarded with contempt by the new leaders of Japan, Germany and Italy.

At the end of 1931 the Japanese invaded Manchuria; early next year they landed at Shanghai, but these acts of aggression brought forth no more than futile remonstrances from the peace-lovers of the League. By 1933 Hitler and his Nazis were in power and the Calvary of the German Jews began. In 1935 one hundred thousand German children swore 'eternal enmity' to the Jews. In October of that year Hitler's Axis partner, Italy, attacked Ethiopia. Once again the League failed to penalize the aggressor, any more than when, in March 1936, Germany occupied the Rhineland.

Then, in July 1936, tragedy hit Spain. The Civil War, originally a domestic affair, quickly blew up into a cruel and bloody international conflict which gave Germany and Italy a heaven-sent chance for testing out the tanks and guns and aircraft they were preparing for World War II – of which the Spanish Civil War was the curtain-raiser.

The war started with an insurrection of the army in Spanish Morocco, led by General Franco. Next day army garrisons on the mainland mutinied. At Toledo the rebels (Franco's 'nationalists') withdrew into the Alcázar. For two months the world followed with bated breath the siege of the Alcázar, whose defenders, under Colonel Moscardo, became legendary heroes.

The defence of the Alcázar is regarded, however, very differently by Arthur Koestler, then correspondent of the London *News Chronicle*, who calls it one of the most preposterous gangster exploits of our day. The garrison numbered 1,100. Besides them were four hundred women and children, of whom two hundred and fifty were hostages, including 150 eight- to ten-year-old cadets of a military academy.

All attempts to persuade the rebels to release the four hundred women and children failed. On the contrary, Colonel Moscardo received orders from the rebel government in Burgos not to release them on any account but to expose them to the full view of the enemy. During air-raids they were locked up in the cellars. 'The most terrible thing of all,' said an eye-witness, 'was the shrieking of the women, the crying and whimpering of the children.' One day 'in that hole of a cellar' a child was born, while around there was chaos. Three women went mad; three more killed themselves. Another howled the whole time 'like a dog baying at the moon'. A fourteen-year-old kitchen maid, Zara Gonzalez, escaped by crawling through the sewer into the town, where she collapsed in a pool of blood. In hospital she somehow managed to explain that she had been raped by nine of those heroes of the Alcázar. Four days later she died.

In a further attempt to get the women and children released a mediator, Colonel Rojo, was sent to parley with the defenders. He returned two hours later. 'They refused,' he reported. 'They declared that they would all die and that the women and children would die with them ....' Then the Abbé Camarasa was admitted to the Alcázar to plead for the women and children, but Colonel Moscardo still remained adamant. 'No one shall leave this place.' Finally the Chilean ambassador, doyen of the diplomatic corps in Madrid, agreed to intervene. He travelled to Toledo, where Moscardo refused to receive him. So his offer to facilitate the evacuation of women and children was conveyed by Colonel Barcello, commanding the government forces. The offer was rejected. After a sixty-seven-day siege the Alcázar was relieved. Eighty-three of its eleven hundred defenders were dead. Nothing more was heard of the fate of the women and children hostages.

During the Civil War both sides rivalled each other in terrorism and atrocity, with no quarter shown for non-combatants. Spanish children of the thirties will for ever be haunted by the horrors they witnessed.

Teresa, daughter of Count V, was one of them. She was ten when there began 'that horrible thing they call Civil War'. She and her young brothers and sisters lived in Madrid with their father; the elder children were with their mother at Seville. The 'nationalists' rebelled on 19 July – it was her father's birthday and he took the children to see a film. Next day he told them, 'There is war everywhere in Spain. Madrid is in the hands of the government troops. We are prisoners.' A few days later Teresa's twenty-six-year-old brother arrived on leave. Barely an hour after he had entered the house a member of the secret police and seven armed militiamen burst in and arrested him – he had been denounced by the concierge. The soldiers forced him down the stairs leading to the street. At the bottom one of the militiamen shot him in the back. Teresa's last glimpse of her brother was as he lay there dying.

A few days later the militiamen came back to arrest Teresa's father. At the sight of them her sixteen-year-old sister went out of her mind, screaming with terror and rolling about on the floor trying vainly to stop the soldiers entering. They pretended to be friendly, telling the children that the *Señor Conde* would be safer with them than at home, where he risked the same fate as her poor brother. The Count was locked up in San Anton prison, where the children were allowed to visit him once a week – until October, when the visits were stopped. It was on 6 November that Teresa's father was led with three hundred others to a tunnel near the capital. There every one of them was machine-gunned to death. Teresa only heard the tragic news later. Meanwhile she and her little brothers and sisters, five in all, continued to live in Madrid alone with the servants. The telephone never stopped ringing; it was always an unknown voice saying that very soon they would be invited to go for a walk in the neighbourhood, when they would be shot dead.

Then the children were taken in by friends of her parents. But the militiamen kept coming there too, so that they lived in a permanent state of anguish, having to lie low and keep quiet; they could never play and hardly slept. Food began to run out and huge queues formed, and at midnight, braving the military patrols, they would slip out to try and pick up a scrap to eat.

One day the militia came to arrest Teresa's fifteen-year-old brother – who managed just in time to climb out onto the roof where he remained for hours while the house was turned upside down and Teresa and the other children looked on in terror. Food became so scarce that they were reduced to living on sunflower seeds. Then came the nationalist air-raids on Madrid, no doubt carried out by German *Luftwaffe* and Italian *Regia Aeronautica* squadrons. Civil populations were as yet unaccustomed to concentrated bombardment from the air. Teresa still remembers how she used to sit with her brothers and sisters, all of them petrified, for hour upon hour in the cellar, feeling, in her own words 'desperate, forgotten and lost'.

At last, after a two-year nightmare, the children were taken by the

International Red Cross to Seville, to their mother and safety.

Angela, with her parents and two young sisters, lived in a *hacienda* near Mijas, up in the hills west of Malaga. From the white-washed farm you could look down across a plain covered with olive trees to the sandy beaches, burning hot in the Andalucian summer. Forty years ago, Angela recalls, 'there were no foreigners, sky-scrapers or crowds of tourists who invade everywhere without any consideration for the crops, the flowers and the flocks to which we devoted so much trouble and hard work.'

Many men of the village had left to join up with Franco's nationalists. Angela's father, an invalid, and her mother stayed on at the farm with their girls. 'We lived sparsely, simply, as many Andalucians still do today.'

Not far away lived a titled family – the *Señor*, the *Señora*, their two daughters-in-law, and their grandchildren, aged ten, twelve and fifteen. The two sons of the house were away fighting for Franco. For this reason government militiamen often came to the big house to question *el Señor*. For hours Angela would listen to the soldiers shouting and threatening and she was very much afraid. As the soldiers' visits became more frequent Angela grew even more afraid. Her parents begged *el Señor* and *la Señora* to flee with their children into the mountains along paths known only to the shepherds, who offered to lead them by night into Nationalist territory. But the old couple refused, saying they would rather stay on their own land with the villagers whom they loved.

Angela will never forget the morning when the whole of that brave family came running and panting to the *hacienda*. They left a few things and papers with her father saying that they had just heard that they were going to be killed and were trying to escape – alone. They wished no one else to be involved. The children were crying, their mothers pale, dishevelled and out of breath; the grandparents seemed calm. 'We watched them as they walked across the maize fields, through the olive groves and entered the forest.' Two hours later a dozen militiamen came to Angela's house and, after hitting her father and slapping her mother in the face, demanded, 'Where have the rich people gone?' Then they hurried off to join a lot of other soldiers who had already started into the forest. Angela froze with fear. Her sisters were in tears, her parents stood motionless in their anguish. Angela knew only one thing: 'The shadow of death was upon us.'

Many minutes passed, long, long minutes during which all was silent save for the occasional bleating of sheep. Otherwise the birds, it seemed to Angela, had stopped singing, nor could she even hear the murmur of the little brook she loved so much, which ran below the orchard. Then suddenly the silence was rent by the crashing echo of machine-gun fire. A few seconds later there followed several more shots. Angela could bear it no longer; she fainted. Two days went by. Then the foresters came with the bodies; they buried them by night. 'I have never, never forgotten,' Angela says. 'Forty years later I can still see the bodies of the three children, their brains blown out and the body of *el Señor*, his hands crossed upon his breast. I was only nine; but after that I never played with my doll again.'

In Spain during those years no children were safe. Some were even at the front, defying the enemy bullets. George Orwell (author of *Animal Farm*, *Nineteen Eighty-Four* and *Homage to Catalonia* – from which I borrow) was with them in the government ranks. 'We struggled along with far less cohesion than a flock of sheep ... and quite half of the so-called men were children ... sixteen years of age at the very most.' They uttered shouts 'which were meant to be warlike and menacing, but which, from those childish throats, sounded as pathetic as the cries of kittens.' Yet, Orwell says, they were all happy and excited at the prospect of getting to the front. This is one glimpse that he had of them, once there: 'Twelve wretched children ... who had been posted by the Fascist [Nationalist] parapet were ... unable to escape. All day they had to lie there with only tufts of grass for cover, the Fascists shooting at them every time they moved. By nightfall seven were dead ...'

Other children simply cowered, or were blown to pieces, in their own homes under the bombs, most of them dropped by the German *Luftwaffe*'s Condor Legion, sent by Hitler at Franco's request. Its chief of staff, Lieutenant-Colonel Wolfram Freiherr von Richthofen, cousin of Manfred, the 'Red Baron', was said to cherish his squadron's aircraft – which caused such wanton death and destruction – almost as much as his wife and young son. At Durango, on 31 March 1937, his bombers killed 248 civilians. On the 27 April they were to massacre hundreds more.

The day before, von Richthofen had briefed his men: the target, a strategic one, was the bridge of Renteria, on the outskirts of Guernica, a small town of the Basque province of Vizcaya, and the home of Basque liberties. The bridge was a small one, ten metres wide and twenty-five metres long. Yet Richtofen's attacking force consisted of an armada of forty-three bombers carrying a total load of fifty tons of fragmentation and incendiary bombs – the kind normally used to kill people and burn buildings, but not to bust a bridge.

The first man over the target was *Leutnant* von Moreau, an expert bomber pilot, flying one of the *Luftwaffe*'s new Heinkel IIIs. His and his bomb-aimer's reputation for accuracy were well-known. Their bombs fell not on the Renteria bridge but in the station square, several hundred metres away in the middle of Guernica. One bomb cut the façade of the Hotel Julian in two – the crashing masonry buried several children playing below. Nobody knows how many more civilians were killed in the crowded square. Another bomb knocked the fire brigade chief, Juan Sillano, off his feet. From where he lay he saw a group of women and children blown into the air and their bodies disintegrate. 'Legs, arms, heads, bits of everything were flung in all directions.' While the Renteria bridge remained untouched, succeeding waves of German bombers tore the town apart. Incendiaries fell on a confectionery shop whose director saw one of his girl employees transformed into a ball of flame. A high explosive bomb hit No. 29 Calle Don Tello where, with her mother Lucila, Victoria Bilbao was celebrating her fifteenth birthday. The young girl and her mother were recovered dead from among the ruins, on top of which the birthday cake was found intact. Then the German fighters, led by *Kapitän* von Lutzow, dived. As Juan Guezureya watched them flying to and fro a hundred feet up, raking with their machine-guns the fleeing, panicked population, they reminded him of sheep-dogs rounding up the people to massacre them. Juan was searching for his young brother who had fled when the first bomb dropped. He was eventually found two weeks later, along with fourteen other boys, crushed to death by a mass of shattered masonry.

More waves of bombers followed. A bomb fell on the *residencia* Calzada, whose roof was marked with a giant Red Cross. Of the nuns, the aged, the wounded and orphans sheltering there, forty-five were killed. But the Renteria bridge was still untouched. Flight-Commander von Beust later reported that it was impossible to see the target for dust. There was no question, he added, of returning to land with his bombs – it would have been dangerous for him and his crews. So he dropped them on the women and children of Guernica.

People taking refuge in the Town Hall had made just enough room to shelter a group of children who had to squat with their heads between their knees. The Town Hall was hit three times, the roof fell in and three storeys collapsed on those below. More than five hundred women and children had taken refuge in the Church of Santa Maria, believing they would be safe. But the church was hit by incendiaries. For want of enough water Father Eusebio had to use communion wine to help extinguish the fire, remarking that he was sure that the good Lord, had he been there, would have changed it into water.

Then the bombers retired – and still the Renteria bridge remained intact. Of Guernica, however, between the station and the market, little remained. The heart of the town had been torn out. And, far from feeling the slightest remorse, the German airmen celebrated that evening in the Fronton Hotel. Bawdy songs were sung, the brothels opened their doors ... And the evening passed into ultimate oblivion. But the massacre of the innocents of Guernica will never be forgotten. With the gaunt silhouette of its shattered buildings, the dead bodies of its citizens strewn about its streets, its hospitals, churches and schools, Guernica set an unmistakable pattern for future massacres from the air in which no one, young or old, could expect any quarter.

In 1937, while the Civil War in Spain still raged, a new and terrible war broke out on the other side of the world. That winter the Japanese invaded China.

Not long before that Edith Lynn, then only just eighteen, had arrived at Wei-hei-wei as nanny to the British consul's son. Wei-hei-wei was a peaceful fishing village whose quiet was only broken by the rhythmic chug of fishing-boat engines, the laughter of fishermen as they hauled in their nets and the scream of seagulls wheeling above the catch. Sometimes Edith would go sailing to Cat's Eye Bay in a boat hired from one of those fishermen, who was always accompanied by his boy. When the wind dropped and the sail hung limp like the battered wing of a great brown moth the fisherman would whistle, whistle for the wind, while his son gazed silently towards the horizon.

Back on shore, too, the boy was always silent and withdrawn. He never joined the village children when they gathered on the waterfront or when they sang the missionaries' hymn, 'Yes, Jesus loves me'. He never uttered a word. He was a deaf-mute. The only useful thing he ever did was to chase the seagulls who stole the fish his father caught. That he did well. He was always running, running down the narrow strip of sand by the harbour, his faded blue trousers flapping about his brown ankles, his thin arms wildly flailing the air as he leapt and reached for the seagulls. When his fingers closed on one and tightened about its neck he would hold it to him as he scooped a little hollow in the sand, there to bury his enemy beneath a little mound, like those which covered his ancestors' graves dotting the hillside.

He was running on the sand that grey winter's day when the Japanese invaded, when one of their submarines, like a half-submerged crocodile, slithered towards the jetty at Wei-hei-wei and disgorged a party of marines. They scrambled up the slippery steps shouting *banzai* and bore aloft triumphal arches of dark green leaves studded with coloured rosettes. People peered from windows, terrified. Anyone who ran was shot, their heads stuck on poles, their bodies trundled in wheelbarrows through the streets as a warning to others.

The boy was still running, leaping in the air, snatching at the seagulls as the Japanese marines came ashore. One of them slowly raised his rifle and aimed. Edith and the children with her stared blankly, helplessly after the running figure. Then, unable to bear the suspense any longer, turned away. A shot rang out and the seagulls rose in a screaming white cloud. But on the sand lay the thin body of the boy, silent as ever but now quite still.

One of the most moving stories to come out of China during those terrible years of war is truthfully and beautifully told by Alan Burgess in *The Small Woman* or, to give it the title of the film that was made out of it, *The Inn of the Sixth Happiness*. To escape from the war and all its atrocities an Englishwoman, Gladys Aylward, known to the Chinese as *Ai-weh-deh*, led a hundred Chinese children on a two-week trek through the mountains to the Yellow River and beyond, where at last they found safety from the brutalities of the Japanese soldiery.

While forced to live under the rule of the Japanese Gladys had been greatly puzzled that they could behave so barbarously yet at times show so much courtesy and kindness. The soldiers had often shown their fondness for children. She remembered that once a party of them had brought sacks of sugar, tipped them into large water-jars and, with shouts of laughter, handed out cups full of the syrupy liquid to the delighted children. Yet when Gladys walked into Yangcheng after the Japanese had left she found 'a city of hollow-eyed corpses'. Most had been bayonetted and crouched or lay, twisted grotesquely. Many were children.

The decision that Gladys made to lead her hundred children away from these horrors involved her and them in a hard and perilous journey. The end of one arduous day found the children eating a frugal meal of cooked millet. Gladys cupped her bowl between her hands 'embracing the tiny warmth it offered'. Beside her sat two teenage girls, Ninepence and Sualan, 'exquisite little creatures with clear, pale skins and blue-black shining hair'. 'How absurd,' Gladys thought 'that they should be forced to make this long journey to save their lives', and it angered her intensely that the stupidity of men should be the cause of those children's terrible ordeal — which was my own feeling when listening years later to other boys and girls who were still fleeing before the stupidity and bestiality of men in order to save their lives.

While in Spain and China the carnage of civilians – that meant children – increased, Hitler was making the moves which would lead to the global holocaust of World War II. In November 1938 he turned in a paroxysm of fury on the Jews. He had persecuted them relentlessly for the last six years, but now came a nation-wide pogrom, the Week of the Broken Glass.

Forty years later, in Jerusalem, I met El Hanan Schmidt, once a Jewish German, now an Israeli, who escaped from the pogrom in his village of Badersfeld. I asked El Hanan what it meant, as a boy of eight, to be involved in a pogrom. 'We lived in a nice apartment,' El Hanan told me, 'full of the finest things. Then one evening – it was the 9th of November – the door-bell rang. I, as the youngest of the family, went to open the door. There stood a policeman and two SS men. They gave me a terrible fright. All three entered and told my father: *"Herr Schmidt, Wir kommen Sie in Schutzhaft nehmen"* – we are coming to take you into protective custody. And so they went on from house to house taking all the Jewish men. It was only next day that we realized the meaning of *Schutzhaft*, protective custody. My father came home that evening and we saw that he was bruised and beaten all over. He had been ordered to leave town at six a.m. next day.'

So young El Hanan and his family had to leave their apartment and all the fine things in it. They went to stay with an uncle at Gross Krotzenburg. But that same day, 10 November, the SS rang at the door. There was not even time to open it; they broke it down. They were youngsters of eighteen or twenty, armed with sticks and axes. They smashed everything in the house and threw it out of the windows. 'What did you do?' I asked El Hanan. 'We just stood there,' he answered, 'and cried to heaven.' 'Did they hurt you?' 'No, they just broke up everything and we stood there helplessly, crying.'

El Hanan's father put him in an orphanage. He was just nine, and to be separated from his parents was, he said, 'most terrible. I have never got over it to this day.' El Hanan had two sisters, one eleven, the other thirteen. 'Did they go with you?' I asked. 'No,' he replied almost violently, 'they were sent to a camp and there they were killed. When I think about it today I say to myself no one who has not seen it can ever understand.' 'And your parents, did you ever see them again?' 'Four years later,' he said, 'I got a letter from a Catholic lady, a friend of the family who told me what had happened. I am very sorry she ever wrote it,' he said bitterly. He would rather have remained in ignorance of his parents' fate.

As the power and territorial possessions of Hitler's Nazis increased, so did the number of concentration camps. By 1939 places called Dachau, Sachsenhausen, Buchenwald, Mauthausen and Ravensbrück had a deathly ring. Then, on 1 September 1939, German troops invaded Poland, killing, smashing, burning all before them. Less than three weeks later Soviet troops swept into Poland from the east. World War II had begun.

Part Two

CHAPTER FOUR

The Martyrdom of Polish Children

World War II accounted for just about double the dead and wounded of World War I. But statistics are inhuman and cannot possibly tell the tale of human suffering. It would be just as inhuman to make comparisons between the suffering of nations and individuals, when all were so sorely hurt in the universal suffering of World War II. Did not Jesus say, even of the sparrows, 'Not one of them is forgotten before God.'

But in looking for a symbol of that universal suffering it is impossible not to think of Poland – Poland, because she was the first victim of aggression and then from two sides; Poland, because it was the Poles – Slav and Jew – who were the first to be singled out for total extermination; Poland, because from the day of her enslavement her sons and daughters began to fight back against their tyrannical masters; Poland, because from the brutal assault upon her soil and her liberty there radiated a wave of suffering which enveloped nearly sixty belligerent nations – of which two, her original aggressors, Germany and Russia, were ironically the most hard hit. But every nation involved, especially those who suffered on their own soil, was left with a sad and motley host of martyred, maimed and orphaned children, children who, in the nature of things, were destined to perpetuate the human race and in so doing pass on to succeeding generations the fears and infirmities which the war of the preceding generation had inflicted upon them. The process is as old as humanity itself. In the event of a third world war the dying agony of the human race will not be prolonged beyond the decadence and death of our own children and grandchildren.

For Polish children who, that first sunny day of September 1939, were suddenly awoken by the crash of bombs, life as they had known it – the family, the love and protection of parents, home, games, friends – from now on ceased to exist. Terrified by the storm of shot and shell they were driven with everybody else to hide underground, like moles, cramped into dark, damp burrows which passed for shelters, where they found themselves cheek by jowl with people of all sorts and ages, with the sick and the dying, with wailing cats and barking dogs, where scenes of panic and hysteria alternated with heart-rending prayers for salvation. If the children hardly understood what it was all about they felt it deeply. When at last they could quit their shelters they were told 'the war is over'. But all around them were ruins, twisted corpses and the wounded still bleeding and agonizing in the streets. Before even the fall of Warsaw General Frank, Gauleiter of Poland, noted in his diary that he had orders to pillage mercilessly the enemy's territory and reduce its institutions, economic, social, cultural and political, into 'a simple heap of ruins'. The term used by the Nazis for this process was *Neue Ordnung* – the 'New Order'.

Henryka Veillard-Cybulska, then a girl belonging, as she says, to the inferior race (the Poles) who were marked down for extermination by the *Übermenschen*, the (German) supermen, joined up immediately with the Red Cross and the Committee for Social Aid (*Polnisches Hilfskomitee*) – the RGO – the only Polish charitable organization accepted by the Germans. In the autumn of 1940 she was attached to the Polish Law Court at Radom. Later she became a juvenile court magistrate and worked closely with a number of youth welfare organizations. Painful as it was for her to recall that long and dreadful period of the occupation, she has given me an insight into everyday life in Poland under the Nazis. Henryka still bears the traces of her own first encounter with the Nazi administration. Insulted by an official as a 'Polish swine' she replied: 'There is another form of justice besides the German kind.' That defiant Polish girl was hit in the face, knocked unconscious, then kicked downstairs.

Decrees and memoranda were issued. One dated 25 November 1939 and published by the *Rassenpolitische Amt der NSDAP* (the Nazi Party), defined the Party's attitude towards Polish children. According to the 'race theory' an 'examination of race' was made compulsory for children between two and six years of age with the object of making a 'scientific' selection of children who would qualify as Germans on 'racial grounds'. In the relentless child-hunt which followed, children were kidnapped from their homes without mercy and passed on for examination.

The hunt had begun among children in schools and orphanages. Then it became general. The Polish Committee for Social Aid (RGO) took in some of the 'racially non-valid children'. Some had already undergone compulsory sterilization. They were a sad lot who neither laughed nor played. Often parents would come to the RGO searching desperately for a son or daughter whom the SS had stolen from them. When the Germans found that they could not cope with such numbers of small victims they simply put them up for sale. Prices ranged from fifty to one hundred zlotys, but a bottle of vodka or a packet of cigarettes was enough to buy a child.

The 'purchase' would often be handed in to the RGO. One peasant woman brought along a little girl of seven. 'I bought her,' she said, 'as I was searching for my own children who were kidnapped from me. I saw a truck full of children, surrounded by people who were bidding for them. The children shouted "Mister, buy me" and "me, me, Madam, save me!" or "Mister, I can work" or "Madam, I will be very good". The tiny ones were in tears and calling "Mummy, mummy" – in vain for they would never see her again.' The woman went on: 'A little girl knelt down and prayed "Oh, Holy Mother, make someone take me". The truck was just leaving when a boy jumped out and ran off towards the forest. A shot rang out ... then I took off my wrist-watch and gave it to the truck-driver, pointing at this little girl. Since then she has been with me while I have been searching for my own children, but now she is too tired. Take her, please. Maybe her mother is looking for her. I shall go on looking for my children. If I don't find them, nor she her parents, I will take her back.'

Many years were to pass before parents and children – some of them – were reunited. And then, all too often, the children did not recognize their father and mother, nor could they speak their parents' language, but only German. The Nazis had seen to that. After seizing the 'racially valid' children from their parents they sent them to Germany to be 'Germanized' in 'Fatherland schools' (*Heimat Schulen*) or lodged with a family of 'thoroughbred' Germans. The children were made to forget their Polish name (a German one was substituted), their family, their country and the Polish language.

Only a few managed to escape the Germanization process. One was a little tuberculous boy with Nordic features who was released in order to persuade his father to sign the *Volksliste* which would enable them both to become Germans. His father told him 'if I sign the *Volksliste* I can put you in a sanatorium in the mountains.' But the boy only answered: 'Father, if you become a *Volksdeutsch* I shall die of shame.' Both were soon to die, but they died as Poles.

Sometimes, thanks to the selfless courage of a parent or friend, a 'racially non-valid' child was snatched from certain death. Michel, for example. His mother, as if by some strange intuition, dressed her nine-year-old son as a girl. It saved their lives for when they were both arrested, she never relented during a whole week of cross-questioning in her assertion that she and the child were of pure Aryan blood. Had Michel been wearing trousers the Gestapo had only to take them off and the game would have been up.

Louis's father was killed by the Germans in 1943. Louis was then four and he and his mother were thrown out of their apartment. But a kindly Polish couple, at the risk of their lives, took Louis into their home and arranged for his mother to work there as a housemaid. And Louis always had to treat her as such and never call her Mummy. Except at night when everybody was asleep and he crept into her room, into her bed, into her arms.

Then there was Georges. His father and mother had died, victims of the extermination campaign. A Polish family took the little boy and hid him – in a cupboard, all day long, for two years. By the time Poland was freed, the little boy was more of an animal than a human; his case was given up as hopeless. But a friend of the family living in Paris fetched him from Poland and brought him to her home. Then began her fight to save Georges from perdition. For months she gave up everything for him. She managed to get him into the communal school, but had to sit beside him in class, never leaving him for a minute – as if she had been herself one of the pupils. Her patience and devotion were rewarded – Georges in time became like any other of his classmates and is today a brilliant scientist. Which goes to show that love is to a child a form of nourishment every bit as vital as milk. The Nazis lost no love on children whom they considered 'subhuman'.

The Gestapo chief, Himmler, insisted that children must be 'thoroughly persuaded that, among God's commandments, the most important are: obedience to the Germans, honesty, the will to work ...' He concluded: 'after ten years of rigorous application of these measures the population of the Government General will necessarily consist only of individuals who are in every way inferior.' It was on his orders, that not only high schools and public schools were closed down, but libraries and bookshops also. All intellectual, scientific and artistic activity was made illegal. Polish children were forbidden to possess sports equipment (skis for example), photographic or radio equipment, records, motorbikes or bicycles. On the tramways the rear half of the last coach was reserved for 'Jews, Poles and dogs' – the savage dogs of the Gestapo. And as most people lived in the suburbs their children often had to walk for miles in temperatures as low as $-30°C$.

The 'people's schools' (*Volksschulen*) existed in the worst possible conditions – between seventy and a hundred pupils to each class, with poor accommodation and a woeful lack of school books. Every pupil had to know by heart the leading precepts of Nazi propaganda. For example, to the question: 'Which is your worst enemy?' they had to reply: 'Jews, lice and typhus.' When, during a visit, a school inspector discovered that the word 'Jews' had been changed to 'Germans' the entire class was sent out onto the playground where the temperature was −12°C. There they were ordered to remain standing until someone owned up. No one did, so the school was closed down and pupils and teachers sent to work with the construction corps (*Baudienst*).

But neither the pupils nor their teachers were going to submit. Between them they organized secret classes called *Complets* of no more than half a dozen; they learnt nearly everything by heart, for it was too dangerous to take notes. School books had to be concealed, say, in the bottom of a basket of potatoes or coal. Discovery could mean death. A boy who was caught by the SS with a history book and a girl who had kept a map of 'ex-Poland' were both executed. But the courage of the children, both teenagers and younger, was extraordinary. There was never any lack of volunteers for the 'Kangaroos', boys and girls who, at great risk, transported forbidden books in a special lining inside the front or back of their pullovers. Terrorism did not prevent the secret schools from spreading to every town. Every Polish home was a meeting place for the *Complets*, though for safety pupils and teachers had to move continually from one place to another. Their ingenuity, and the help of grown-ups, made it possible for boys and girls to study up to *baccalauréat* standard. There even existed at Warsaw and, after its destruction, at Radom, a clandestine Faculty of Philosophy.

But the risks run by the clandestine schools were enormous. Many children were caught, their teachers deported or executed in public. One seventeen-year-old boy had a very near escape. His *Complet* met in a number of picturesque hiding-places including a loft where his friend raised pigeons. When it was fine they would often go to the 'Old Garden', the only park at Radom open to the Poles. The teacher would sit beneath a tree with the pupils around him. But two boys would always be up the tree on the look-out for the 'death's head' SS. One day the *Complet* met in a private house. Our young friend's main failing was unpunctuality — and it saved him. Arriving a quarter of an hour late he was just in time to see the rest of the class, headed by the teacher, being escorted out of the house by some SS men. 'The poor teacher ended up in Auschwitz,' he said. 'As for my friends, I never heard what became of them. I myself ran away into the forest and lived there until the Liberation.'

The teaching corps showed exemplary courage; they were among the first victims of the *Neue Ordnung*. Two hundred lecturers from Cracow University were deported to Sachsenhausen; Warsaw lost more than two hundred more. The lecturers of Lwow University were bestially murdered by the *Nachtigal* battalion of the SS. Then there was the saintly Dr Janusz Korczak – a medical man by profession but a teacher at heart. He refused, despite his exemption as a doctor, to abandon his two hundred pupils in the Warsaw ghetto. He once said: 'I ask for nothing better than to remain a teacher, to have my little corner in the children's home and two frugal meals a day.' The Nazis closed the orphanage and on 5 August 1942 Dr Korczak assembled his children for the last time. Believing they were all being moved to a holiday camp, he told them: 'There you will be closer to the light, closer to God.' He made them sing and, singing still, they were transported to the death camp where, with their doctor in the lead, they filed into the gas chamber.

If the Nazis forbade Polish children a normal education they had certain educative methods of their own. One of them was to force schoolchildren to attend public executions or at least to contemplate the corpses of their victims swinging from the gallows. Special permission was granted to school teachers to break off in the middle of a lesson in order to lead their pupils to the place of execution, where they could 'study' the methods of the Gestapo. Once, a little boy recognized his father among the victims. A few months later he was again led to the foot of the gallows – which the Gestapo, characteristically, had erected close by the orphanage. Suddenly the boy screamed and fled from the scene. 'They have killed my daddy for the second time,' he sobbed. 'I recognized his pullover which mummy had so often darned.' It was indeed his father's pullover – his mother had given it to a neighbour who in turn was hanged. Among the other victims was an eighteen-year-old girl student eight months pregnant; by her side hung her student husband, her parents and her three brothers and sisters.

Horror, persecution and restrictions and, above all, the break-up of family life, drove children to crime. The juvenile courts were crowded with youthful prisoners. The most frequent charge was theft. Yet, when accused of stealing food, clothes, shoes, coal, cigarettes, drink and money, the reply was invariably on the same theme: 'But what harm have I done if I stole from a German? They have robbed us of everything; we only take back a few crumbs, and it's a risky business. We deserve to be congratulated.'

As time went on the young offenders grew more and more arrogant.

One of them, an impenitent coal-thief, asked the judge, 'You're not going to have me locked up in that foul prison just for a few kilos of coal? Do you want to be taken for a collaborator?' Once again he was released, but not for long. One evening, back at his same old game of coal-thieving, he was shot dead by the railway police.

Another, hauled up for stealing a litre of milk, was told that judgment would be deferred for another two weeks. 'You think that I shall live as long as that?' he exclaimed. 'Put me in prison straight away. At least once a day I shall get a bowl of hot soup – which I haven't tasted since my parents were arrested. And who knows, I might meet them in prison.'

The thought uppermost in the minds of boys was to live for the day of vengeance. Though the idea seldom occurred to Polish girls, one at least wreaked her own particular kind of revenge against the Germans. Like so many of her sisters in other lands at war, she was a prostitute. And like the majority of Polish girls who appeared in court she had venereal disease. She was seventeen, but looked like a very sick woman of thirty. Accused of contaminating two Germans with her disease, she replied defiantly: 'Those two boys have got what they deserved. What's more, I'm proud of myself for I have given the same little present to a score of German soldiers. I'd be even happier if I could have done likewise for a hundred more, but I have no more strength left.'

Following Russia's treacherous attack on Poland in 1939 two million Poles were deported into the depths of Russia. Masses of them died. Then, in June 1941, Germany invaded Russia. Despite the past, the Soviets and the Poles became, at least on paper, friends again and the surviving Polish prisoners were released from bondage. They were evacuated to the Middle East, East Africa, India and across the Atlantic. In *The State of Health of Poles Evacuated from Russia to Persia, 1942*, Dr Michael Kruszynski describes the arrival of the first batch at Tehran on 28 March 1942. 'Two buses stopped outside the hospital buildings and out of them shuffled a group of bedraggled skeletons dressed in what had been white night-shirts, now stained with blood and dirt, and black caps ... these were very sick children ... all were covered with excrement, having lost the will to keep clean. Their ages ranged from four to fourteen.' Hundreds died, from typhus, cholera, malaria, dysentery and a multitude of other diseases including measles, mumps, scarlet fever and hooping-cough. Hundreds more were saved, thanks to the skill and extreme courage of the doctors and nursing staff of the Polish General Civilian Hospital in Tehran.

From Russia, bound for India, came more Polish refugees and their children. Seven hundred of them were aboard a British ship bound for Karachi. Also aboard was a Nursing Sister, Lilyan Field. Today after all those years those children are to her still a most painful memory, children of tender years sitting around with faces drawn and wrinkled, looking like little old men and women; children who did not laugh or cry or fight or play with each other. When given a toy they drew back in fear. War, planned, declared and directed by the great, had turned these nameless innocents into mental and physical wrecks.

Alas, it was only in thousands that the Russian trains brought the Poles to freedom, while other trains – German ones – transported them in millions to slavery and death. Of the countless thousands of children among them, I recently met one, Zvi Gill, who described to me the terrible journey he made to Auschwitz, and beyond.

Zvi's father was a prominent businessman, his mother the matron of the local hospital. Zvi lived with his parents and two younger brothers in a small town near Lodz. There, one morning in 1942, the Gestapo ousted them from their home and ordered them to assemble at the cemetery. This was the usual rendezvous. There, covered by German rifles, they were split up. Zvi found himself with his grandfather. He did not know where his father was, or his mother and brothers. Then his grandfather was torn away from him. He tried to run after him, but the Gestapo hit little Zvi with their rifle-butts and stopped him. 'You know, I was used to German brutalities; we used to live on the main square and there I saw hangings and shootings. And I don't remember even crying, because it was exactly as if I were being driven from civilization into the jungle and among the wolves.'

There was Zvi in the cemetery, beaten to the ground and ordered to lie down like all the others. It was terribly hot and he was thirsty. He got up to go and look for water, but bullets whipped past him. On the second day his mother, crawling among the supine figures, managed to find him. 'My mother was glad to find at least one of her boys alive. For don't forget, there were black lorries coming and going all the time and I knew what that meant. The Chelmno concentration camp was not far away; they dug graves there in advance. The lorries were entirely closed. Inside them cyanide gas could be turned on. People were herded towards them, loaded like cattle, pushed inside. Most often they were gassed on the way.' Zvi stayed with his mother. 'Somewhere else,' he went on, 'were my father and brothers, my grandfather and uncles.' He was never to have any further news of them.

'What does it feel like,' I asked Zvi, 'when you are fourteen and you know that at any moment you may be loaded into one of those lorries and gassed. Are you afraid?' 'No, not at all. I think it's because you feel you are doomed – you feel a sort of helplessness and you can do nothing about it. But I couldn't understand why it should be that I should have to leave my father and brothers. I didn't know where I was going and I wanted to be with them. I thought of my two young brothers and hoped that at least father was with them.'

I asked Zvi: 'Did you feel like running away?' 'No, not at all,' he said. To run away and expect to live was hopeless. 'At a later stage,' he went on, 'I did escape – from a train. But at that point it was different: I was so cold then that I was frozen – it was like having a tooth pulled, when you are given an injection and everything freezes up. It was like that in the camp; your body was frozen – you just breathed. Except for breathing I don't think you were alive at all.'

'And all those people,' I asked, 'who were led into the gas chambers. Do you think they just went on and had no feeling?' 'Yes, I guess so,' Zvi said. 'Because if you have feelings, if your mind functions, then inevitably your first thought is "How can I get out of this? What can I do to make *them* pay for it? How can I jump the Gestapo or a German soldier, any German? I'm going to die anyway, so let them die with me." And I believe this tremendous feeling of being stunned, this total apathy, was the main reason why people did not react. You see, people didn't cry. I didn't cry, though I was very young, because if somebody is crying it means he has emotions; he can reason and his mind starts to function. But if all feeling has gone there is no desire left. I don't think,' Zvi concluded, 'that people who died felt any basic desire for survival.'

After that tragic day in 1942 when Zvi and his mother found themselves alone they went to live in the ghetto at Lodz. Zvi was then sixteen and found life in the ghetto what he called 'realistic'. 'All around you,' he said, 'are barbed wire and sentries in the garden and you go out into the moonlight with your girlfriend as if you were in Acapulco or somewhere like that. It's another planet.' The 'realism' became grim when, in 1944, the Gestapo staged another round-up. After hiding for twenty-four hours in the house, Zvi and his mother gave themselves up. Soon after, they found themselves crammed in a sealed cattle-wagon and on their way to Auschwitz. In Zvi's wagon people were dying of thirst and suffocation. 'It was a matter of breathing,' he told me. 'We were so crowded that your only hope was to force your way to the side of the wagon and try to suck in a little fresh air.' People in the train knew where they were going; they knew that on arrival at Auschwitz they would be sent either to the gas-chambers or to a labour camp. 'I knew what was ahead of me – in complete contrast to what happened two years before I now felt a grown-up man and I knew exactly what I was going to do. I didn't want to die now.'

At Auschwitz he saw his mother led away, but not to the gas-chamber. She was watching, unknown to Zvi, when he himself was marched off to a labour camp. 'In other words, I was taken to life and not immediately to death. For me the problem was to stay alive; I had made up my mind to survive. I was determined not to stay in Auschwitz. I did not want to have a number tattooed on my arm.' People were being selected to be sent to a labour camp at Baden, Bavaria. 'I tried very hard to get selected,' said Zvi 'and was!' I asked Zvi about the selection process. 'In my case there were a thousand people lined up. Then the prison officials came in and examined us body by body, looking for people fit to work. Some of the prisoners tried not to be selected because they suspected that if they were they would be taken to the gas-chambers. It became a sort of psychological game that everyone played differently. Everybody was guessing, but nobody knew the answer. On the whole, I would say that most people tried to be selected and not to stay behind.'

After a few weeks at Baden Zvi was moved on to a forced labour camp. It was December and despite the freezing cold the prisoners wore the scantiest clothing. 'Because I was a youngster,' Zvi went on, 'I was given easy work.' 'What kind?' I asked. 'Every evening I had to carry frozen corpses out of the camp and throw them into graves.' 'But a corpse is heavy?' 'Yes, but with a child walking in front and another behind it was considered to be easy work for us. And sometimes we were lucky – there was an old *Werhmacht* sergeant who seemed to be fond of us kids. He gave us crusts of bread and other titbits.' I asked Zvi, 'Why did people die?' 'Because,' he answered 'they were hungry, tired and frozen – the body couldn't stand any more. I don't know to this day how I managed with only a thin prison uniform to wear in temperatures of 15°C below zero.' One day while working in the forest he was so cold and exhausted that he just broke down and cried. 'I couldn't stand it any more.'

I asked Zvi, 'Did you live in constant fear of the gas-chamber?' 'Of course, I certainly did. They were always there. But I wasn't really scared because I was determined that I was going to make it, get out of the camp. There was a tremendous urge, part of myself, to overcome and take revenge. I don't know if other people were scared; they were panicky but that's not quite the same thing. There certainly must have been some people who were scared because the longer you wait the more time you have to think and then the more you fear.'

Zvi, with a lot of others, fell ill with a high fever. They were put on a train and travelled all day until after dark when, somewhere near Landsberg, Bavaria, the train juddered to a standstill. The RAF was overhead. Down below, the train guards panicked. In the confusion Zvi 'took off' and, with four others, ran for the woods. More soldiers arrived and began firing blindly in their direction. When the shooting stopped they split up and went their own way. Zvi spoke German fluently. The fever was still on him and he was as thin as a scarecrow. A German family took pity on him and for several months he worked as a farm-boy, sleeping in the hay-loft.

The Allies were advancing. Then General Leclerc's division reached Landsberg. Zvi was saved. 'I was adopted by the French boys. They gave me rations – chocolate and so on.' In time Zvi was able to contact the Zionist Youth Aliyah, who brought him to Palestine, then still under British mandate. There he received news that his mother was alive.

CHAPTER FIVE

To Hell by Train

When Russia, faced with Finland's refusal to cede part of its territory, attacked that country in November 1940, the Finns organized, with the help of the Swedes, another kind of deportation – of Finnish children, most of them under ten. In Stockholm, I talked to Anna Edvardsen, herself a Finn, who had got to know many of the children and has told their story in her book, *Finnish War Children, 1939–45*.

Anna explained to me that when Russia attacked Finland nine thousand Finnish children were 'deported' to Sweden. The 'winter war' ended in March 1940, but Finland again found herself at war when, in June 1941, Germany invaded Russia. Between then and 1948 a further fifty-five thousand children were transported to Sweden, where it was hoped they would grow up in safety. Many, like Pirrko O'Meara, did. She was four and her brother three when they were sent to Sweden. The war over, her parents asked for the children to be sent home to Finland. One day her Swedish 'grandma' showed her a photo of a very beautiful woman. 'She said it was my mother in Finland. I did not cry but I held the picture hard in my hand the whole evening and just looked at it. I could not understand that she was my mother.' Pirrko was thrilled at the idea of meeting her parents again. On the train to Finland a man came and sat beside her. He had a dictionary and tried to talk to Pirrko and her brother. Pirrko goes on, 'A woman told us that this was our father. That young man our father! I could not understand it.' Their mother, their real one, met them at the station. 'Mother was so slim and beautiful. She looked just like a young girl, not at all as we imagined mothers should look.' That night they all slept in the same bed. 'Father and Mother wanted us to experience the feeling of togetherness, despite the language difficulties.'

Unhappily, Pirrko's experience was not always shared by others, for whom the good intentions of the Finnish and Swedish authorities paved the way to prolonged hell. Anna Edvardsen thinks that the system itself was wrong and inhumanly cruel; children were sent to and fro between their Finnish parents and their Swedish foster-parents. They felt neither Finnish nor Swedish and did not know where they belonged. They were sneered at and humiliated by children of both sides. Separated from their real parents, the need for security – basic in all children – went unsatisfied. Without a proper knowledge of their mother-tongue they became not bi-lingual but half-lingual. Some ceased altogether to speak either Finnish or Swedish.

Anja's story is typical. Born in 1942, she returned, after two wonderful years in Sweden to a small village in North Finland. 'Nobody, including my family, could speak Swedish. I did not understand Finnish and so I was beaten. My mother was ashamed of me and tried to hide me.' When her sister was married, Anja was locked up in a room. 'I had to stay there when the others feasted and made merry.' When she was eighteen she ran away from home, back to Sweden. 'I immediately married a Swedish boy. Not from love, but from pure astonishment that somebody cared for me. I was so desperately starving for love. I feel neither Swedish nor Finnish.'

More pathetic still is the story of six-year-old Risto who, with his younger brother and sister, were carried away almost by violence to be sent to Sweden. Their mother promised to accompany them. Risto tells what happened at the quayside: 'She left us in a room saying she'd be back, but instead slipped away. I cried terribly and shouted that Mummy should be with us, but they just pulled me on board despite my desperate resistance.' In Sweden they continued by train. On arrival at the terminal station they all sat, holding hands, Risto in the middle, on a bench in the waiting-room. 'I had been told,' Risto explained 'that in wartime soldiers were very dangerous. So I nearly went out of my mind when a man in uniform, with sable boots and all, came up and grabbed my brother. "Risto, Risto," he cried, and stretched his arms after me.' But all Risto and his sister could do was to watch through the window as his little brother was put into a big black car. Then a woman came and led his sister away. 'Same thing with her – into a car and off.' Risto wondered, 'Does nobody want me?' and started crying. A little girl, about two years old, gave him a banana. 'That,' says Risto 'was the first kindness since I left home.' She was his future foster-sister.

No one seemed to realize how cruel was this system of selection, as if the children were like so many cattle. Juhani, then seven years old, related how, after the de-lousing station at Uppsala, he and other Finnish children were put on a train for the north. At each station the train stopped; the children were made to get out and people made their choice.

Juhani was still wondering if anybody would ever take him when the train reached Lapland. At last a couple took him. They had brought with them an empty pram. 'Probably because they hoped to get a baby,' Juhani remembers sadly. 'I had to push the pram all the way back to my foster-home.'

In the spring of 1940 Hitler launched the big offensive which would make him master of Europe. Neutral Denmark and Norway were his first victims.

Thirty-eight years later, almost to the day, I listened in Oslo to Randi, wife of the former Norwegian Prime Minister Trygve Bratteli, as she recalled the German attack on the capital in the early hours of 9 April 1940. 'Even today I experience the same feeling of terror and complete hopelessness which possessed me during the first hours of the attack,' she told me. Her terror was only natural, for she was then fifteen and very much in love with life. More than anything, Randi felt *safe*, safe with her parents and brothers, safe with her friends. Only one thought plagued her continually: some time before a man had come to visit her father. He had only recently been released from Oranienburg, one of Hitler's most infamous camps. 'He told us the most dreadful things,' Randi said. 'And long after I had gone to bed I would lie in the dark thinking about them. I felt so lonely and thought how painful and incomprehensible it was that human beings could plague and torment their fellow-beings like that.' But these black thoughts vanished with the dawn of another day and life again felt as wonderful as ever – until the small hours of that morning of 9 April, when the screaming of the sirens woke Randi.

She and her brothers all tumbled out of bed and their father told them, 'Dress as quickly as possible and go down to the shelter' – an improvised one rigged up in the cellar of their block of flats. Randi was trembling so much with fear that she could hardly get her clothes on.

Her father, director of Oslo's biggest newspaper, disappeared into the darkness saying he was going to the office, and she wondered when she would next see him. Later that morning, as black-crossed German bombers swept low over the city, Randi clutched her mother, weeping. But a fire began to kindle within her. 'I felt a burning, boundless hatred towards Hitler and his men, towards the traitor Quisling.'

Next morning, as Randi and her mother wandered from room to room of their flat, there was a ring at the door. They stood transfixed: the Gestapo, so soon? But no, it was a friend to warn them to leave Oslo. They packed but the barest necessities; Randi took with her photos of ski-ing holidays, happy memories which she feared the war would destroy. She cried as she left the flat, sure that she would never return. (She did, and her parents are still living there.) They managed to get on a train going to Hamar. There they found Randi's father again; he had already organized a radio news service with the help of his staff, who had fled with him. One of them was Trygve Bratteli, Randi's future husband. Another was Rut Brandt. Randi told me she will never forget how kind and helpful he was in those dark days when the Nazis invaded her country. After the war he became world-famous — as German Chancellor Willi Brandt.

Randi went on, 'We fled further north, sleeping in corridors and on living-room floors, feeling people's solidarity. We wept over the places that had to surrender, over the towns bombed to smithereens.' When the train stopped at a wayside station called Harpefoss her father left them. He was going farther north to continue the fight. After a night spent in a wash-house Randi crept out at daybreak to find she was in a deep valley whose steep sides sloped up to the blue sky. 'The beauty of it was overwhelming.' It obliterated all the terrors of the last few days. With her mother she stayed in that valley all summer, listening to the news bulletins, hoping, trusting. But by June all was over; Norway had to capitulate. Her brothers had to flee to Sweden. Randi returned to Oslo, where she found her father again. Two years later he was arrested and sent to Germany — by train, of course, one of those trains of sealed cattle-wagons bound for a concentration camp. All these years after, Randi remembered vividly how she felt, as a teenage girl. She told me simply, 'Nothing in the whole world was safe any more.'

And so for five years those dreadful trains, crammed with thirsting, starving, suffocating and often frozen human beings rounded up in Norway, Denmark, Holland, Belgium and France, rolled eastwards towards Germany and the concentration camps — and back, for yet more victims.

Mme D. and her husband were members of an escape-line, handing on Allied prisoners to neutral frontiers and freedom, until one day there came the hammering on the door that everyone dreaded. Before the Gestapo led them away she was able to whisper to her ten-year-old son, Francis, 'Listen to me carefully, *mon chéri*; you know nothing, you've seen nothing. We shall be back.' But her husband was to die — kicked to death — in Gross-Rosen camp. When, after three years in Ravensbrück and Mauthausen camps, she herself returned, her boy shrank from her in horror. 'That's not my mother,' he screamed. 'I never had a mother like that. It's a scarecrow.' Mme D. weighed less than six stone.

In 1940 Edith K. was living in Brussels with her parents, Polish Jews who had immigrated eleven years earlier. On 10 May, the day that Hitler violated Belgium's (and Holland's and Luxemburg's) neutrality with his Panzers and parachutists, Edith's father told her gravely, 'We are at war.' Edith, who was only seven, did not know what 'war' meant; but she realized that something terrible had happened. Her parents decided to flee and they all left Brussels in a goods train. When it stopped near the frontier they continued on foot towards France. Not far away they saw Dunkirk burning. Soon after, they were captured by the Germans and sent back to Brussels. There, for two years, Edith's father, who was a linotypist, worked with the clandestine press – until one day he was denounced and arrested. Ten days later two men in civilian clothes – they seemed to Edith very polite and kind – called at the flat to see her mother, who left with them, telling Edith, 'They are just friends of Papa.' But Edith understood immediately. She never saw her parents again, only long afterwards she received, through the Red Cross, her mother's wrist-watch. It had been recovered from Auschwitz. 'They could not have survived long,' Edith thinks, 'for they were in poor health.'

From the train which took them to Auschwitz her parents had managed to throw a postcard on which they asked Edith's grandparents to hide her in the country. She spent the rest of the war at Famenne, in the Ardennes, with a baker and his wife. Edith felt not the slightest embarrassment in telling everyone she met that she was Jewish. She had no idea what significance that word had, but simply wanted to let people know so that they could get to like her. Her foster-parents explained the great risk that both she and they were running and implored her never again to mention the word 'Jewish'. 'But it was more than I could do to hide the truth. And anyway the nuns and the villagers were all so kind to me.'

After the war Edith lacked the money to realize her dream of a university education, and as she grew up she experienced that strange phenomenon among survivors, a feeling of guilt at not having perished with the rest. She reproached herself that she had not died with her parents at Auschwitz. For years it made her miserable. Then at last she found happiness with the man she loves. 'I wept as I wrote this to you,' Edith confessed to me, 'but perhaps it will be of some use.' I know it will and that is why I tell Edith's story.

CHAPTER SIX

Raïa, the Girl with the Yellow Star

They were numberless, those boys and girls who suffered under the Nazis. In France, whole families were seized, packed into 'Black Marias' and transported to one of two sorting camps: Drancy or Pithiviers.

Drancy, in the northern suburbs of Paris, was good for all sorts, Jew and Gentile, rich and poor, elegant young women, students, schoolchildren and babes in arms. The camp commandant, *Kapitän* Brunner, had one obsession: to load his deportation trains to capacity. A 'passenger' who fell sick at the last moment was replaced on the spot. Failing that, Brunner himself would scour the streets in his own car and grab a few Jews, adults or children, it did not matter, to fill the gaps. Failing everything, the sick deportee was dispatched willy-nilly. If he, or she, died on the way that was none of Brunner's business. He had loaded the train to capacity, that was all that mattered. Many children were delighted as they climbed aboard the train and screamed with excitement when the whistle went and it chugged off.

Pithiviers, a picturesque small town north of Orléans known in happier times for its *pâtés d'alouette*, honey and almond cakes, had become a place of dread. Pithiviers was essentially a camp for mothers and children, or more specifically where children, clinging to the skirt or even the breasts of their mothers, were torn from them, never to see them again. Every two or three days a train, fully loaded, left for Germany. To the fiends in charge of loading this human cargo, it mattered nothing if a mother was despatched alone without her children, or whether it was she who remained behind the barbed wire while her children were locked into the cattle-wagons. As at Drancy, the essential was that the wagons should be packed full. If any room remained, the orphans' *crèche* would supply the necessary bodies, small though they were, to fill the vacant space.

Then there was the Rothschild Foundation Hospital, the only one which the Nazis had left open to Jews. But the hospital was not the refuge that the Nazis pretended it to be. It was more like a charnel-house where men and women, boys and girls, whether they were Jewish or not, were dumped after staggering forth from the Gestapo's torture chambers, to be resuscitated or just to die.

Many were those – teachers, curates and others – who took enormous risks to hide threatened children. One little girl – call her Jeanne – Probably owes her life to *Pasteur* Jean J. of the Mission Populaire Evangélique and his helpers. Jeanne was as happy as could be until 1940 when the Nazis entered Paris. She was ten and from then on everything changed. 'Besides that frightful yellow star we had to wear, there were all the *verboten* things: forbidden to ride with other passengers in the métro – only the last carriage was for us; forbidden to go to the cinema and the theatre; forbidden to shop at the same time as other people – we had to wait for hours and, needless to say, there was hardly anything left.' The whole family lived in constant fear of being denounced, of hearing that dreaded thumping on the door which announced the Gestapo.

In 1943 Jeanne's three elder brothers slipped away and joined the *Résistance*. But Jeanne, now thirteen, and her little brother and sister were too young to leave. Jeanne's mother, in case the worst happened, had prepared a little bag for each child. 'We were ready,' said Jeanne '*pieds et poings liés* [tied as we were hand and foot], for no one could help us. We knew we could count only on ourselves, like those ill-fated heroes of the Warsaw ghetto.'

In 1944, to add to the round-ups, the terror and the restrictions, came the daily air-raids. Jeanne says: 'And then out of the darkness there came for my mother, my sister and me a gleam of light: someone had found us a refuge.' In a marvellous château, surrounded by a great park, *Pasteur* Jean J. and a handful of teachers, both men and women, were defying the Gestapo and hiding a hundred Jewish children. 'They had accepted this terrible responsibility to enable us to escape the death-camps and survive until the day of liberation. Each of us had a false name, a forged ration card and little did we realize what a terrible problem it was for them to feed us all, to keep us warm, to hide us and, above all, create an atmosphere in which we could forget the past, learn again how to live and to play. Thanks to our *Pasteur* we were there to welcome the Americans when they arrived at the end of August 1944. At last we were safe from those black vultures of the Gestapo and the SS. Life began again.'

Another little girl, saved with Jeanne from the Nazi terror, said to me years later: 'Who can ever forget those marvellous years of youth, when everything seems possible and life is good and love seems to reign in the world. In me these feelings were completely killed.'

And then there was Raïa. She lived at Tours with her mother, her fifteen-year-old sister and her baby brother. Her father had just died. In 1941 the family were summoned to the Police Commissariat where they were each given a yellow star. Only her brother, aged two, was excused this humiliation. Raïa's star had an extraordinary effect on her schoolmates – even those she had known all her short life and whose parents were friendly with hers. Now they simply turned their backs. (Only later did she learn that they did so because their parents were afraid that their children might be arrested with their Jewish friends. The Gestapo were not too particular when it came to details.)

With all the anti-Semitic propaganda and restrictions, the family was reduced to poverty. The curfew kept them at home after six p.m. They lived permanently in fear of their lives. Then came the first deportations; Drancy became a dreaded name and hatred crept into people's hearts.

At six p.m. on 15 July 1942, when the curfew fell, Raïa and her family shut themselves in. Her mother, who was ill, was already in bed when they heard the sound of tramping boots outside. The Gestapo were there. Her mother had to get out of bed to pack a few things, 'just enough for the journey,' said the Gestapo officer. 'You will be given all you need later.' Raïa's mother pleaded, 'I'm ill, please let me stay with my children!' 'They will be going with you,' came the curt answer. And the little family was led outside. Seals were set on the door.

Exactly the same thing was going on one floor above with the family of Raïa's friend, Annie. (Annie's father had already been deported.) The two families were assembled in the street and loaded into a bus. But there was not enough room. 'Wait there,' the Gestapo man ordered. 'We'll be back to fetch you.' So Raïa and her baby brother, thirteen-year-old Annie and her brother, aged nine, were left behind. Raïa continues, 'What could we four children do? I won't go into the screams and the tears and all the rest of it. I will leave you to imagine what a human being, be he father, mother or child, feels in such a situation. When you are a toddler like my brother you are still very dependent on your mother. I thought my little brother would never stop crying.'

So there they were, two teenage girls with their small brothers. 'We were very lightly dressed because of the heat; never before had our parents left us alone; we could not get into the house; we had no money. The instinct of self-preservation made us decide to run for it before they came back to look for us.' But where could they go? The best thing seemed to be to make for the banks of the Loire. So off they went, hugging the walls, trying to hide their yellow stars. 'I had the greatest trouble keeping my brother quiet,' said Raïa. 'He had wet his pants and was crying for Mummy. We were terrified that he would attract attention, so we hid behind a pile of scrap metal.' Annie and Raïa thought of all the non-Jewish people they knew who might help them. Finally they decided to call on a Polish family. But the Poles, terrified at the sight of the children, slammed the door in their faces. So they returned to the river bank and there spent a sleepless night.

After another council of war an idea struck Annie. When her father was deported his *patron* had been very kind. She would go and see him. Some hours later the children had been spirited unseen into the house, thoroughly washed and their filthy clothes exchanged for new ones. Then one of the firm's lorries took them to a quiet village where they were hidden in the school. In the evening men would call on the schoolmistress and Raïa would hear them singing, very loudly, the 'Volga Boatmen'. She then realized that the singing was merely to cover the BBC news from London. They were members of the *Résistance*, which explains why, after a week, the schoolmistress told the children they must leave.

They returned to the riverside. As Raïa's little brother refused to leave her side Annie went alone to see the lady at the creamery in Tours where their mothers always went. She returned with a huge omelette and a loaf. And so on, day after day, until the creamery lady found them a *passeur*, a guide. He agreed to take them secretly into unoccupied territory. Disguised as a priest he met them at the bus terminal. The children had no idea where they were going, but when, after driving some way, they saw the priest making ready to get off they knew that they, too, must get off at the next stop. It was only then that Raïa realized that the score of people who got off with them all belonged to the priest's flock. As the bus drove away he explained to them that, to avoid German checkpoints farther on, they had now to walk another thirty kilometres across country.

That walk was pure torture for fourteen-year-old Raïa. She had to carry her small brother all the way. No one else offered to do so – even if they had, he would have refused to leave his sister. After a while he fell asleep, but that only made him feel heavier to Raïa who lagged more and more behind. She caught up only when the others stopped to eat. As they opened their packets of sandwiches the children watched, having nothing to eat themselves, though someone was generous enough to give them half a tomato to share.

Night fell and the *passeur* told them, 'Stick together, for if someone sees us in the distance they'll take us for a tree or a bush.' They moved on and Raïa's torture began again. She had eaten practically nothing and was exhausted. Her sandalled feet, cut by the bristly corn-stubble, were sore and bleeding. Her brother felt heavier and heavier and in the pitch dark she kept on losing contact with the others. By peering ahead into the obscurity she could just discern what looked like a tree moving and she knew it was one of the party. To add to the terrors of that night the alarm was often raised as they passed close to a village. Dogs barked, whistles blew and occasionally a flare rose into the sky. Everyone would then flatten themselves on the ground and Raïa had almost to suffocate her brother to stop him screaming. Yet those terrifying moments were in one way a blessing – they allowed her time to regain her strength.

Finally the *passeur* halted them. 'We are now three hundred metres from the demarcation line,' he told them. 'I have pointed out the road to this young couple. Just follow them.' As soon as he was gone the couple told the children, 'We grown-ups are going to rest a bit here. As your pace is slower than ours you go ahead and we'll catch you up in ten minutes.' And they showed them the direction. The children set off but as after some time there was no sign of the others they retraced their steps to where they had left them. But there was nothing to be seen, save an umbrella that one of the party had forgotten. The children were aghast at having been left in the lurch. Then it struck them. 'We suddenly realized,' Raïa told me, 'that the grown-ups had sent us off on purpose in the wrong direction. They wanted to get rid of us, the weak ones of the party for, who knows, we might have ruined everything at the last moment.'

Not knowing where to go they just walked on and on until at last they saw houses ahead. Help at last! But suddenly every dog in the neighbourhood began barking. 'In a panic,' Raïa said 'we knocked at one door after another, but no one answered. Yet as I knocked I called out, "We are only children so don't be afraid. We are lost . . ." Finally, from behind a door, came a man's voice, "You are five kilometres from the line. Be careful – a patrol comes this way every two hours. There's nothing I can do to help you."' So the little ones staggered on until, on the outskirts of the village, they found a barn. There they sank into the hay utterly exhausted. And the barking of the dogs died away.

At dawn next day a farmer appeared and threw them out. All day they lay hidden in the undergrowth by the roadside. Once a German soldier came past on a horse and Raïa trembled. 'Once again I nearly had to suffocate my brother for fear he might cry.' They were all in a sorry state, clothes torn and bodies covered with scratches which drew swarms of flies. They pushed on and Raïa spotted a farm which somehow looked friendly. A young woman welcomed her, sat her and her brother down before two huge bowls of milk. She was so sweet that Raïa poured out her story. The young woman pointed to a house with a red roof. 'It is in the unoccupied zone. You have five kilometres to do without a scrap of cover. You must try it during the midday meal when the Germans are less alert.'

So those two brave, obstinate little girls, Raïa and Annie, with their charges, set off on the last perilous stage of their journey to freedom. Raïa's brother refused to walk – he was too tired. So was she. But he was a piece of baggage she could not abandon. She lifted him up and stumbled on across the rough, parched fields. The midday sun was scorching and she felt a terrible thirst. More and more often she had to stop and rest so that soon she was far behind Annie. Then the famous red roof came closer; she could even make out the house. Annie and her brother were almost there. Watching them Raïa knew she could go no farther. She collapsed and sat there on the ground, her brother beside her, for she knows not how long, unable to make any movement. Raïa thought it was the end. 'From the red-roofed house Annie and her brother were waving. They were saved – I felt I could never make it. I got up slowly, picked up my brother and began walking, but only very slowly. The house seemed a little nearer, when I saw some men on a haystack waving frantically. I don't know how I reached them, for the next thing I knew was people all around me. Someone was washing my feet. They told me that I had crossed the road just behind five German soldiers with two dogs. The peasants were terrified they would devour us.'

The children were safe though Raïa's ordeal was far from ended. She, and her brother clinging to her, were passed on from hand to hand – at fearful risk to themselves and their saviours – until the war ended. It was only then that Raïa heard about the German extermination camps. Until then she had never lost hope of seeing her mother and elder sister again. But the only trace of them that ever reached her was an official paper which said: deported from Tours, 15 July 1942. Died at Auschwitz, 20 July 1942.

Raïa and her brother had escaped a similar fate because there was no room in the Gestapos' bus. Modestly, but with complete truth, Raïa says: 'There's nothing extraordinary about my story. All those who escaped the Nazi man-hunt owe their survival to a variety of miracles.'

Not every child was able to endure as much – like the two French war orphans, a boy of four and his two-year-old sister. Since birth they had known only the atmosphere of the battlefield and bombardments. In September 1943 they were smuggled across the frontier into Switzerland. Frightened, half-starved and exhausted, they were taken in by a baker of Delemont, near Basle, and his wife, who washed and fed the children and put them to bed. Hand-in-hand the children fell asleep. When morning came the couple went to wake them. There lay the two little ones, still holding hands, sleeping on – for eternity. The heart of each one had broken under the strain.

CHAPTER SEVEN

The Children of Jastrebarsko

Until the Nazis' murderous air attack on Rotterdam on 14 May 1940, the British and German bomber forces had mutually withheld their fire on inland targets. But after Hitler had himself initiated the bombing of Rotterdam, Churchill, next day, 15 May, ordered British bombers to attack industrial targets in the German Ruhr. It was an open invitation to Hitler to bomb London and anywhere else in Britain he chose.

From then on the war against children was to be carried by both sides into the heart of towns and cities. However hard the bombers tried, and sometimes they didn't, to hit well-defined military and industrial targets, their bombs were bound to kill and maim civilians and their children. Tacitly the Allies acknowledged as much; the Germans were more specific. In Berlin, on 4 September 1940, Hitler told an audience of frenzied, applauding women, 'When they [the British] declare that they will increase their attacks on our cities, then we will *raze* their cities to the ground.' And the objective was clearly defined by the *Luftwaffe* Commander-in-Chief, Goering: 'Progressive and complete annihilation of London.'

'Complete annihilation' meant that every building in London was a target. One of them, the school at Ardgowan road, Hither Green, was the target annihilated one day in September 1940 while fifty children were in class. Constable Ernest Hooper was among the rescuers. 'The carnage was indescribable,' he said. 'There were children lying all over the playground, some dismembered, some partially buried, some simply blown to pieces. One little girl was crying all the time because she had blood in her eyes and couldn't see. She had nothing left to see with.' A little girl about the same tender age as Goering's pretty daughter, Edda. But no such thought occurred to Goering. He was in raptures as, from his headquarters at Cap Gris-Nez, he telephoned to his wife. 'You've heard already, Emmy? Yes, it has been a wonderful day. I've sent my bombers to London. London's in flames!'

And not only London, for his bombers were killing children in important towns up and down Britain. And not only important towns. Petworth, the sleepy Sussex market-town, had no importance whatever, at least militarily. But one day a low-flying German bomber dropped a stick of bombs across it. One made a direct hit on the boys' school, killing twenty-nine pupils.

Defenceless, without protection – that is the predicament of children when armed men make war against them – which they did with increasing ferocity on land and in the air until the end of World War II. Though the assault on London continued until 1944, the most savage of all attacks was launched on the night of 10 May 1941 by five hundred Nazi bombers. High-explosive and incendiaries engulfed the city in fire – or, rather, 2,200 separate fires – and 1,436 civilians died.

Less than four years later the Anglo-American bomber force, with greater numbers and improved techniques for blasting and burning, was able, at Dresden, to immolate nearly one hundred times that number. Of the wind sown by Hitler the unfortunate Germans and their children were left to reap the appalling, fiery whirlwind.

1,436 civilians killed by Nazi airmen in a night. By an odd and mournful coincidence exactly that number were murdered by Nazi soldiers in one afternoon, in the small Greek town of Calavryta. They included all the male citizens over fifteen years of age. Fifteen, when a boy is on the verge of life and his head full of dreams – the last of which is to be placed against a wall and be killed by a bullet in the heart.

In November 1940 Benito Mussolini had launched the assault on Greece. When his legions were checked, then repulsed by the Greeks, his friend, Hitler, came to the rescue. By the end of April 1941 the Greeks were overpowered. The Nazis then set about them. Train-loads were sent to Auschwitz, while thousands more Greek patriots were exterminated on the spot. At Distomon the Nazis varied their sadistic style: there, fourteen babies and forty-two children were among the two hundred victims of an abominable massacre. Those able to escape fled to the mountains where they lived in caves. When rescued later the children had become like animals, unable to speak a human language.

In order to attack Greece, Nazi forces had to pass through Hungary, Romania and Bulgaria. The latter two sided wholeheartedly with Hitler; Hungary, after many vacillations, did likewise. The three countries came under Hitler's domination. From them, in April 1941, Hitler's troops invaded Yugoslavia, marching on into Greece to give the *coup de grâce*.

The characteristic signs of Nazi occupation were soon evidenced in

Yugoslavia. Gallows were set up, concentration camps built. As usual, children received no mercy: they were imprisoned, executed or sent to concentration camps. They were thrown alive into rivers and chasms, massacred or done to death in gas chambers. Before their eyes, their parents, brothers and sisters were tortured and killed. Twelve-year-old Dora Sekulić, fleeing with her mother and young brother and sisters, saw what happerend when, at night, they took refuge in a hut. 'I could not sleep. Somebody screamed and I raised my head. The hut was on fire.' Mother and children ran outside. Only to be confronted by Nazi soldiers. As the hut burned Dora noticed that the flames were reflected in the Germans' eyes, giving them a bloodshot look. 'They stared at us and seemed to pierce us with their eyes.' The Nazis then ordered the children and their mother to jump into the blaze. 'We held Mamma's dress tightly. A Nazi threw her into the snow, shouting, "Wait, you old sow, the little ones are going to burn first."' A soldier then grabbed Dora's little sister and dragged her towards the fire. 'The staring eyes of the little one were looking towards Mamma.' It was at that very moment that shots rang out close by. The partisans had arrived! The Nazi fiends disappeared into the dark. 'We left,' Dora said, 'as if we had risen from the dead.'

Pursued by the Nazis another mother, Boja, tried to destroy, with her own hand, her children and herself. When the Nazis killed her father and set her house on fire she fled with her five children. As she came to the river Una she told them, 'We are all going to drown ourselves so that the Nazis won't catch us alive.' Tearing herself loose from the clinging arms of her two youngest she flung them into the river. The other three clung to her skirts, held her by the knees, pulled her back. 'I struggled thus with my life and theirs.' The children were too strong for Boja. 'Mamma, let's flee into the woods and find our way to the partisans.' They found them and Boja worked in a partisan children's home until, in 1944, she died of typhoid fever.

The Nazis took it upon themselves to set up so-called children's homes in Yugoslavia. The three most notorious were at Stara Gradiska, Sisak and Jastrebarsko. Under a scheme called 'Removal of Refugees from Danger Areas' Yugoslav children were sent to these places, which were run by the Ustashas, Yugoslav collaborators. Stara Gradiska received children with their mothers, who were then forcibly separated from their offspring and sent on to forced labour in Germany. If a mother was stubborn she would be allowed to board the train with her children who, *en route*, would be seized, leaving her to continue on her way to the German labour camp. But normally the separation would proceed to the satisfaction of the Ustashas, who lodged the little ones in a cellar or attic where, without food or care, they died or were 'rescued' to suffer some other fate. Dragica Habazid, a Yugoslav Red Cross nurse, visited Stara Gradiska on 9 June 1942. She was shown into the 'hospital for children' in which she found the young inmates lying on the bare floor. 'In the corner there were chamber-pots and on each squatted a child looking like a ghost or a corpse.' Coming to a door, Dragica opened it, then drew back in horror. 'Little skeleton-like corpses of children came rolling down into the "hospital".' Behind that door was the 'store' for dead children, who were carried out and deposited there by their sick comrades.

One of the internees of Stara Gradiska, Ljubica Bobrinic-Saga, records: 'Tomorrow is the Poglavnik's birthday. It must be celebrated becomingly ... tonight one hundred Serbian children were butchered as well as five hundred Serbian women who were unfit to work in Germany.'

When Yugoslav Red Cross nurse, Jana Koh, visited Sisak she was told by Dr Najza, the administrator, that the children lodged in the Salt Works were 'healthy'. Their state of health is described by Jana: 'They had not eaten all day. They were covered with sores and scabs.' The children stank unbearably, their eyes were inflamed and the sound of their weeping sent a melancholy echo among those cold, salt-encrusted walls. In the Quarantine Block, on the bare floor, lay four hundred children, crying inconsolably for their mothers, who lay but a few steps away, guarded by Nazi sentries. They had come to nurse their children for the last time. When they were brought together the little ones flung their arms about their mother's neck, sucked greedily at her breasts and, sated, fell asleep. The mothers departed in silence, save for a few words whispered to the Red Cross workers: 'Take care of our children ...' That night another train, full of childless mothers left for Germany.

The 'Children's Home' at Jastrebarsko was there before the war; it was run by nuns of the Congregation of St Vincent de Paul, under the direction of the Prioress of the Convent, Pulherija Barta. Professor Kamilo Bresler vividly remembered the arrival, in July 1942, of the first children from Stara Gradiska, where they had been taken from their mothers. 'When the doors of the cattle-trucks were opened ... we saw a hundred childish forms squatting or lying in heaps on the floor ... As soon as we took them out ... and put them on the ground they would squat like terrified birds.' When carrying the children the professor was struck by their lightness. 'They were living skeletons. In their armpits they carried pieces of bread – they were too weak to eat it.' The Professor and his colleagues tried to find out from the children their names in order to inform their parents. But when asked, 'the children looked at us in terror', said the professor, 'and hid under the blankets without answering.' This reflex came from bitter experience: their names would give away their fathers and relatives who had joined the Partisans. So the Partisan children remained silent till they died, unknown victims of Nazism.

The religious brethren and sisters used to press the children to declare their religion, their pretext being that, if they were not Catholics, they could not be buried in a Catholic cemetery; Prioress Barta had taken care to have a hole dug beyond the cemetery walls for the 'Partisan vermin', as she called them. Each evening the dying children were subjected to an inquisition.

A girl of fifteen lay in Ward Three; her body was so emaciated that she seemed lighter than her pillow; her two bright eyes, following every movement around her, were the only sign that she was alive. The sister in charge, Lina Padovan, asked her name. 'It does not matter,' murmured the girl, 'I'm going to die anyway.' But the following night she called for Lina. 'My name is Danica; I'm from Cerovljani,' she whispered into Lina's ear. But the prioress had overheard. That evening the priest, cross in hand and muttering inaudibly some incantation, entered the ward. Behind him a nun swung a censer, filling the room with reeking smoke. A shrill cry went up from the children as they buried themselves under the bedclothes in terror. Only Danica lay there calmly and with her big eyes stared at the priest as he clutched the bedrail and, his body swaying back and forth, intoned incessantly, 'Danica, return, back to God . . . tell me when you last received Holy Communion . . . when you last confessed. Danica . . .' And he stressed the name that the girl had refused to utter . . . except to Lina. But Danica just kept on staring at him and did not utter a sound. At last the priest withdrew and Lina hurried to Danica's bedside. She took her hand, begging her not to believe that it was she who had betrayed her. But in Danica's eyes were only reproof and contempt. She snatched her hand away from Lina's and turned over, facing the wall. That night, her face still to the wall, she died.

With Western Europe, the Balkans and Greece secured and the invasion of Britain postponed *sine die*, Hitler was now ready to realize a long-cherished dream – the conquest and colonization of Russia, which naturally involved, on the Führer's orders, the 'destruction of the Russians as a people'. As part of this attempt, Hitler's men reduced to ashes nine thousand Russian villages.

In the titanic struggle which began in June 1941 two cities, Leningrad and Stalingrad (now Volgograd), have a special significance: they withstood the invader. Stalingrad symbolizes the valour of the Russian fighting men, Leningrad the heroic steadfastness of the Russian people, its children included. The city was encircled and besieged from August 1941 until January 1944, nearly two and a half years. Leningrad did not surrender, though starvation alone killed well over half a million of its citizens – that means tens of thousands of children. The stories of a handful of them were told by Ales Adamovich and Daniil Granin in *The Blockade Book*; extracts from this were reprinted in *Sputnik*, 1978, under the title 'Children and War'.

Cold, fear and above all hunger were the most impelling forces, to which children reacted in their own way. One little boy took life – and death – quite philosophically. L. A. Manykin describes how, leaving his home one day, he found the boy huddled by the gate. 'What are you doing here?' he asked him. 'I've come here to die,' replied the boy. 'To die? But just look at you! If you could walk here you're not dying. Where do you live?' 'On the Moika,' the boy told him. 'Our yard is very dark and it's dark inside the flat. But look how light it is here! So I came here to die.' Manykin and his daughters took the boy into their house, gave him warm water to drink, some small crusts and joiner's glue. The boy told them, 'If I live I shall always eat this glue.'

The privations suffered by the citizens of Leningrad drove them to both the basest and the noblest actions, though discipline and self-sacrifice prevailed, not least among the youngest. Irina Kuryaeva was in the children's hospital when another little girl was brought in and laid next to her. The girl, who was dying, said to Irina, 'Please eat my bread [a meagre ration of 125 grams]. I won't live till tomorrow.' Irina goes on, 'I couldn't sleep all night because I was thinking: "Should I take the bread, or shouldn't I?" I was terribly hungry and it was an awful struggle with myself. I didn't take it in the end. The girl died and the piece of bread remained under her pillow.'

Throughout the siege most people tried to keep up the pretence of a normal life and this helped them to survive. Marina Tkacheva's mother made her children brush their teeth every day – not with tooth-powder, of which there was none, but with charcoal. The family's proudest act of self-denial was to resist eating the cat – which became so scrawny anyway, that it was practically uneatable. But that did not lessen the family's joy at their own and the cat's survival.

On 7 December 1941, six months after Germany's invasion of Russia,

Japan attacked the U.S. fleet at anchor in Pearl Harbor. Within a few months the Japanese had overrun the Philippines and the British and Dutch colonies, from Hong Kong and Burma to Borneo and beyond; from Singapore to the Celebes, Sumatra and Java. Apart from the Allied fighting men who fell into Japanese hands thousands of civilians and their children were interned, generally in the harshest conditions.

When, in February 1942, the Japanese invaded Java, Jeannette, a Dutch girl, then six years old, was living with her parents in Surabaya. The Japanese soldiers, at bayonet point, drove her and her mother into an enclosure. Shortly afterwards they and other families were put into a train and transported to a camp at Semarang. Though the distance was only seventy-five miles they were on the train for several days – in a temperature of 40°C with hardly anything to eat or drink. Halfway, they stopped and were shut into a Roman Catholic church. There, the boys, ten years old or more were dragged away from their mothers amidst hysterical scenes, to be sent to a camp for men. Some mothers tried to kill their boys and themselves, but, Jeannette told me, 'The soldiers did it for them.' She went on, 'After the boys had been dragged away there remained an atmosphere of panic and horror. I am reminded of it to this day whenever I enter a church.'

The train moved on to Semarang. Jeannette, who often saw women beaten and raped, thought 'The Japanese must be the worst oppressors.' But, with no experience then of other oppressors, she could not know that they are all, in the end, as cruel as one another.

When Jeannette was finally liberated she was ten years old. Disease had ravaged her small body and she was now a skeleton. She had never been to school. So traumatized is she still that she concludes, 'I am still very frightened at the idea of another war. Should there ever be one I should kill myself and my children.'

When, early in 1942, the Japanese landed at Sangihe, a small island then belonging to the Dutch, North of the Celebes, in the Indonesian Archipelago, they did not at first bother the Europeans, among them fourteen-year-old Emma Csesko and her parents. But, because Emma's father had helped some wounded Allied soldiers, the Japanese put him in prison, where he died. Then they arrested Emma's mother. They forced Emma to look on every day for two months while her mother was tortured. When, finally, she was decapitated Emma was present.

So Emma was now left alone to look after her younger sister, Eva, and her two small brothers, Guyla and Joseph. The four children were the only whites on the island but, with the help of a kind Indonesian woman, Emma managed somehow to find enough for them to eat. Then, one day in March 1945, the children watched amazed as a Catalina flying-boat alighted just offshore. Out of it came soldiers and an Englishman, Richard Hardwick. 'He said he had come to rescue us,' Emma explained – as if it were necessary!

Richard Hardwick, so a friend of his, Hazel Furzey, tells me, was a wonderful character. Although in his sixties he was chosen for these hazardous missions to rescue people like Emma and her family under the very noses of the Japanese. Of Emma's rescue Richard Hardwick said, 'We could hear the guns of the Japanese a few miles away. The children were so weak that they had to be carried. On the beach we were surrounded by the locals, begging to be taken aboard the "Cat".' In the end, the flying-boat was so overloaded that it only took off at the third attempt. 'By then,' said Hardwick, 'the Japs had arrived. No doubt they killed all those we had to leave behind on the beach.'

The last chapter of Emma's story is the most touching. Before the war her parents had been very friendly with a missionary couple, the van der Beeks. Between them the families had made a pact that if anything happened to the parents of one, the other couple would adopt their children. It was thus that Emma, her brothers and sister were brought back to Holland by the van der Beeks. 'I had known their eldest boy, Gerard, since we played together in Sangihe,' Emma related. 'I think I must always have loved him, because as soon as I saw him again in Holland I felt certain we would get married one day.' And that is exactly what happened.

After Pearl Harbor the Japanese rounded up civilians of the Allied countries living in all the Chinese provinces they already occupied. That is why a little girl, not quite five – we will call her Josette – found herself with her father, a Belgian, her Russian mother and her small brother behind barbed wire at Weihsien, about three hundred miles south-west of Peking, along with other Belgians and French, English and Americans. There began for Josette the happiest time of her life (though not for her mother and father).

At Tientsin, where the family lived, Josette had been woken up in the middle of the night and told she was off on an unexpected journey. She was delighted, the more so because her father was coming too. At the station she played happily among the crowd who waited, sitting on their baggage looking emptily into space.

The camp at Weihsien was a one-time Protestant mission, now surrounded by a six-foot wall topped with electrified barbed wire, with watch-towers at convenient intervals. Two thousand prisoners lived in the camp, the only place, with Hong Kong, in the whole Pacific where families were allowed to remain together. With her friends and the games they played together Josette felt that she was part of a happy family. The Japanese soldiers, who obviously loved children, were always kind to them. 'We teased them, creeping up behind them to touch them. They always laughed and gave us drawing chalks which we loved, for there were no pencils or paper available. So, with the chalks, we used to draw pictures on the walls.'

Now six, Josette became fascinated by the wall, which fascinated everybody. For the prisoners two worlds existed: one within the walls, the other beyond. The Chinese would come and sell them eggs and other supplies, pushing them through holes in the wall, or throwing them over the top. One day Josette climbed up the wall. 'But all I could see was fields and Chinese children playing.' It seemed to her that the grown-ups were even more obsessed by the 'outside'. One of them climbed to the top of a very tall tree so that he could see as far as possible. The branch broke and he was killed. Josette was also fascinated by the birds. '*They* could fly over and beyond the wall. What luck! Jays, magpies and most of all the golden oriole, rarer than the others, and oh! what a beautiful sight against the setting sun.' Soap bubbles had the same fascination, as they floated upwards on the warm evening air as high as the tree-tops, then drifted away beyond the wall. Aeroplanes, too, had the same magic.

One day after nearly three years inside the walls Annie, a tall young Dutch girl, came running. 'The war's over!' she shouted, and Josette remembers so well her long legs and her excited voice. No one would believe her, but a few days later confirmation arrived in the shape of a huge silver aeroplane which zoomed over the camp. Josette had a strange feeling and everyone in the camp, she noticed, began to behave in the strangest way. They all yelled and jumped in the air, laughed crazily, cried, rushed through the camp gates into the fields – free at last from the prison walls. 'I too cried – because my lovely world had ceased to exist.'

Josette still feels that, as a child, her life was a normal and happy one. There were no tortures and all the worries and anxieties were borne by the grown-ups. The children, thanks to the International Red Cross, had all they needed in the way of rations. They were free to play as they wished, surrounded as they were by the wall. They formed a real little society with its laws and its games. It was only when, with her parents, she left the camp that Josette felt sad.

Josette's story is really the story of everyone who knows of a world, blissful and safe, protected by a wall against outside things. Within is heaven. A heaven you can enter only if you are a child.

CHAPTER EIGHT

Aharon in the Underworld

On the Western front the tide of war had begun to turn in the autumn of 1942. In North Africa, at El Alamein began the long campaign which would drive the Nazis out of Africa and Italy and finally liberate the whole of Western Europe. From the banks of the Volga, out of the smoking ruins of Stalingrad, the Russian army surged westwards towards the Balkans and Berlin. Of what they saw while advancing, an eighteen-year-old Polish boy, Venceslas Lipinsky, spoke before dying of starvation, to a friend of mine. Venceslas's family were peasants; his parents, his two brothers and his young sister had disappeared during the battle which raged across their land. Venceslas decided that his only hope was to follow the Russian troops pursuing the Germans. Many of them were young boys like him and he made friends with them. In the evening he would listen as they sang and talked about the Nazi occupation. Venceslas repeated the story that one of those young Russian soldiers had told him: 'During our advance towards the Polish frontier we passed through village after village, all of them burnt to the ground and deserted. But of all the frightful things we came upon the worst were the *isbas* which were still left standing. To the door of each one a child had been fastened by a long nail driven through his head.' In such manner was the Nazis' 'New Order' brought to the Russian people.

However, as the Russians re-conquered the Ukraine the slaves of the 'New Order' were freed. One of them was a small boy called Aharon Appelfeld. Today he is one of the best-known authors in Israel. In Jerusalem, in the offices of the Youth Aliyah, the Jewish immigration agency which brought him, like so many orphan children, to Israel, Aharon told me his story.

In 1940, when he was eight, the Germans had deported his parents and him from their home in Romania to a camp far away in the Ukraine – a labour camp which soon became an extermination camp. He was taken from his parents and never saw them again. He has no illusions as to their fate. Women and children were being killed every day, 'in a simple brutal way,' Aharon said. 'The Nazis had not yet introduced mechanized killing – gas-chambers and crematory ovens – so those people, my mother and father too, no doubt, were shot by the Germans with the Ukrainians helping.'

I asked Aharon, 'What did you feel, as a boy, being afraid every day you might be shot and seeing others being killed before your eyes?' Aharon replied, 'I cannot exactly say. It was easier for children than grown-ups because with us it was animal instinct more than reason. The impulse was to escape, so like animals we children, several of us, dug a kind of tunnel through the snow and escaped.' Aharon never knew what became of the others.

Aharon became a shepherd boy. 'Rather an idyllic life?' I asked him. 'Not exactly,' he smiled. 'I spoke the local Ukranian dialect and my face wasn't looking too Jewish. But I was very conscious that I *was* Jewish and Jewish means that you are circumcised and if the peasants find out they will kill you. The peasants were even more dangerous than the Germans.' I asked Aharon what religion the peasants professed. 'Fundamentally they were communists but in their homes you could find pictures of Jesus, Stalin and Hitler – their faith was very primitive.'

As a shepherd boy, Aharon wandered from place to place. He had to. 'If you remained a long time in one place people would ask awkward questions. It was dangerous to remain more than two or three weeks in the same place.' I asked him, 'How did you feel having lost your parents? You were a very small boy. Were you terribly lonely?' Aharon answered, 'It is strange and hard to say so, but I completely forgot my parents. You survived as an animal because you were motivated by fear, by bad dreams even. You acted instinctively. Parents were no longer a symbol of the family; slowly they disappeared from your conscience.'

So, for five years, Aharon continued his wanderings, always frequenting what he called 'non-established people' – thieves and other criminals. 'They adopt children, you know,' Aharon explained. 'Unknown children, dubious children.' I asked him if they ever got him to do a 'job'. 'Oh yes,' said this now celebrated man of letters. 'I did a lot of jobs for them. They belonged to the underworld, so did I. We had a common language.' 'And were they kind to you – any one of them in particular?' 'Oh yes, many were kind. There was a prostitute, a very nice woman. She gave me sweets and she let me live in her house' – not that it went further than that. Aharon was only ten and the lady had her own business to attend to.

When, in 1943, the Russians came, he, like many other deportees, followed the Red Army westwards, through the Ukraine, into Bulgaria and Romania until some months later he came finally to Yugoslavia.

From there, Aharon was brought in one of the Youth Aliyah's ships, the *Haganah*, to Israel – illegally, of course. Intercepted by the British Navy, they were escorted to Haifa. 'Then we met English people – they were nice to us compared with the Germans. But still, seeing soldiers made us think of the German Army.'

I asked Aharon, 'How old were you before you first fell in love?' He replied: 'None of my friends of my age is married because, through force of circumstances, we became deeply suspicious, withdrawn into ourselves. You cannot trust yourself, nor your friends. You cannot trust a woman – it was a very deep feeling.'

'Do you think,' I asked, 'that your experience as a shepherd boy has inspired the extraordinary finesse of your writing, your sensitivity about the earth, the sky, nature?' 'Perhaps,' he replied. 'But deeper than all that was this fear that the peasants or the Germans would discover that I was Jewish.' Aharon felt then, but no longer, that the world was divided into Jews and non-Jews, with the Jews, for many reasons, the victims. 'Even though I have the same face as you, the same smile, even though my speech is friendly, there is a certain mystery about me, because I am Jewish. I do not exactly understand the significance of this mystery; all I know is that the others, the non-Jews, smell it. They know that I'm Jewish and so I become a victim because I have a special smell about me.'

In conclusion, I asked Aharon what he felt for the men in Nazi Germany who had done so much evil to children like him. He just said, 'Suddenly out of Europe, which we believed so safe, there sprang a beast. It was unbelievable, in view of European culture, German culture. It was more than an evolution; it went very deep.' 'Do you think there is a beast in every man?' I asked him. Aharon thinks so. 'We have in the Jewish culture a respect for other cultures, races and religions. The Jewish people,' he went on, 'are characteristically rather timid and withdrawn. Yet there is a beast in them that can be roused and make them the most redoubtable fighters.'

Early in 1944 the Russian Army fought its way back across the Polish frontier. Auschwitz lay 220 kilometres to the west; among its thousands of starving inmates who prayed for deliverance was a fifteen-year-old boy, Avrham Schdeur. I met Avrham in Israel; stockily built, his dark-rimmed glasses and small black skull-cap stood out against the pallor of his face and his sparse, greying hair. Clearly Avrham had greatly suffered. In his quiet voice he told me how.

In 1942 Avrham and his family made the dreaded train journey to Auschwitz. There, the family was broken up; Avrham was led to the barber to have his head shaved. As he sat there the barber pointed towards the crematorium and casually remarked, 'You know, son, your mother is in there at this moment.' The remark knocked Avrham quite senseless. He simply could not realize that, as he sat there in the barber's chair, his mother, a few yards away, was being burnt alive. 'That same night,' Avrham told me, 'I had a number tattooed on my left arm.' It was then that he bared it and showed it to me. The figures were quite small, blue, indelible; *A11667*. He and all the others were told: 'From this day on you are no more human beings; you are just a number.'

Meanwhile, the immediate fear that gripped Avrham was that he, like his mother, might be sent to the crematorium. He told me, 'I knew I could only save myself by my will to live and, if possible, to fight.' And he found that, as long as he worked, he thought less of the crematorium. So Avrham, though only a boy, did more than a man's work; that alone saved him.

He was liberated by the American Army. Avrham was now fifteen. His mother had been murdered, practically before his eyes. His father, his brother and his two sisters had disappeared without trace. He fled from the past to a new life in Israel.

I asked Avrham if he could explain how it was conceivable that the Germans could have thus treated the Jews, civilized human beings like themselves. He replied, 'We talked about this endlessly among ourselves, but never found the answer. All we know is that it happened.'

The allied campaign in North Africa had begun with the British 8th Army's victory at El Alamein in 1942. One of the men that were there, Private S. Hopkins, told me, 'Many things happened at Alamein, but it's a funny thing, I always remember best something which happened many months before.' He went on, 'I was on guard duty one night. It never got very dark, but in the shadow of the boundary wall it was impossible to see anything.' About two a.m., Private Hopkins had the feeling he was being watched. 'I picked up my rifle, put one up the spout and advanced towards the wall. "Come out of there," I shouted, "or I'm going to fire." Out of the shadow came a little Arab boy – he could not have been more than six – trembling with fright, his hands held above his head.'

After Private Hopkins had led him into the guard-room and made him some cocoa the boy told his story: he had gone out begging as usual that morning, but when he returned to his mud house near the camp his parents were gone. No one came to fetch him. 'With my broken Arabic and his halting English we struck up an instant friendship,' said this hard-bitten, soft-hearted soldier. Every evening, after the day's begging, the boy came back to the guard-room to sleep.

On pay-days Private Hopkins used to spend the evening in Cairo. But one day, after settling his debts, he was broke. So he stood in for one of his mates on guard duty. The Arab boy was surprised. 'Why haven't you gone for a drink?' he asked. 'Because I haven't any money,' replied Private Hopkins, and rattled the few piastres remaining in his pocket. 'Here,' said the little boy, 'take this,' and, holding the surprised soldier's hand, emptied into it from a goat-skin pouch the whole of his worldly belongings – 'just enough for one bottle of beer,' said Private Hopkins. He gave the money back with a few of the coins in his own pocket. Next day, the boy returned with a worried look. He took the Private's hand and into it put a ten-piastre coin. 'You gave it me last night,' he said. 'Yes,' replied Private Hopkins. 'But I'm your friend, aren't I? So we share and share alike.'

One night the little Arab boy did not come back. Private Hopkins told me: 'When I speak of him to my grandchildren they always ask "What happened to him?" and I tell them "I have no idea. All I know is that he was a war victim and I shall never forget him." '

Three little Italian boys were more fortunate. The Germans were still holding out in Rome, in July 1943, when Colonello Rodolfo Lodi's beautiful Spanish wife gave birth to her third son, Diego. The other two boys, Luigi, four, and Rodolfo, two, were at home. Just as Diego was due to arrive in this world American bombers also arrived overhead. So close did their bombs fall to the clinic where Signora Lodi was in labour that an injection was given to help the terrified young mother, and a priest called. Diego was born amidst the crash of bombs; meanwhile his father, back home, was persuading his two other sons, that they were not bombs at all but just a huge thunderstorm. The boys immediately asked to go outside and watch.

The Colonello and his wife were determined that the boys should believe that the war was a huge joke. In Rome, Jews were being hunted and every day an elderly gentleman came to hide in the Lodis' water-tank. The children were curious, so their father told them, 'But haven't you seen how clean he is? He comes to take a bath every day.' 'Then why doesn't he take his clothes off?' chorused little Luigi and Rodolfo.

The Colonello, rather than stay in Rome and defend a lost cause, obtained permission to conduct his wife and family to her home in Spain. They arrived at their first stop, Poggibonsi, just as the railyard was being bombed and Diego started yelling for his bottle. So far the other boys had had the run of the train, which was empty as far as Nice, where French refugees crowded aboard. Luigi and Rodolfo sat on their father's knee until Marseilles, where the locomotive was blown up by partisans. Everybody was ordered off, but the Colonello refused to budge. With three small children and nine suitcases, what else could he do? 'At last,' he told me, 'the baby could have his first bottle quietly, the boys re-conquered the space they had lost and my wife and I, still very much in love, exchanged a long tender kiss.' The train began to move and everything seemed fine – until, at dawn next day, the Lodi family found they were back in Nice.

There, after downing an 'exquisite' glass of Sauternes, the Colonello managed to procure a car. It ran on coal. Cruising at eight miles per hour they pressed on to Nîmes. No one was worrying. 'Our two elder sons were thoroughly enjoying themselves. The baby got used to eating and sleeping.' At the entry to Nîmes, three bodies swung from a gallows by the roadside. 'What are those men doing?' asked the two boys. 'Oh, they're just doing exercises on the ropes,' their father reassured them. 'But they didn't look too convinced,' he told me. Rodolfo, spotting in a shop-window a dressmaker's dummy in a pink frock and broad-rimmed straw hat, insisted on taking it along with him.

At the frontier, the German officer glowered suspiciously at the Colonello and his strange little family, then told them, 'Go away – get lost.' Which is what they did – into Spain. Colonello Lodi told me: 'My sons have very pleasant memories of the war. Without fear or suffering they remember a long, amusing and romanesque journey.'

CHAPTER NINE

Bombs Cannot Discriminate

With the Allied invasion of France in June 1944 and the creation of a 'Second Front', the fate of Hitler's thousand-year Reich was – after only five years – sealed. But for many months yet the tide of battle was to flow over northern Europe, sparing no one in its path, least of all civilians and their children.

Hellyett Lemoigne was nineteen when, in July 1944, the battle raged around the farm near Avranches, Normandy, where she and her family had taken refuge. All day long bombs and shells fell around them. 'We were all terrified and my eleven-year-old sister never stopped crying in the arms of my mother.' In the midst of the inferno a figure, almost that of a child but dressed in German field-grey, mud-bespattered, without helmet or rifle, stood in the doorway. Then, rushing towards Hellyett's mother and crying 'Mamma, Mamma', he threw himself at her feet. The boy somehow made them understand that he had been forcibly enrolled in the German Army, that he was sixteen and a Russian, Nicolai Kondratiev!

The massacres she witnessed as a girl have left Hellyett with bitter feelings. 'Heads of state sip champagne together, manufacture arms and sleep in peace,' she protests. 'They alone are responsible for the atrocities of war by allowing the arms' traffic to continue.'

Raphaëlle L. is another who, still deeply affected by the fate of her childhood friends, feels 'a repulsion for war which goes to the depth of my being'. It was a conversation at dinner that inspired her to tell me what happened. The other guests were predicting a third world war in 1985. 'As I listened to them pouring forth their endless inanities,' she said, 'my mind went back to August 1944.' On the road from Grenoble to Lyons, forming part of a convoy of German ambulances, were two private cars, between them carrying a French family – seven children and two women. The convoy was machine-gunned – by French partisans. Of that family a girl of eight died after a few days' agony;

another, five years old, had to have her right arm amputated. A boy of eleven suffered severe brain damage and had to be trepanned. When that one-armed girl reached the age of eighteen she became, deeply, morbidly conscious of her infirmity. 'Once vivacious and intelligent she now went from one nervous depression to another,' Raphaëlle told me, adding 'I shall do everything in my power to prevent my own children from being involved in war which is the most appalling of all man's stupidities.'

It was not always easy for the Allied forces, in their long, gigantic battle to liberate the occupied countries of Europe, to discriminate between friend and foe, combatant and non-combatant. Four-year-old Jeannine was living in Argenteuil, a western suburb of Paris, when Allied bombers, British, French and Canadian, attacked a nearby factory. Jeannine was in her mother's arms when the house was hit. Splinters tore her small leg clean off and ripped open her mother's thigh. More splinters hit Jeannine's fifteen-year-old brother in the eyes, blinding him for life. It was thus that an unknown and doubtless well-meaning young airman, pushing, in the dark, on a button several kilometres above the earth, grievously wounded a child of four and caused her to suffer for the rest of her life. Not to speak of her blinded fifteen-year-old brother.

One night in June 1944, Allied bombers attacked the marshalling yards at Le Mans. It was two a.m. when Mme Crenn, whose house was far from the target, was awoken by explosions and the splintering of glass. She rushed to get her seven-year-old daughter Andrée and with her husband made for the cellar. Just before they got there a bomb hit the house, burying the family beneath the ruins. A beam lay across the back of the little girl who kept repeating, 'Papa, Papa, I'm suffocating.' Her cries grew fainter, then ceased. Andrée, her mother told me, was 'so affectionate, so intelligent and pretty'. But a bomber crew high above the earth could not let themselves be deterred by such thoughts. That bomber returned to its base in England, each of its crew to a well-earned beer. For bombing was a very risky business and the men engaged in it showed the highest courage, no matter whether they hit industrial targets or children.

In fact, I well remember one of the bravest and most distinguished of all bomber pilots, as we talked of civilian casualties. He thrust his pugnacious little face into mine and said with immense feeling, 'We must bomb the men and the women and the children, too, the little bastards.'

CHAPTER TEN

At Hiroshima and Nagasaki

Hitler, who, less than five years before, was master of all Europe, now saw his frontiers invaded, in the east by the Russians, in the west by the Anglo-Americans and their allies. The twilight of the Nazi gods was at hand and the German people were to pay a cruel price for the crimes of their leaders.

But, well before the Allied armies had overrun Germany the Anglo-American bomber offensive was ravaging German cities with fire and high explosive – and with little regard for the civil population. In July 1943, in a series of attacks on Hamburg, fires were burning over eighteen square miles of the city, with up to five square miles of concentrated fire. Three hundred thousand dwellings were destroyed, 750,000 people made homeless and – no one could count them in that fiery carnage – up to 100,000 people were killed, among them tens of thousands of children.

As the Allied armies closed in on Berlin the capital was mercilessly pounded. Late one evening the pastor of a village not far from Berlin heard a knock at the door. There stood a boy, thin as a rake, his hair dishevelled. On his back he carried a heavy sack. The pastor led him inside and the boy laid his sack carefully on the ground. 'How old are you?' the pastor asked him. 'Six,' the boy answered, 'and my brother's three. Yesterday the bombs destroyed our home. My parents were killed so I put my little brother in this sack and just kept walking as far as I could from the city.' Stooping down the pastor opened the sack. The infant boy inside it was already dead.

Though the pretext for the air-raid on Dresden, on 13 February 1945, was the same as the one for the raid on Guernica – that the city was a 'main communications and railway centre' – 135,000 people, the great majority civilians, died in the flames which consumed the city. How many children would that be? Twenty, thirty, forty, fifty thousand? massacred in a few hours. Children like the baby boy identified by the papers found in his dead mother's bag, like the two train-loads of twelve- to fourteen-year-old evacuees, like the two little brothers, of eight and ten, who were found clinging tightly to one another, stark naked, their legs, stiff and twisted, sticking out of the ground in which their faces were buried; or like those whose small bodies had been piled up in mounds, one on top of the other, in front of the Central Station. Many of those dead children were wearing the carnival costumes which they had put on to meet their parents at the station. Most were victims of the 650,000 incendiary bombs dropped on the city – hardly, as at Guernica, the most suitable bombs to use against road and rail communications. They had been choked to death by hot gases and smoke, poisoned by carbon monoxide fumes, asphyxiated through lack of oxygen. Such details were by now commonplace. During the previous five years children had died in the same way in the ruins of British and German cities, by order of the warlords in Whitehall, Washington and the Wilhelmstrasse.

Japanese children fared no better. The Americans, in their incendiary-loaded B-29s, burnt the heart out of the largest Japanese cities. In March 1945 they reduced to ashes seventeen square miles in Tokyo. In six hours they burnt 85,000 people to death – the great majority, as usual, being civilians and their children. The climax came on 6 August 1945 when, at 8.15 a.m., one bomber dropped one bomb, the first atomic bomb which, in a few seconds immolated over 100,000 people, mostly non-combatants, in Hiroshima.

Basically, it was argued that it was better that they (and a comparable number at Nagasaki) should die in one fell blow, rather than that the American forces should run the risk of far greater casualties in an outright invasion of Japan. Colonel Paul Tibbets, a courageous and extremely skilful pilot, was at the controls of the B-29 bomber. He had called it after his mother and on the front painted her name, *Enola Gay*.

Down below, in Hiroshima, was Sachiko Habu, aged five. Her mother was, as she put it, 'turned into white burns' by the heat of Colonel Tibbets' bomb. Another five-year-old, Ikuko Wakasa, heard Colonel Tibbets' B-29 flying high overhead. Then there was a flash of white light. 'After a little while a lot of blood came out of my ears.' Ikuko looked at her mother. 'She was all bloody below the hips.' Yet another girl, Kikuko Yamashiro, described how, the day after the explosion, her brother told her, 'Mother has died.' Kikuko called: 'Mother!' But no matter how much she called, her mother did not answer. 'I fell across her chest,' said Kikuko, 'and cried and cried.' The mother of Keiko Sasaki, a girl of six, was living in Hiroshima, but Keiko lived with her grandmother in the country. After the bomb, the old lady set out for Hiroshima. A week later she was back, carrying a rucksack. Out of it she took a little box; it contained a gold tooth and a single bone. That was all that remained of Keiko's mother. The name of Colonel Tibbets' mother will for ever be associated with the mothers of Hiroshima who lost their children, the children who lost their mothers, the mothers, fathers and children who were killed by the bomb dropped from *Enola Gay*.

Hiroshima today is once more a great and prosperous city. Its streets are broad and busy and in its parks thrive fir trees and maples, shrubs and shady lawns. I met in Hiroshima two people who were schoolchildren on the day that the entire city was reduced to dust and ashes. One, Hiroshi Yoshioka, was then a fifteen-year-old schoolboy. *Enola Gay* brought death to his mother, too, a slow, agonizing death; and to his young sister. Hiroshi himself had a lucky escape.

He was a good pupil and loved school. But in those days there was less time for school – the children were organized in groups to clean the streets and cultivate the land. He and his friends were assigned to digging potatoes on a plot near the station. That morning he had to be there at 8.20, but he arrived early, round about eight, dressed as usual in khaki denims, which the students wore instead of school uniform. Hiroshi told me, 'The all-clear had gone, so we spent those few spare minutes frolicking around.' Then to Hiroshi came the sound of an aeroplane; he looked up and saw not one but three. Two of them (the photographic and the instrument-carrying planes) were higher than the third (which was *Enola Gay*). The third was more clearly visible and Hiroshi recognized it as a B-29. Calling to his friends he pointed to the sky. 'Look, boys, an old B-29 and it's flying well below the others.'

Hiroshi was still pointing skywards when suddenly there was a blinding flash – it looked more like a fire-ball. He was knocked off his feet and his lunch-box blown away. He fetched up some yards off. Lying there in the grass he had the impression of being in the midst of a sea of flames. 'I don't remember feeling any blast,' he said, 'but I felt as if the bomb had gone off next to me.' Luckily his clothes were not blown off him, but his left sleeve was scorched and the burn went through to his arm, which, with his left cheek, was burnt and blistered. As he looked at his arm the flesh was already swelling and suppurating. After the heat-flash everything seemed dark for a few minutes. Later came the fall-out – 'debris, bits of paper and wood came down from the sky' – and it began to rain, black rain, but that did not last for long.

Hiroshi picked himself up and started to run home. 'But coming towards me was an enormous rush of civilians so that I couldn't get by.' Most of them had their clothes ripped off; their flesh was red, 'the colour of a boiled octopus', said Hiroshi; their skin had been torn off and hung from their fingertips. Some soldiers were so badly burnt in the face they could not see. They were roped together and led by another who could. There were many children, terribly burnt; a youth with no legs was trying to crawl, a mother dragged a corpse so burnt that it was impossible to recognize its sex. 'That solid river of humanity,' Hiroshi recalled, 'was the most horrible sight I have ever seen.' The whole city was 'wrapped in fire' so he could not get home that day. Next morning he set out with two friends. They walked along the tram rails. On both sides of the road houses were burnt and smouldering, corpses were stacked up in heaps. On the three boys went, 'past the arms and legs hanging from the windows of the charred trolley-car, the piled-up schoolchildren in the water-tanks, the burned bodies floating like logs in the Ohta river.' Hiroshi found that his house was 'completely burnt and gone without a trace'.

No trace either of his mother and sister. For days Hiroshi searched, 'weighing the endless walking, the bad smell, the wretchedness' against the joy of finding them again. Then, quite unexpectedly, he ran into his father, who had come back from Osaka where he worked. He told Hiroshi that his mother was only slightly injured. 'Nothing in my whole life made me so happy.' But his joy was short-lived. His mother's injuries healed but her body simply wasted away. In three weeks she was dead — from radiation sickness. 'This is how tenaciously that devil was haunting us, sucking the marrow from our bones.' Of Hiroshi's younger sister no trace was found.

Miyoko Matubura could hardly speak to me, so overcome was she still by the memory of that dreadful day. Miyoko did not lose her mother but, from the moment the bomb exploded, her mother lost a carefree, vivacious daughter. Miyoko was twelve and working that morning with a student labour battalion one and a half kilometres from the epicentre. It was after the all-clear that she felt a 'sharp flash' and was knocked out. When she recovered she got up and began to run home. At the Tsurumi Bridge a woman was trying to beat out the fire which had taken a hold of her clothing. Miyoko was badly burnt too and with scores of others in the same plight she jumped into the river. People were calling for help. Only fifty-five out of 320 students managed to swim to the other side; the rest were drowned.

For months Miyoko was treated for her burns, but was left with keloid scars on legs, arms and face. Temporarily, she lost the use of her arms but did exercises to prevent them stiffening. Every time she moved them they bled at the joints. Often she would ask her mother for a mirror, but her mother refused. When Miyoko finally looked at her face she was horrified. 'When I was not able to get a job because of the scars on my face I would cry. I would cry when I did not have the strength to go to school. I would cry whenever I thought I could not get married.' Miyoko's mother often cried too. 'I should have been burnt instead of you,' she would tell her daughter, 'for I am older and it is easier for me to die.' Or she would say, 'It would have been better for you if you had died when you were burned.'

This brave, martyred woman, Miyoko, has suffered atrociously since her girlhood – thirty-three years ago. 'We survivors,' she says, 'never want the millions of people in the world to suffer the same tragedy as we had.' She asks, 'Please say with a loud voice we don't want war any more and NO MORE HIROSHIMAS.'

President Harry Truman, on hearing that the A-bomb attack on Hiroshima had been successfully accomplished, exclaimed: 'This is the greatest thing in history.' Greater, presumably, in the President's view, than Christ or Krishna or Confucius, greater than Moses or Mahommet, greater than Buddha or the Bible. Greater, because while their acts and thinking have taken centuries to influence humanity and are still far from accomplished, the atom bomb was great enough, in a few seconds, to destroy the years of toil and suffering that a city and its tens of thousands of inhabitants represented. Great enough indeed to destroy the human race. Only when it does so will it really deserve to be called the greatest thing in history. Because then there will be no more history left.

Presumably, the President considered the next greatest thing in history to be the atom bomb which, three days later, on 9 August, destroyed the city of Nagasaki and 70,000 of its inhabitants. Nagasaki is a beautiful city today and had been, before the bomb, a centre of culture, learning and industry and for centuries the only Japanese city open to the West. All its historical past was pulverized in a few seconds, its inhabitants scorched, cremated, asphyxiated. This time, it was not *Enola Gay*, but *Bockscar*, the B-29 piloted by Major Sweeney, which delivered the bomb.

Living in Nagasaki at the time was Sakue Shimohira, she was eleven and people called her Ako Chan. I met Ako Chan in the prefecture at Nagasaki. She took me to a window and pointed out where her home once stood, a two-storeyed wooden house with a concrete façade. It was five hundred metres from the epicentre of the A-bomb explosion, today marked by a black marble column. The steelworks to the north and the arsenal to the south are both about a kilometre and a half away – the distance by which the bomb fell wide of these two legitimate military targets. But what did that matter with a bomb so powerful? The targets were destroyed and so were tens of thousands of Nagasaki citizens living in the vicinity.

Ako Chan was fifth in a happy family of six children. Her father was in the army. Her elder brother was a medical student, the two other brothers pilots in a kamikaze unit; they were both killed on active service early in the war. Ako Chan's elder sister had just become a mother; her other sister was younger than she. Now that the bombing had become very heavy in Nagasaki, Ako Chan no longer lived at home but in the shelter, for about thirty people, which had been set up in a cave on the mountainside about a kilometre away. That morning of 9 August the air-raid siren had sounded the all-clear and about sixteen people left the shelter, among them Ako Chan's elder sister, who went home to fetch food for her baby and her younger sisters. Those who remained behind were all children. Ako Chan was so afraid of the bombing that she never went far from the shelter.

At two minutes past eleven in the morning the atom bomb burst on Nagasaki. In the prefecture is a battered clock which was rescued from the ruins. Its hands are stopped at 11.02. At that moment a blinding yellowish flash, like lightning, lit up the interior of the shelter. 'After the flash,' said Ako Chan, 'there was a tremendous blast and the ground was covered with *tatami* [reed mats] which had been blown helter-skelter.' Ako Chan was knocked out. When she came round she saw all around her people who had been burnt; some of them had actually been blown out of the shelter and those who could crawled back into it again. Ako Chan described to me the terrible burns, blister burns all over the body. The flesh swelled up immediately; the eyes of some people were actually hanging out; some had their arms blown off, others their entrails blown out. Among the dead outside the shelter was a young woman lying face downwards on the ground, her hands covering her face. Her body was completely charred, but her face, covered as it was by her hands, was unburnt. Ako Chan recognized it as the face of her elder sister. Farther away lay a woman, a dead baby in her arms. It was Ako Chan's aunt. She had been in her house which had collapsed on top of her; she was burnt black all over and in her struggle to free herself from the debris her throat had been gashed by nails and splinters. In this state she had made for the shelter before which she now lay, as dead as the baby in her arms.

Little Ako Chan remained for another seven hours in the shelter. The wounded were crying out for help and begging for water. Ako Chan told me, 'We had to tell them no, we can't give you water because if we do you will die.' And they implored even more desperately, 'Give us water – it doesn't matter, we would rather drink and die than not drink at all.' Ako Chan happened to have a flask on her. A man, burnt almost beyond recognition, grabbed her by the legs and tried to wrest it from her. Other people whom the bomb had scorched crawled outside, pushing aside the dead bodies, to a little pool full of muddy water in which they thrust their faces and drank.

Towards evening Ako Chan's father appeared at the shelter. He had walked the thirty-five kilometres from Isahaya where he worked. Although by now the smell in and around the shelter had become unbearable Ako Chan was told to wait a little longer while her father went back to the house. Some time later he reappeared. He told Ako Chan that he had found her mother. Of her there remained nothing recognizable save her gold teeth.

The mother of Michiko Seto was one of those 'little folk' among whom are to be found more heroes, anonymous ones, than in all the annals of heroism. In the prefecture at Nagasaki Michiko told me what happened that day of the A-bomb when she was nine.

The family, parents and seven brothers and sisters, lived in a wooden house, near the centre of the city. Michiko and her sisters were happy girls. They loved playing at housekeeping and their mother let them use the household cups and saucers and utensils. Michiko went to the elementary school, but August was holiday time.

On the morning of the 9th all the children were at home; Michiko's father was out driving his horse and cart on his delivery round. After breakfast, of rice and *miso shiru*, her mother told the girls to be good and play while she went out into the fields to look for egg-plants. She told Michiko to have the *shichirin*, the portable cooking-range, alight by eleven o'clock, when she would be back. But Michiko was so busy playing housekeeping that she forgot to light the fire. 'Was your mother angry with you,' I asked her, 'when she got back?' Michiko looked at me and said quietly, 'There was no question of her being angry. She had other things to think about.'

It had just gone eleven when Michiko, who was inside the house, saw a dazzling yellow flash – she thought at first it was lightning. Then there came a terrific explosion and she felt as if the house was being lifted off its supports. She must have lost consciousness for when she came to she was lying in the debris beneath the bamboo supports and a lot of tiles. A big cut on her head was bleeding profusely.

Michiko and her two sisters managed to extricate themselves, but the baby sister, two-year-old Itsko, was still under the ruins, crying at the top of her voice. Nobody could get her out, so the elder girls went for help and returned with six sailors who dragged away some of the wreckage. But Itsko, though uninjured, was still pinned under a big beam which no one could move.

Michiko now saw a terrible apparition staggering towards the house – a body completely stripped of clothing and burnt beyond recognition. It was only when she heard a voice asking thickly, 'Is everybody all right?' that she recognized the apparition as her mother, her hair burnt off and her arms scorched to a dark purplish black. Despite her terrible injuries her first thought was for Itsko. 'We can't lift the beam,' the sailors told her. So Michiko's mother crawled beneath it, put her shoulder to it and somehow succeeded in heaving it aside. Itsko was free. I asked Michiko, 'What then happened to your mother?'

She began to sob, looking at the ground and wiping away her tears with her hand. Then she collected herself. 'My father and brothers took mother to a shelter and laid her down. She kept crying, "It hurts, it hurts so much".' She was suffering atrociously when Michiko lay down to sleep. When she woke up next morning she went to her mother. She was dead. And Michiko, again in tears, sobbed: 'I saw she was all swollen up like a pig.'

Michiko says that when she told her mother's story to her own teenage daughter, she replied, 'The world would be a better place with more people like her.' Especially among the ranks of those who rule nations and run the world's affairs.

President Truman would have been right if he had said, 'This is the greatest massacre in history.' He had found the formula for the perfect massacre: one bomber, one bomb and about one hundred thousand human beings (if you include, as you must, those with their children and even their grandchildren who are dying today, thirty-five years later, of atomic disease caused by the bomb).

Three days later World War II ended. It was time. During six years it had killed fifty million people, maimed as many more. Think how many children that means.

People were sick of slaughter and dreamed of a world free of war, a better, a cleaner and a safer place, especially for children.

Part Three

CHAPTER ELEVEN

Post-war 'Peace'

The illusion of peace was short-lived. All those millions crushed beneath the war juggernaut were not enough to stop it. World War II contained the seeds of future conflicts. The partisans and insurgents who had fought the German-Japanese 'New Order', the freedom fighters who opposed oppressive and imperialist regimes, now wanted to install, by force, 'new orders' of their own. As the fires smouldered out amid the ruins of Hiroshima and Nagasaki, new fires, smaller to be sure, but fierce in intensity, were kindling elsewhere. One, in Greece, had already burst into flames.

The Greek civil war really began when, in March 1944, the communist-led National People's Liberation Army (ELAS) set up a political committee in opposition to the Greek government which had been driven into exile in April 1941. By the time the latter returned, in the autumn of 1944, ELAS was strong enough to contest them and the British troops supporting them. Fighting broke out, but peace was restored in February 1945. In the autumn of 1946 the Democratic Army, led by 'General' Markos, resumed the civil war in earnest, terrorizing towns and villages which had received loyalist troops, burning, pillaging, kidnapping. Thousands of Greek children were orphaned, thousands more carried off to neighbouring communist states.

The Greeks had a word, *paedomasm*, collection of the children, for this form of kidnapping, which was initiated by a Balkan youth conference meeting in Belgrade. There, it was decided that in 'free' (i.e. rebel-held) areas of Greece all children of between three and fourteen should be taken away and cared for in the neighbouring communist countries. Neither the children nor their parents had any say in the matter, unless luck was with them and they managed to escape. But against ten men with guns what can a child of three do? Nothing, nor could his mother, from whose arms he was snatched.

Fortitude, not luck, is the theme of the tragic story of Felicity, a sixteen-year-old orphan girl. In a cottage in the Eurytanian mountains she looked after her two young brothers. One evening she heard men's voices outside and, guessing what they meant, woke up the boys, dressed them hurriedly and rushed outside into the snow. Following the goat-tracks which she knew, she climbed above the village. But the snow was so deep that in the darkness, hour after hour, Felicity had to fight her way through the drifts and the thorny scrub, her two brothers in her wake. Where she had passed, the snow was stained with blood. At last she and the boys reached a military outpost at Karpenisi, where the soldiers found her half-naked; the front of her body formed a single, bleeding wound. That same day she died.

To avoid capture a hundred thousand children of school age fled from their mountain villages to the towns where 'children's cities' were set up. The flight became a wholesale migration southwards, the children, with labels around their necks, singing as they went: 'Whoever does not want God, King and family, we'll pay his expenses and send him to Bulgaria.'

The reverse side of the *paedomasm* coin was described by Kenneth Matthews in *Memories of a Mountain War: Greece 1944–49*. He visited a children's hostel at Plovdiv, Bulgaria, where he found 170 Greek children singing: 'We're giving the death-blow to Fascism; we're marching to civilization'. But Stathoula, a pretty four-year-old girl, did not join in. She just cried, without stopping, for her mother who was far away in Greece.

To the question, 'Why do you like General Markos?' the children chorused, 'Because he gives us liberty.' When they were asked, 'What is liberty?' one girl piped up, 'It means go back home and eat cherries.'

In China, the enmity – bordering on civil war – between communists and nationalists had been put aside to form a united front, however precarious, during China's struggle against Japan. But, Japan defeated, a fratricidal war began in 1946 between the opposing factions. It was to last until the end of 1949, when the communists captured Nanking, the nationalist capital.

Marching in the ranks of the Red Army were the Young Vanguards, boys from twelve to seventeen years old, nicknamed the 'Little Red Devils'. Organized and disciplined by the Communist Youth League, they received compulsory education in reading, writing, athletics – and politics. Here is a portrait of one of them drawn by an eye-witness (Edgar Snow in *Red Star over China*). The boy was a fifteen-year-old bugler, rosy-faced, with shining eyes. He wore tennis shoes, grey shorts and a faded grey cap with a red star on it. His family lived near

Changchow, in Fukien province. They possessed no land and were very poor. In summer the boy cut wood in the mountains; in winter he went there to collect bark. With it the family made soup for they never had enough to eat.

When the Red Army came to Changchow he applied to join up. They gave him plenty to eat and sent him to school. No wonder he liked the Red Army; they drove out from his village the landlords, money-lenders and officials and gave his family land.

Most of the little Red Devils wore uniforms too big for them with sleeves reaching down to their knees and coats trailing on the ground. An exception was a thirteen-year-old lad who served as orderly to a high official in the foreign department. The boy soldier wore a Sam Browne belt over a perfectly fitting uniform. Beside him Mao Tse-tung looked a tramp. The Red Devils did a variety of jobs – orderlies, mess boys, buglers, radio operators, water-carriers, spies. Many had fought in battle, charged with bayonets fixed. Unfortunately, they were so small and light that the enemy soldiers just grabbed their bayonets and pulled the little Red Devils into the trench. Two hundred of them had been captured and thrown into a filthy gaol at Sianfu, where they stuck it out with amazing fortitude.

Commander of the Youth Brigade was Chu Ling-wei, a smiling boy of eleven – the 'little Red Colonel'. The spirit of his 'men' was superb. They were cheerful, hardworking, heroic. They made Edgar Snow think that China, rent as she was by civil war, was not hopeless: 'No nation is more hopeless than its youth.'

After helping to defeat Japan's imperialist ambitions, Britain immediately set about the dismemberment of her own empire. In 1947 she handed over the power she had enjoyed for nearly two centuries on the Indian sub-continent to two new sovereign states: India and Pakistan. The process was accompanied by a savage conflict between the two communities, Hindu (which included the Sikhs) and Muslim.

In August 1946, exactly a year before Independence, there began in Calcutta, an orgy of killing. Then it spread to Noakhali, in eastern Bengal. Before the blood-lusting Muslim *goondas* (hooligans) Hindus fled westwards to Chandpur where the railway station seethed with weary, terrified fugitives, women clutching babies and men, many of whom had panicked and run for safety, leaving wives and children to their fate.

The fury of killing spread to Bihar. There, on 'Noakhali Day,' Hindus wreaked vengeance on Muslims. More than seven thousand were butchered or burnt. Women and their children were cut to pieces. At Paigambarpar a woman had seen her baby cut in two; another gave all her savings in return for a promise that her children would be spared. They were then murdered before her eyes. Some infants were slain as they sat on their mothers' knees. At Bikatpur mutilated children lay dead beside the corpses of their mothers; at a nearby village mothers and their children had been stripped naked before being burnt alive. A few weeks later, at Garhmukteswar, near Delhi, the fair was in full swing when, in the middle of the fairground, a mob of Jats, a Hindu people, fell upon the Muslims in the crowd, spearing and strangling them, ripping open pregnant women and tearing the babies from their wombs, bashing out their brains; they seized young Muslim girls, raped them and tore their legs asunder, while Jat women howled encouragement to their men.

Kanda, a Hindu, told me how, as a seventeen-year-old boy, he watched aghast at Jullundur Station when the Johore train pulled in to Number One platform. It was full – of dead; in front of Kanda there passed an old man, moaning, as he dragged a handcart in which lay the dismembered body of his son.

Into the little Punjab village where Kanda lived there flowed a stream of refugees. They told appalling tales of Muslim brutality; of babies who had been snatched from their mothers, hurled into the air then caught on spears; of children whose feet had been hacked off and, the shoes still on them, handed back to their parents.

For weeks after Independence (which entailed the partition of Bengal and the Punjab) the massacres continued. At Simla in the Punjab, once a prim and pleasant English hill-station, a Sikh tea-merchant, Niranjan Singh, was confronted one morning by one of his oldest clients, a Muslim, who screamed, 'Kill him, kill him'. A dozen *goondas* set upon Niranjan, severed one of his legs, then slew his son. As he lost consciousness the Sikh saw his daughter being carried away, screaming, on the shoulders of his faithful client.

But the Sikhs were as vicious killers as any. In a Delhi street a Sikh, with his bare hands, tore the door of a dwelling off its hinges. Out rushed a little Muslim girl holding in her arms her baby brother. Other Sikhs closed in on her and, with hockey-sticks, poles, hatchets, spears and swords beat her to the ground, where she lay, trying in vain to protect her brother's body with her own. The swords and axes of the Sikhs cut them both to pieces. Then the Sikhs found her parents, her twelve-year-old brother and her sister and, beating their bodies, hacking at their limbs, left them dead.

British officers kept repeating that even in World War II they had never seen such terrible, sadistic slaughter. Yet the Sikhs and Hindus on one side and the Muslims on the other were equally bestial. From a roof-top Guldip Singh, a fourteen-year-old Sikh boy, saw Sikh women who chose, for themselves and their children, to be immolated by fire rather than violated. The women watched as their men were dragged out and killed. Then they climbed onto the roof of a house which the mob immediately set on fire. As it burnt beneath them, the Sikh mothers gave their breasts for the last time to their babies. Then they threw their children into the blaze and jumped in after them.

Children sometimes joined in the killing. In a Calcutta street six teenage Hindu boys, shrieking 'Muslim Muslim', attacked two middle-aged men. Unconvinced by their protests, the Hindu boys tore away the folds of the men's *dhotis* to find that, like all sons of the Prophet, the men were indeed circumcised. Their young captors then drove them down to the banks of the Hooghly river, pushed them into the muddy water then, with crowbars, beat them senseless. As the two inert bodies floated away downstream the teenagers raised a cry, '*Kali Mayi Ki Jai*', Long live the goddess Kali!

After partition, Muslims and Hindus (including Sikhs), caught on the wrong side of the demarcation line, had but one impulse – to flee to the other side. Trains packed to the roof with refugees plied hither and thither. They were easy prey for the killer-bands of both sides and in many of them only a few passengers survived the journey.

Millions more refugees made their escape on foot. For hundreds of miles, in columns miles long, they tramped on in the heat, throats parched, stomachs empty. Parents who no longer had the strength to carry their children simply left them by the roadside to die. A little boy was seen sitting beside his lifeless mother, tugging at her arms, not knowing why they no longer moved to embrace him.

Following a column of a hundred thousand refugees was a station-wagon for the dying and the new-born. A midwife took care of the women in labour. The vehicle stopped just long enough for a mother to deliver. Within hours she and her infant vacated their crude maternity ward and took to the road again.

And so the first generation of Indians and Pakistanis were born, Hindu or Muslim as befitted their case. And until someone told them they would never realize they were different.

On 29 November 1947 the U.N. General Assembly voted for the partition of Palestine. The British mandate, after twenty-five years, was to end on 15 May 1948. A Jewish sovereign state (Israel) was assured – unless the hostile Arabs could nip it in the bud. Soon after the U.N. vote fierce fighting broke out among Jews and Arabs.

Among the hills on the western outskirts of Jerusalem was a village of stone-cutters, Dir Yassin. At 4.30 on the morning of 9 April 1948 it was attacked by a force of the Irgun Zvai Leumi, aided by a unit of the Lechi, the 'Stern Gang', in all some 130 strong. The men belonging to these two groups were known to themselves as 'freedom fighters'; Ben Gurion, the Jewish leader and chief of the official organization, the Jewish Agency, and of its private army, the Haganah, disapprovingly called them 'dissidents'. To the world at large they were known as terrorists. The leader of the Irgun was Menachem Begin, 1978 winner of the Nobel Peace Prize.

Naturally, accounts of the Dir Yassin attack vary. Begin says, in his book, *The Revolt*, that Dir Yassin was a strategic village, and that before the attack started the inhabitants were warned by loudspeaker to withdraw. He claims that the 'lying propaganda' which told of Jewish atrocities 'helped us. Panic overwhelmed the Arabs of Eretz Israel ... the Arabs began to flee in terror ... It was not,' he argues, 'what happened at Dir Yassin, but what was invented' that put the Arabs, who outnumbered the Jews by about 1,300,000 to 700,000, to flight.

What then did happen at Dir Yassin? There is the account of Dominique Lapierre and Larry Collins in their *O Jerusalem*, whose main evidence was taken from Jewish, as well as British and Red Cross sources. To begin with, the Haganah commander-in-chief, David Shaltiel, has observed that there was no military advantage in Begin's plan. As for the warning to the villagers, it was not heard by them; the armoured car equipped with a loud-speaker had fallen into a ditch some way from Dir Yassin.

Now for the eye-witnesses, whose testimonies coincide with the medical evidence of a doctor and nurse of the Government Hospital in Jerusalem. Twelve-year-old Fahimi Zeidan told how, after all her family had been lined up against a wall, 'they started shooting at us. I was hit in the side, but most of the children were saved because we hid behind our parents. The bullets hit my four-year-old sister Kadri in the head, my sister Sameh [eight] in the cheek, and my little brother Mohommed in the chest.' All the others against the wall were killed.

Haleem Eid saw one of Begin's men shoot her sister Saliyeh, who was nine months pregnant, in the neck. Then the freedom fighter cut her stomach open with a butcher's knife. And a youth, Mahommed Jaber, saw from where he was hiding under a bed, the 'freedom fighters' drive everbody else outside, line them up against a wall and shoot them.

Next day, the delegate of the International Red Cross, Jacques Reynier, escorted by a member of the Irgun, visited Dir Yassin. He saw people carrying sten guns, pistols, rifles, knives, running in and out of the Arab houses. 'The bodies were strewn about,' he wrote – 254 men, women and children. The Irgun man explained to Reynier, 'We're still mopping up.'

The report on the Dir Yassin survivors written by Richard Catling, Assistant Inspector-General of the Criminal Investigation Department of the Palestine police, contains references such as: 'There is no doubt that many sexual atrocities were committed ... Many young schoolgirls were raped and slaughtered ... Many infants were also butchered ...'

When the Jewish 'official' army, the Haganah, took over Dir Yassin from Begin's 'dissidents' one of their leaders, commander of the Gadna, the youth organization, described the scene as 'absolutely barbaric'. Almost without exception the dead Arab villagers were old men, women and children.

Whatever difference there may be between what really happened at Dir Yassin and what was invented, there is no disputing the consequences. The immediate one was a sense of shock – felt as much by the majority of Palestine Jews as by anyone else. The next, four days later, was reprisal. Yelling 'Dir Yassin', Arabs attacked a Jewish convoy on its way to Jerusalem's Hadasseh hospital and the Hebrew University, killing seventy-seven doctors, nurses and teachers. The ultimate consequence to which Arabs unwittingly contributed by broadcasting the gruesome details, was the headlong flight of a million Arabs from their mother country, Palestine.

The tragedy of the Palestinians had begun.

CHAPTER TWELVE

Hong Pae and the Will to Survive

Thousands of miles away from Palestine, the defeat of Japan had resulted in the liberation of the Korean peninsula and its division, by the 38th parallel, between North and South under the influence respectively of the Soviet Union and the United States. The show-down between communists and capitalists came in June 1950, when the North Korean army invaded South Korea, converging on Seoul, the capital.

The first thing that sixteen-year-old An Yong Cha knew of the North Korean attack on Seoul, where she lived with her parents, three sisters and a brother, was when some South Korean soldiers ran past the house shouting that the area was unsafe. The soldiers were retreating; Yong Cha, however, went to school as usual that morning, only to be told to go home – and it was then that she realized that there really was a war on.

Yong Cha originally lived at Puiong Yang in North Korea, where her father owned a soap factory. Rather naïvely she told me, 'He was co-operating with the Japanese when they occupied the country and as nobody liked the Japanese he was ousted at the same time as them.' That is how Yong Cha, a North Korean, came to be living in Seoul, at present under attack by her own North Korean countrymen.

Until then she had felt that life as she knew it – the circle of her family and friends – was very stable and great fun. She dreamed of becoming a famous dancer. The war shattered all that. A few days later North Korean tanks came rolling down the street and soldiers knocked at the door asking for information. This put Yong Cha's family in difficulties; the North Koreans have a strong accent and the family were terrified lest it betray them. Her father kept well clear of the house, returning only now and then.

Very soon Yong Cha and her family were going hungry. Then they moved to a farmhouse on the outskirts of Seoul. The road there was littered with corpses; to Yong Cha, who wanted to give her whole soul to dancing, that desolate scene was a dreadful shock. Dancing, she told me, was an art in which the whole body found its most gracious, its supreme expression; and those still, bloated corpses made her think that once the soul has left the body the body becomes just an ugly piece of rubbish.

The house in Seoul was destroyed by bombs, so the family moved farther south to Pusan (where I met Yong Cha). There, she said, life became really hard. The family, once well-to-do, were short of money. Yong Cha went to a secretarial school. She got a good job with the U.S. Army. Yet she was sad. Why? I asked her. 'Because we Koreans like stability and peace and we are very much attached to our homes.' Yong Cha's job took her far from home. Not only that; she always missed her home in North Korea. 'It was a very nice place to live.' she said. 'If only the North and South can be reunited then I will go back to North Korea where I belong.' How did she feel, I asked her, about being driven from her own home by her own people? 'Well,' she answered, 'I just don't like the people who call themselves communists. It is they who drove us out, not the North Koreans with whom I always feel the closest ancestral ties.'

When, in the summer of 1950, the North Koreans captured Seoul, Chin Sok Yang was nine. He was the son of a middle-class family – six boys and a girl. It was not Chin's father but his grandfather who was acknowledged head of the family. He was a man in his sixties, 'a very playful man', as Chin described him, and when the children were scolded by their parents, grandfather would step in and save them. 'I have really big images and good memories of my grandfather. He was the family's provider.' The home was comfortable and, added Chin, 'we were well fed'. That is perhaps the most important thing in a small boy's life.

Chin's past contact with the North Koreans was, he said, 'not so bad'. The soldiers tossed him biscuits and sweets. 'They weren't as good as what the G.I.s gave us when they came, but they were not too bad.' 'So you weren't frightened of the communist soldiers?' I asked him, and he answered, 'Not a bit – until the day they took my grandfather away.' Chin was there. Four men just walked straight into the house. 'What were they like?' This is how Chin saw them: 'A harsh, and very serious kind of men; they wore plain clothes – such distinguished outfits that they couldn't be other than members of the communist party. They wore pistols. They frightened me very much.' The four men walked straight down to the basement where his grandfather was hiding and told him to come out. 'Did you ever see him again?' I asked Chin. He answered quite simply, 'No, that was it.'

All the same, little Chin could not at first believe that his beloved grandfather would not return. But as the days passed he grew more anxious. 'I had,' he said, 'an enormous question in my mind: Why? What had he done to be taken away from us? I'm certain that my own anti-communism is entirely due to that dramatic experience I witnessed as a boy.' From now on life became very hard. The day came when there was no more to eat and, while Chin's father was away for three days searching desperately for food, Chin, once so well-fed, suffered the pangs of hunger. 'The first day wasn't that bad,' he told me, 'but from the second day I felt as if my whole stomach was just crunching up.' He tried drinking water but only threw it up. On the third day, as he put it, 'I clearly saw the so-called death before my eyes.' I asked him, 'Were you frightened?' 'No,' he said, 'I didn't even have the strength to be afraid. It just seemed so natural that I knew how it was going to be, how to reach the so-called death.'

Sitting on the floor (as they do in the east), leaning up against a wall, in one position – just simply sitting with nothing to do was what Chin called 'a powering thing'. He meant, I think, overpowering. He was 'overpowered' by weakness, for when I asked him the obvious question: 'Didn't you think of lying down?' he told me, 'I didn't really have the strength to push myself to lie in a comfortable position.' He just leaned to one side and slid on to one shoulder and stayed there. Unable to bear that position any longer, he somehow pushed himself back into a sitting position. Then, on the third day, long after dark, his father returned, bringing food.

From now on the family somehow kept alive, though the basic food, rice, was very hard to come by. What little they had was mixed with barley or wheat or beans, and mainly corn. Chin told me, 'As I talk to you now, the taste and the smell of corn comes back to me and it makes me feel quite sick.'

When Seoul was retaken by the Americans the food situation eased. Chin said they lived on the left-over food of the troops. It was all dumped into a cauldron and boiled up. It tasted something like vegetable soup. I asked Chin what were his feelings about the Americans filling themselves with food while he was half-starved. He replied, 'I was too hungry to have any feelings. I was only too pleased to eat what they threw away.' The soldiers threw chewing-gum and candy bars to the Korean children, and that made Chin wonder: 'How is it possible that the Americans are so rich that they can throw things away without feeling it?'

Chin's family never left Seoul, even when, later, the North Koreans returned. Nine-year-old Chin got mixed up in the street fighting. It went on right in front of the house. Chin called that 'a rather interesting experience'. A rather ghastly one too, for one morning as the children walked outside 'we found,' said Chin, 'a gigantically huge body lying right in front of the house; he was a big man, enormously big.' The children were very frightened and, as nobody took the corpse away, Chin's mother, 'a very religious person', covered it with a blanket. During the night the family had to remain indoors in one room, lying down – because of the firing. Next morning when they went out an even more horrible sight confronted them. The blanket had been removed from the dead giant, who had been stripped of all his clothes save for his T-shirt and underwear. Chin saw tears in his mother's eyes. 'How in the world,' she sobbed, 'could humans do this to another human?' And Chin, though 'not knowing what the dead were, but realizing the difference between dead and alive', shared his mother's feelings.

Somehow the macabre sight of that giant corpse – it was, in Chin's words, 'white by race' – struck the boy more forcibly than did the small corpses of children of his own race strewn among the bombed-out ruins. But Chin's experience did not stop at these anonymous dead. His second brother, a boy of seventeen, left home one day at noon to see a friend. He never came back. Chin can only suppose: 'He was picked up off the street, loaded into a truck and taken away for the so-called "basic training". And that was the end of that.'

Then Chin's little brother started 'a weird ailment'. The vague expression he used merely reflects the fact that there was no doctor available to diagnose it. 'His stomach was swollen up, so big.' 'Prior to the war,' said Chin, 'my grandfather would have done everything to save him.' But now there was a war and no grandfather. 'That bothered me more than anything,' said Chin, pathetically, that his little brother had to be left, helpless, to die. 'He was one of my favourites,' he told me. 'When he died I cried so much, I couldn't eat anything.'

All the time his own survival was getting harder. 'We had to live poorly and often skip meals.' Chin went out on the street selling chewing-gum, cigarettes and candy, but his takings did not help much. So he became a shoe-shine boy and one day shone the shoes of some British soldiers who took him back to camp, made him their mascot. These 'mascot-children', the most pathetic of all, were often found clutching the photo of some friendly Tommy or G.I. who had abandoned them when their unit moved on. But Chin was luckier. The Tommies nicknamed him 'James', and the sergeant, Chin told me – his name was Butler – 'was so kind and friendly' (I only hope the Tommies thought so, too). And he remembers, 'Whatever they got from home in the mail –

like cookies – they gave to me.'

I asked Chin, 'Can you explain why soldiers, who are generally so kind to children, are capable of killing them mercilessly?' He reflected for some moments then said, 'I don't think soldiers really want or intend to kill children. But in war children are the victims of circumstances.' 'And indiscriminate air bombing?' I pursued. 'Do you think that is a justifiable act of war?' 'Yes and no,' Chin replied, unperturbed. 'My theme is the same. The bombers are not aiming at children; they are always victims of circumstances whenever conflicts erupt.'

Chin's reasoning is idealistic, but not faultless. Warfare, psychological or armed, is, as we have seen and have yet to see, sometimes aimed specifically at children. But when, finally, I said to Chin, 'So, logically, the only way to avoid hurting children so terribly, as you yourself have been hurt, is to refuse to make war,' he gave the only possible answer: 'That's right,' adding, 'From what I saw throughout the Korean conflict, the invaders of my country were willing to sacrifice children's lives to win their war, to satisfy their ego.'

When the south-west port of Samtcheon-Po fell to the North Koreans in August 1950, Si-Hong, a restaurant-keeper, fled with his family and a number of others to the sea-shore five kilometres away. His six-year-old daughter, Yung-Soon, clutching a bag of food, rode all the way on the shoulders of her father, who also carried under one arm the baby girl, Yeong-Ee. Si-Hong's wife carried their four-year-old boy, Yeong-Kap. Why, I asked Si-Hong, did he run away from the communists? It was from pure fear, he told me; the story had spread that when they captured a town many people were executed and Si-Hong feared a massacre. Yung-Soon was very frightened, too, but once she reached the sea-shore her fear went. In fact she had a lovely time even though, during the day, the whole family had to hide among the rocks. At night they slept out on the beach and Yung-Soon always found some time to play in the sand. The days were hot and there was no shelter, but this did not worry her. The communists were her only fear.

For her parents those two weeks camping on the beach were far from care-free. Food was scarce and after the two weeks no more remained, so Si-Hong decided to make for a village, Seokkae-Ri, up in the mountains, where a relative lived. It was a walk of ten kilometres. As before, Si-Hong and his wife carried the children. On the way the family had repeatedly to take cover, both from the communist tanks hidden in the woods on each side of the track and from the American aircraft which were bombing the communists. As they lay huddled together in the undergrowth a bomb splinter smashed into Si-Hong's arm. A tourniquet, fashioned with his belt, helped to staunch the profuse bleeding. He forced himself to struggle on and then, about halfway to the village, collapsed. Poor Si-Hong. He was now too weak to lead his family to safety. He sent his wife on to the village with Yeong-Ee, the baby girl, while, with Yung-Soon and Yeong-Kap, he waited for help. Yung-Soon told me how sorry she felt for him as he lay there bleeding and in pain. After an hour her mother returned and with others helped Si-Hong to stagger the rest of the way to the village where, with nothing available but a tin of balm, the arm healed into a mis-shapen claw.

Two months later Si-Hong returned alone to Samtcheon-Po, now recaptured from the North Koreans. He went back to his restaurant but found only a charred ruin. There, he pitched a tent for himself and set up as a grain-dealer. But he could not make enough to keep his family, who were still in the hills, so they all moved to Pusan, a great city. The head monk of a Buddhist Temple took pity on them and gave them shelter in a store-house. But so poor was Si-Hong that he could only feed his family on thin soup. The children began to waste away. Yung-Soon, now seven, went out daily to the port to glean the few grains of rice which fell as the sacks were being unloaded. She told me: 'This was a very hard time. Not only did I glean rice at the port; I went out into the fields to pick up cabbage leaves and I also went begging in the streets.' As she spoke, she became very moved and lowered her head as if she was going to cry. Then she looked up at me again and smiled. She had been overcome, she said, by the memory. Because she was so young people pitied her and were kind. She never felt the least shame at begging – it was the only thing left to do, she was so hungry.

Back at their home in the store-house Yung-Soon's mother baked cornflour cakes and the little girl would carry them on a platter on her head into town and sell them. Eight kilometres there and back. Yung-Soon told me how strange it seemed to her that she was selling all this food to others while she and her small brother and sister had only thin soup to drink. I asked Yung-Soon if she thought, too, of the contrast between her former happy life and the subsequent state of things and she replied, 'Well, the memory of those happy days faded before our desperate need to survive.' And she sighed and passed her hand across her forehead and again I saw that she was deeply moved.

Despite all their efforts and the left-over cakes which were given to the children, hunger gained on the family and began to devour it. Yeong-Ee, the baby girl, was the first to die. Yung-Soon was at her bedside; in a quiet voice she said to me, 'She did not suffer too much.' It was otherwise with Yeong-Kap. Si-Hong remained with his dying son until he could no longer bear to watch his suffering. Then he left the house and only came back when he learnt that the boy was dead. Yung-Soon watched over her brother for days as he lay, covered with sores, scratching at them so that his mother had to tie his hands. 'He suffered terrible agony,' Yung-Soon said and broke down completely at the thought. After a while she went on, 'The world felt empty after the death of my brother and sister and it seemed to me, and still does, so unjust that my family, once so happy, should have suffered such misfortunes.'

Si-Hong told me, 'When I think of my two dead children, of another, born later, who had half his hand blown off by something he had picked up during the war; when I look at my own arm and think of all that my family went through – I can never forgive the men responsible. Were it not for them I, and thousands of others, would still be living happily in our homes.' Yung-Soon agrees: 'They were the worst possible enemies,' she said.

For Yung-Soon the struggle continues to this day. A widow, with five children, she is determined to provide them with the food and the education that she so sorely lacked. She earns but $60 a month, including overtime, but is quite ready to work harder if only she were better paid. 'I want to devote my whole life to my children,' she told me; and the children do not yet know what their mother suffered for them. When they do, will they care? Perhaps; perhaps not, for the unanswerable argument of a child is: my parents, not I, are responsible for my birth.

Outnumbering by far the invaders from the North were the refugees. After three years of war they totalled some four million. During the exodus, thousands of children lost their parents, who often did not try to find them again. Or they simply abandoned them; the rate in Pusan reached four waifs found every night.

Yi Hong Pae was one of those North Korean refugees. In Pusan, late into the night, he told me his story. Hong Pae lived in Sinuiju, near the mouth of the Yellow River, with his mother and grandparents. His father was in business in Peking and only came home twice a year. His mother died, and Hong Pae, then seven, and his younger brother were brought up by their grandparents.

When, in 1947, his father went to settle in South Korea, at Seoul, he wrote asking the grandparents to send the two boys to join him. They allowed Hong Pae to leave, but not his brother – it was the tradition for the head of the family (in this case the grandfather) to keep one son so that the succession be assured. Hong Pae felt sad and resentful at being separated from his young brother, whom he greatly loved. He was not even allowed to say goodbye to him.

North Korea being under communist control, Hong Pae had to travel clandestinely, accompanied by an uncle.

At last, at Seoul, Hong Pae found his father. It was three years since they had met and they hugged each other warmly. But not long afterwards, his father died. Hong Pae, now sixteen, with no funds and no friends, was on his own. He took to selling newspapers, barely making enough to buy two meagre meals a day. Then he turned to selling cosmetics and this took him into cafés and night-joints and into the company of entertainment girls. 'Don't think it was any fun,' he said to me, 'I was only thinking of survival, not of the girls.'

In May 1950, just before war broke out, Hong Pae, with nowhere to sleep, went along one night to the Presbyterian Church in Seoul. 'I have nowhere to sleep,' he told the Minister, who sent him to an orphanage. Hong Pae felt homesick and miserable.

Seoul quickly fell to the North Koreans and the orphanage directress was replaced by a communist 'Kommissar', who summoned the elder boys, including Hong Pae, and told them that he counted on their help – in return for which he gave them bags of rice. Half-starving as he was, Hong Pae's overnight conversion to communism mattered little to him. He was not a communist for long, for a few months later Seoul was recaptured by the U.S. and South Korean forces, and the directress returned. She begged him to stay on. But Hong Pae longed for his home in Sinuiju and especially his brother. He decided to follow the army northwards and, hopefully, back home.

But, said Hong Pae, 'This did not work out.' The American advance slowed up; winter was coming on and both food and lodging were hard to come by. So Hong Pae quit being a camp-follower, returned to Seoul and took to selling matches. He had heard that, in the countryside, they were good barter for rice. He hopped a lift from Seoul in a freight train to Cho Chi Won, 200 kilometres away. From there he walked another forty kilometres till he came to a small village. By the end of the following day Hong Pae had traded his twenty matchboxes for sixty kilos of rice. Humping the heavy sack, he trudged back to Cho Chi Won, where he sold the rice. Then back went this sixteen-year-old lad to Seoul, bought more boxes of matches and twice again made that gruelling return trip.

By December 1950 all Hong Pae's savings were spent. He was destitute – and the Americans were on the retreat. The North Koreans soon recaptured Seoul. By then Hong Pae was fleeing with thousands of other refugees south-east, by train, to Taegu. From there he began walking – back, to find the Americans. He walked for a week; it was February and bitterly cold, 10°C below zero. He managed to keep alive on roots and water. One night he came to an empty farmhouse, scraped up some firewood and fell into a long sleep. Then he walked on for another week and came at last to the front at Yang Suri. By then he was starving, so he called at an American unit where a sergeant gave him food. Hong Pae told him he was desperate. 'I need a job,' he said, and when the sergeant replied, 'Okay,' Hong Pae burst into tears. He washed off the filth of two weeks and changed his rags for the G.I. fatigue outfit which the sergeant gave him. Then Hong Pae went to work as a kitchen help.

From then on, said Hong Pae, 'I began to blossom. Life took on a different colour and my spirits rose.' He has been working with the Americans ever since. That once unhappy orphan who had endured loneliness, danger, filth and poverty is now impeccably dressed. I asked him if he regretted all the hardships and suffering he had been through. 'Not a bit,' he answered. 'There's a Korean proverb which says more or less that you must experience hardship when you're young – you get it free; when you're old you have to pay for it.' When his children are old enough to understand, he will not hesitate to expose them to hardship – under his protecting arm. And so Hong Pae and his younger brother, once so close, are now, despite themselves, widely separated – both by the imaginary line and the differing ideologies which divide North from South Korea. Hong Pae is a capitalist, his brother a communist.

HV40.4.E7 H2
Hammond   LLLF

940.53.L797 N6
Lobel   Jw.

H1.A4 v.S15 LLLF
           Fern

HQ784.W5 053
           LLLF

Marten
gen gen.
Bunia, Af, (Colomb, Bosnia

conn.
K039.C041 LLIR

Fen.
↑
H1.A4V.575   LLIF
_____

Bruno
↑
HQ784.W3 M93 LLIF
_____

(colomb)
↑
HQ784.W3 Y68
LLIF
_____

V34W.874   L3
Brett

CHAPTER THIRTEEN

'The Winds of Change'

In Africa, the 'winds of change' were rising. The rebellion of the Mau Mau, the secret society of the Kikuyu tribe in Kenya, against the whites, owners of the best land, led, in 1952, to an outbreak of bestial killings. White farmers living in isolated areas were attacked, sometimes by their own household staff, and slain. The Rucks, a popular young couple, fought a desperate but vain battle in their garden against a marauding band of Mau Mau.

From inside the house their six-year-old boy had been watching, petrified. Then, as he cowered in his bedroom, he heard the murderers enter the house. He listened, breathless, as their footsteps, their wild, excited voices, drew nearer. Then that small, white boy saw the door burst open and a number of men, big and black, rush upon him. He saw the cruel blades of their swords and knives slash above his head, then fall, hacking at him. That, after a short life of love and toys and cosiness, was the last thing the little boy would ever know.

Four years later, in 1956, Kenya's northern neighbour, the Sudan, declared its independence. For nearly two decades the new state was to be torn apart by civil war – north versus south. Towards the end of that time General Joseph Lagu wrote to the Pope: 'Already more than five hundred thousand men, women and children have perished.' Men and women: their sufferings almost defy belief. Children: either they died with their elders or were tortured and butchered separately.

During the 1955 rising in the south, northerners, including children, according to the report of the subsequent commission of enquiry, quoted by Cecil Epril in *War and Peace in the Sudan, 1955–1972,* were 'whipped and skinned and hung from trees'. Such a sentence in the language of the violence of our time, or any other time, sounds almost banal. But come closer to the execution place, and what do you see? A girl or boy is dragged screaming to a post and tied. A brute raises a leather-thonged lash, brings it down on the child's back, raises it again and brings it down again and again and again. The skin breaks and bleeds. Then the brute, or another, takes a knife, presses the blade to the weals and flays the skin from the child's back. The flesh is raw, the pain consuming, beyond feeling. The sun beats down, the vultures wheel above. The child – it could be yours, or your brother or sister – is already half dead. A rope is fixed round its neck, thrown over a branch or gibbet and the youthful, mutilated body hoisted off the ground. The vultures glide down. The agony of that child should hurt you, too. Imagine your own child in its place.

Or put yourself in the place of the father of a certain Sudanese boy of six. You are attending the trial of a police sergeant who explains to the District Commissioner, presiding over the trial, that he shot your boy, who was playing with others, because he mistook the children for monkeys. The District Commissioner turns to you and says, 'The case is simple: the sergeant could not tell what he was shooting at.' He then tears the sergeant's stripes off his arm and says to you: 'There, I hope you are happy, now I have demoted the sergeant.' And he offers you £20 in compensation for your dead son. Doubtless you would do what the poor father of the little Sudanese boy did – express your utter contempt, return home and, far from the cruel indifference of men, mourn your beloved son.

The agony of the virgin Sudanese state was consummated in the massacre at a village called Banja. A patrol of northern soldiers burst in on the Christian congregation while they were at prayer. The worshippers – half of them children – were tied with thick rope to their chairs. The officer commanding the patrol jeered: 'We're shooting you in your house of worship. Let your God come and save you.' In the name of freedom and independence the pitiless custodians of the so-called enlightened, democratic civilization of the twentieth century, with their tommy guns and grenades, made a mockery of the right of sanctuary as practised by the earliest civilizations as well as the most primitive tribes.

Tibet was also to swell the growing multitude of refugees in the post-war world – that world for whose betterment fifty million had sacrificed their lives.

After the annexation, in 1951, by communist China of the mountain kingdom, the resentment of Tibetans against the Chinese grew steadily until, in 1959, it broke out into open revolt. The god-king of Tibet, the twenty-four-year-old Dalai Lama, was requested to use his army against the rebels. He refused. On 10 March 1959 the Chinese army commander invited the Dalai Lama to his headquarters for a theatrical performance. This time it was the people, suspecting foul play, who refused: a gigantic parade prevented the Dalai Lama getting there. Street fighting broke out and the Dalai Lama fled towards the Himalayan passes followed by thousands of his people. Three of them, who as boys had survived that terrible flight, told me about it in Delhi. Caisang at the time was ten, Yuda was nine and Dashi thirteen.

Both Caisang and Dashi agreed that the Chinese, when they first came to Tibet in the early fifties, were very pleasant and polite. 'They were especially nice to children,' Dashi told me and Caising agreed: 'Being very small, I used to like the Chinese soldiers. They gave me sweets and often came round to the house for a chat. They were very friendly, *loshang*, as they said. But my parents didn't believe them, they didn't like them.' Both boys were in time to find that their parents were right.

Yuda happened to be on the spot when the rebellion broke out. He lived at Dejong in central Tibet and with his family had gone up to Lhasa for what he called 'a big ceremony'. It was on 10 May 1951, the day the Chinese planned to capture the Dalai Lama. 'Everybody rushed into the streets and tried to protect him,' said Yuda. 'The Chinese shot many, many cannons at the Dalai Lama's palace. It made a terrible noise, many smoke and dusty. I saw many people in the road; some are dead, some dying. I was very afraid. I ran away with my parents. Many, many Tibetans were running away.'

I said to Yuda, 'Before those events people used to say that you Tibetans were the happiest people in the world,' and he replied, 'Yes, that may have been true. I was very happy. In my heart I wanted to become a monk.'

But his desire to enter the priesthood – at so tender an age – did not stop Yuda having fun with his friends. His two favourites were Beri and Kumchoktenpa. 'And what did you three get up to?' 'Oh,' he said, 'running and jumping and things like that. We had great games with the horses; we rode without saddles and raced each other. And we went swimming in a pond.' But Chinese cannon had ended all that. Yuda was being driven from his beautiful land.

His family fled on foot, then they found horses and made for the Himalayas. 'We could see far away the Chinese following us,' Yuda said, 'but they did not catch us. We ran very hard.' Yuda was frightened – and hungry – during the week's trek through the mountains to Sikkim.

It was going to take Caisang one whole year to reach safety. His village, where the elders had met and decided on flight, was Akhong, in north-eastern Tibet. The night that Caisang, with his parents and four of his brothers, fled they left everything behind. On horses and yaks, they wound through the deep gorges of the Himalayas, avoiding the well-trodden tracks for fear of the Chinese. But after a month or so the Chinese caught up with them, and attacked their camp. In future, the women and children camped in the mountains, clear of the beaten track, while the men went out to look for food. During one of these foraging expeditions, Caisang's father was killed. 'He was a kind man and very gentle. He never fought anyone.'

Such, for Caisang, was life for the next year, as the refugees moved on through the mountains, often climbing to 15,000 feet, though this did not worry him too much for he had lived all his short life at that height. No, the main problem was food; on the high ground they were weakened, often tortured by hunger. When they camped in a valley they risked attack by the Chinese; that made Caisang very afraid.

One evening, nine months after they had fled from Akhong, Chinese soldiers were sighted approaching the camp. During the night nothing happened, but at dawn the Chinese started shooting. 'We were very lucky,' Caisang told me. The valley was narrow. 'As they shot we ran up the mountainside and our men had the advantage of shooting downwards.' They were pursued all day. Caisang was up in front on a horse, 'because I was small', he explained. 'The men were always behind, protecting the herd.' But Caisang was all the same very frightened that the Chinese would capture him. 'They were good soldiers, very disciplined,' he said.

At last, after a full year's travelling, they reached Nepal. Then India. What were Caisang's feelings about the Chinese who had driven him from his home, broken up his family? 'Our feelings are very bitter, of course. India is not my home. I miss my home, my grandmother, and two of my brothers whom we had to leave behind. We have no news of them.' The separation hurt most when he was sent far, far away – to Norway, although he liked the cold climate, the mountains, the snow, which were some compensation for his far-off Tibet. Caisang believed that he could have lived to the end of his days in Norway. The Indians had been very kind, but their character was different. But, far more, it was the heat of India that Caisang finds so unbearable. Indeed, all of us, as we talked, were in a muck sweat; outside it was pouring in sheets. The monsoon had just broken.

Dashi's flight to freedom across the Himalayas lasted three gruelling months. It started at his home in Sangakcholing, in southern Tibet. The family heard the news of the Lhasa rising on the radio. For two days they travelled by yak and on horseback. Then, avoiding the routes used by traders – and police and army – they abandoned the animals and began a three-month march through trackless jungle inhabited by primitive tribes.

Vividly, Dashi described them: 'They are completely naked. They eat human flesh and are very fierce. They have no ordinary feelings of mercy and compassion. If they are angry they just pick up their swords and kill anyone they come across, even their own people.' 'You, Dashi,' I asked him, 'a boy of thirteen, were you afraid you were going to be eaten?' 'Yes,' said Dashi gravely, 'very afraid,' especially as after a day his feet were blistered, leeches fastened onto his flesh and he began to lag behind. He felt weak too, from hunger.

Then they came to a fair country, sown with maize and rice and potatoes. At last they could eat. But a danger more menacing than the wild tribes now loomed – the Chinese. They were closing in on the Tibetans; Dashi said he could even hear them calling. So close did they come that, as the Tibetans reached the Indian frontier, the frontier guards opened fire on their pursuers.

From the lofty altitude at which he had crossed the frontier, Dashi was transferred to a transit camp in the plains, at Missamari – 'unfortunately one of the hottest places in India'. Tibetans, coming, as Dashi put it, 'from a colder planet', died there by the score, despite all the Indian government did to alleviate their sufferings. Children, said Dashi, were better off – they could play in the water. But the older ones, he continued, 'had inhibitions about changing their very thick clothes for light ones'. And so through an absurd tragedy those poor people died, still thickly clothed for the airy heights of Tibet, in the torrid heat of India.

All three of those boys, Dashi, Caisang and Yuda, were soon to meet face to face their revered god-king, the Dalai Lama, reincarnation of the Buddha, Chenrezi, 'the compassionate', at the school he had started at Mussoorie, two hundred miles north of Delhi. I asked Dashi, 'How did you feel meeting His Holiness for the first time?' 'Well,' he said, 'it was very emotional, difficult to describe.' 'Try,' I said. 'Did your heart beat?' 'Yes, yes, I couldn't control it,' Dashi replied. 'And Yuda: you were nine. Tell me, how did the Dalai Lama look to you.' 'His face,' said Yuda, 'was shining with inside light. His eyes, too, were shining and bright. I felt very happy – and sad too.' Today Yuda is a monk – though you would not think so when you meet him – in his T-shirt and slacks. 'Like this it is easier to stay with the common people.' He changes back into his yellow robes, of course, in the monastery.

Caisang showed me a photo of the Dalai Lama. 'When I first met him,' he said, 'I just cried. There were so many of us children crying that he couldn't very well just come and pat each one of us on the head. But we knew his compassion was always with us.'

Caisang had missed his vocation. He had started – at five years old – studying for the monkhood. 'If I were still in Tibet I would be a monk,' he told me. But the Chinese had messed up his young life. 'Right now,' he smiled, 'I'm in the carpet business, and doing fine!'

Dashi went to work in the Tibetan administration at Dharmsala, where the Dalai Lama lives. 'His Holiness is a very informal person,' he told me. 'He's interested in everything and, unlike with many other great men, you feel very much at ease with him.'

I asked Dashi, 'Is there any organized resistance, any terrorist activity, among Tibetans?' and he admitted: 'There are a lot of young Tibetans who advocate terrorism. They quote the Palestinians. Our own cause is no less justifiable than theirs and many of us feel frustrated because it gets less notice. But His Holiness is opposed to violence, to any terrorist approach. He would not support such activities.' 'And do you think that those young Tibetans would accept the discipline of the Dalai Lama?' 'Certainly,' was Dashi's firm reply.

The boys all dream of home. Dashi's elder brother, Jigme, was left behind in Tibet. 'I doubt whether he is still alive,' he said with resignation.

Yuda, in his mind, clearly sees his house, the village, the fields and the valley and the snow-capped mountains. His friends, too. 'Do you know what has become of Beri and Kumchoktenpa?' I asked, and Yuda replied wistfully, 'I suppose they have become Chinese coolies, eating little and working much.' It makes him sad when he remembers those happy days with his friends.

CHAPTER FOURTEEN

Nkusi in Exile

A mountain paradise like Tibet, though on a comparatively mild and miniature scale, Ruanda-Urundi, on the eastern border of the ex-Belgian Congo (now Zaïre), had lived the 'colonial experience' as a United Nations Trust Territory administered by Belgium. But it was the departure of the imperialists not, as in Tibet, their arrival, that caused *ikiza*, catastrophe. In 1962, when Ruanda-Urundi achieved independence, there came into being two separate, neighbour states: Rwanda and Burundi. In each the two main ethnic groups were the Tutsi, a wealthy, powerful minority, and the Hutu, country folk who account for four-fifths of the population. With the coming of independence the Tutsi in Rwanda and the Hutu in Burundi became victims of savage persecution by the other tribe. In Burundi's capital, Bujumbura, a fair and flowery little city, I heard from both Tutsi and Hutu about the terrors of their childhood, for the first signs of tribal warfare had come before independence.

In 1960, five-year-old Nkusi lived on a hillside in what is now Rwanda. There, as in Burundi, there are no villages as such; the dwellings are dispersed on the hillside, and a 'hill' forms a community like a parish. Below Nkusi's home there ran a river. Young as he was, he already felt a deep love for his hill and the beautiful country around. One day was as happy as the next: he rose at six and ate a plate of beans (which, with cereals, potatoes, green bananas and wild fruit, forms the staple diet). All morning Nkusi played with his friends and his little sister.

His father was a small farmer – he owned half a dozen head of cattle and a sizeable herd of sheep and goats. At mid-day, when the sun beat down, Nkusi would fetch the cattle in and, after a quick bite and a big bowl of milk, he would then take the goats out on the hillside. That was his main job, looking after the goats, which he would bring in at sunset. There was no bed-time hour; when he felt sleepy he slept. 'Life was really heaven,' Nkusi told me.

Then one night he was woken up by a peculiar warning cry – a kind of high-pitched hollering – followed by shouts for help. He saw his father grab a spear and rush out into the dark. After he returned, Nkusi heard people saying that a lot of killing was going on – yet he could not understand why. But when some nearby houses were burnt down he began to feel afraid, the more so because some of the neighbours were leaving, driving their flocks before them.

His parents tried to explain, but still Nkusi could not take it all in. Until one day he saw figures approaching – to little Nkusi they looked like monsters – with faces coloured red and white, yelling and brandishing spears. Terrified, Nkusi watched as they rushed up to his hut. His mother seized him and his baby sister by the hand and they all fled. His father, though badly beaten up, got away. From where they hid they watched their home going up in flames – the big hut in which they lived and the two smaller ones for the goats and cattle. 'It was terrible,' Nkusi said, 'to hear my goats crying and it broke my heart that they and the cattle were dying in the fire.' Yet still Nkusi could not understand. The men who had done these dreadful things were neighbours, of the Hutu tribe it was true, but friends. His parents knew them, so did he.

Worse happened next day. A helicopter hovered overhead showering leaflets. Then it landed and out got some Africans led by a European, a small man dressed in white and black. Someone told Nkusi that he was a priest, but he must have been a gendarme. Nkusi ran off and hid – just in time, for the white man started shooting. 'He shot at people from both tribes because they had been fighting. Three were killed on the spot and another dozen or so lay on the ground. I saw people hit and fall into the river. I now realized how bad things were. It was the first time I had seen people dead.' Nkusi told me that he had only seen one white man in his life, the local priest, who was kind. But that man who had done the shooting made him afraid of white men. In fact, after that massacre, he was afraid of everyone. He felt frustrated (as he put it), too. 'There were no more beans, no more potatoes, not a single cow or goat was left. I was out of work.' Nkusi was eight. He managed, however, to occupy some of his time looking after what remained of the neighbours' cattle which were put to graze down by the river. But 'floating about in the river were people, dead people, my own tribesmen. It made me feel quite sick to look at them.'

School promised to solve Nkusi's unemployment problem, but there he was worse than frustrated. He was persecuted. On the way to school Hutu boys would beat him up, little boys who were urged on by bigger ones and even parents. 'They told the little ones to hit us because we were Tutsis.' Gradually Nkusi's friends fled with their families to Burundi, until he had to walk to school all alone, under the attacks of the Hutu boys. Finally he no longer dared to go to school. 'It was the first time I had been persecuted in my life,' Nkusi said, and he was still only eight. It was to continue, with a few years of peace in between, for more than ten years until, in 1973, when Nkusi was in a secondary boarding school, the offensive against the Tutsis reached a climax. 'Everyone had to sleep with a stick or a knife by his side.' He was often beaten with sticks; some of his friends were knifed. 'It was a real martyrdom that we had to endure,' he told me, 'and for nothing as far as we could see. We were innocent; my father was a peasant – not a chief, or a doctor or an official – just a simple, honest peasant.' And what puzzled and disgusted Nkusi most was that even his own Hutu friends beat him up. 'Doubtless,' he said, 'they had no idea why. They were ordered to chase us out, to make us run for it.' Which is what Nkusi did.

He said a last, regretful farewell to his family, looked for the last time out across the fair hill where, rightfully, he belonged and whose sweet influences he would always feel. Then, secretly, with a few friends, he fled his beloved country. Though the Burundi frontier was normally only three hours' march away, it took them, in pouring rain, two days and two nights, lying up during the daytime, groping their way through the dark.

Nkusi and his friends were among thousands of refugees who were generously welcomed in Burundi. He quickly picked up his studies and made friends, both Tutsi and Hutu. 'It's all the same to me what they are.' 'And the young Hutus who treated you so badly in your own country?' 'It was not because they really hated us,' replied Nkusi, 'but because they were put up to it by others.'

Wherever in the world I spoke to victims of conflict, this was the ever-recurring theme. Ordinary folk can get on with each other. It is their leaders who plant in them the seeds of hatred and evil. It is not possible, Nkusi thought, that men, by sitting round a table, will ever find a solution to human conflict. 'I think that the persecution of man by man is universal.' 'But is it eternal?' I asked. 'Frankly, I think so,' said Nkusi. 'Eternal, because the reason behind it is man's selfishness, his greed, his egoism.'

Nkusi admits a streak of bitterness. It is natural, considering his love for his country, his childhood memories. 'Memories are so precious when they are happy ones. And mine are, at least of my country, those lovely hills, and their winding paths, where women carry their babies on their backs, the children who all played happily together – everyone was so friendly and sociable. And then, looking after the cows and goats – life was very pleasant.' This idyllic vision, Nkusi thinks, has been shattered by the implantation of Western civilization. 'I am not against civilization, be it European or African. Every civilization has its attractions. With us, for example, the cow, with its long, curving horns, is a symbol of beauty, of happiness – a culture symbol you might say. It's not that I want to prevent a farmer today from raising cows for profit. But for me the cow is a beautiful image and the reminder of happy, blissful days. I think of it with sorrow, too, because it conjures up visions of my country and my home which I have lost, probably for ever. That makes me feel bitter.'

'You have the soul of a poet, it seems?' I asked Nkusi. 'We are poetic people,' he replied. 'Every Rwanda dreams of becoming a poet and some of our finest poetry is in praise of that beautiful creature, the cow!' Nkusi, that happy little cow-herd, is today a sensitive and a sad young man; sad above all, because his country, which he so dearly loves, no longer wants him.

Since the day in 1959 when Marie, a young Tutsi bride, heard her neighbours shouting, 'Tutsis, run for your lives! The Hutus are attacking,' she has come through hell. Marie, in a billowing cotton dress, white with blue flowers, was a strikingly beautiful woman. With her was her only surviving son, Joseph Ndoli, a lanky, good-looking boy of fifteen.

Marie and her husband, both Catholics, lived in a wooden house, surrounded by banana-trees and eucalyptus, on a hill near the Ugandan border. He was deputy-chief of the hill and owned twenty head of cattle. The 1959 troubles sent them and other Tutsis fleeing across the border into Uganda, where Joseph Ndoli and two younger boys were born. Then, in 1963, they moved on into Zaïre, hoping to find better land. But Marie's husband, lately a prosperous deputy-chief, could now find only a modest job as scribe. During those hard times two more boys were born to Marie.

In 1972 the family was ordered back to Rwanda. Marie's husband, convinced that would mean certain death for him, escaped to Kenya, while Marie and the boys returned to Rwanda. Guarded by soldiers they were crammed with other Tutsi refugees into a lorry, taken to the frontier and handed over to the Rwanda authorities.

They were then transported, still under armed guard, throughout one whole night, to a refugee camp. There, they were roughly treated and showered with insults. Joseph Ndoli remembered very well – 'they blamed us for being Tutsis,' he said. Luckily, after two weeks, relatives came and took the family away, to a hill near Butari where they were lodged in a hut and where they lived quietly for a year.

Early in 1973, the troubles flared up again and one evening in April one of Marie's neighbours warned her there would be a massacre next day. So, that night, Marie and her boys, with other Tutsi families, fled into the bush and, led by guides, made for the Burundi frontier. There, they had to cross a river: they reached the other side safely, but Marie, in the dark, lost contact with the other refugees.

Carrying her youngest boy, and followed by the other four, she began walking through soft mud. The mud became heavier, deeper underfoot; in the dark Marie and her brood were heading straight into a swamp which stretched for miles. They laboured on through a day and a night, then another day and another night. By then their food had run out and they were exhausted. Joseph Ndoli, a shy boy who stammered slightly, told me: 'My brothers and I kept asking, "Mummy, where are we? Where are we going? Give us something to eat. Mummy ... we're so tired."'

Marie, as she remembered those dreadful moments, was overcome. Then, regaining her composure, she went on with her story. 'In the swamp,' she told me, 'were trees with long thin branches – we had to struggle through them, seeing nothing. But we could hear the toads' ceaseless croaking and the occasional roar of a hippopotamus. In the misty damp, the children never stopped coughing. Their faces were covered with leeches.'

Marie knew her children were soon going to die. One after another they fell, exhausted, without uttering the slightest cry nor even a single word – the second son, the third and then the fourth. The fifth, the baby, whom Marie had carried all the way, was the last to succumb. He died in her arms. Only Joseph Ndoli remained with his mother. They had covered with leaves the body of each boy as he fell. Then for another two days they struggled on until at last they emerged from that dank, cloying hell. When found by villagers their clothes were in rags, their bodies covered with mud and leeches, They were too exhausted to speak.

The villagers cared for them; then came a lorry and brought them to Bujumbura. For weeks Marie was nearly out of her mind. But people were kind to her, nursed her, helped her. She has regained the will to live and only waits for her husband's return. It is hard to tell, but Joseph Ndoli, who is so quiet, now seems indifferent to the horrors which have invaded his young life. He told me that he is crazy about football; he dreams of becoming a great player. Perhaps that has helped him to forget.

Marie had not ceased to astonish me. When I asked her whether she could accept, in obedience to God, her frightful sufferings, she replied without hesitation. 'Yes, I am a believer. I know that God inflicts such terrible trials on us. I gladly accept all I have suffered.'

In Burundi, the rivalry between Tutsis and Hutus led, in April 1972, to a Hutu rebellion. The repressive measures quickly degenerated into a general witch-hunt and the massacre of Hutus.

A young Hutu, another Joseph, told me how he narrowly escaped. Joseph was born in Bujumbura, the youngest of a family of two brothers and two sisters. He was devoted to his parents, though his mother had a weakness for the bottle. 'That did not prevent my loving her, though I did my best to keep her away from her favourite drink, beer.' His mother in turn spoiled Joseph, being the youngest.

He was eighteen when, at the end of April 1972, the trouble started. Until then Joseph's family had been a close-knit, happy one. Since he was six he had been at the Frères de la Charité school, where he was happy. Curiously enough, though, Joseph used to be afraid of white men. 'Their white skin frightened me,' he told me, though he found the Belgians kind enough, especially as they gave him all he needed for school – books, pencils, india rubbers and so on. All the same, he resented, as a black, being made to live apart, in a township, while the whites lived in town. Meanwhile it was black men who were going to instil much greater fear in young Joseph's heart.

He was then at the *école artisanale* (technical school), where the pupils were both Hutu and Tutsi and everybody got on well together. Joseph was learning to be a mechanic. One evening in May 1972, he was with his friends in the dormitory when the Director, accompanied by four soldiers, walked in. Reading from a list he held in his hand, he called on four pupils, all boys in their teens, to step forward. The soldiers immediately led them away. The remaining pupils fell to discussing anxiously among themselves: were those four being taken up for a reprimand or – far more sinister – might it be something to do with the Hutu rising against the Tutsis?

Next day the pupils were paraded and informed that the situation was very serious; they were forbidden to gather in groups of more than five. That evening Joseph and one of his Hutu friends decided to get away, fast. After a hasty meal both boys made for Joseph's home to say goodbye. On the way they met a neighbour who told Joseph, 'Something's been going on at your home; they've taken away your father and mother.' Joseph now felt very afraid – like everyone else.

Nobody knew what was happening.

The two boys separated and Joseph hid at the house of a friend, who told him, 'Listen, they're looking for two of your friends who have left for Zaïre.' Joseph told me, 'By now I was so frightened I couldn't even eat.' Then he had an idea. He got in touch with a Zaïrian friend, a truck-driver called Laurent, who made a regular run between Bukavu (Zaïre) and Bujumbura. They met at the port (Bujumbura is on Lake Tanganyika), where the truck was loaded with sacks of corn. Joseph squirmed in among them – he had two sacks on top of him but that was not too bad – at least to start with. Then the truck drove off towards the customs post, forty-five minutes away. By then Joseph was nearly suffocating, but the customs check went off all right and the truck drove on towards the frontier. After a while Joseph heard his friend shout 'Here we are, we've made it,' and Joseph crawled out, hardly able to breathe, but happy. At Uvira they stopped and Joseph bought his friend a beer, to celebrate.

The truck, Laurent still driving, brought Joseph to Bukavu, where he obtained a refugee card and found shelter at the college of Notre Dame de la Victoire. For two months it was hard living for Joseph – one meal a day, in the evening. Nothing in the morning, nor at midday. In the evening he was ravenous for his simple meal of beans and potatoes. But he (like the hundreds of other young refugees) felt safe – that was lucky for him. For from friends at home he received news that no more had been heard of the four boys taken away from the technical school. Others had been arrested – just because, like Joseph, they were Hutu.

He wondered what had become of his father. Then he felt he had to accept that he was dead. Indeed he had half done so before leaving, because people always said that if someone was taken away and did not return within three days, it was certain they had been killed. And the three days were up for his father before Joseph left Bujumbura. 'But what was his crime?' I asked Joseph. 'Just to be Hutu?' 'That's all,' he answered. He was eventually to be reunited with his mother – but not for three more years, and hard years they were, for Joseph. He longed for one thing – to return home; and though letters from his family cheered him they always said: don't come back yet, not until things have settled down. So Joseph kept hoping, and working.

Then one day he fell ill. Malaria. He was taken to hospital. He felt lonely – and hungry. He noticed that a young Zaïrian girl came every day with food for her mother. Joseph asked her one day, 'Would you be so kind as to bring something to eat? I will give you money to pay for it.' The girl, she was fourteen, was so kind that she even did some cooking for Joseph. Gradually the two young people fell in love. They were married, in 1974, at the Catholic cathedral in Bukavu. Some months later, in August 1975, Joseph received the green light from his family. Joyfully, with his wife, he returned to Bujumbura, where the couple, with their two little girls, have lived happily ever since. Joseph told me – and I admire his generosity, considering all he suffered – that he can forgive the Tutsis for all the harm they caused him. All that, he said, belongs to the past.

One evening, during those days when Joseph had to flee, a girl of sixteen – she was a young Hutu mother – was feeding, at her breast, her few-months old baby Edmond. Her name was Jeannette. When I met her in Bujumbura she sat there talking to me, her breast bared to another baby, André. This basic and beautiful mother-son connection continued throughout our conversation, interrupted only when André was switched from one of Jeannette's breasts to the other. The little boy, Jeannette confided to me, was her only son. Edmond and his father had been murdered.

Jeannette was an attractive girl who smiled hugely every time she spoke. For reasons of discretion, she preferred not to be seen talking to me. So, as I had to drive to the airport, I persuaded her to come with me. Jules the driver, a Zaïrian, interpreted. Jeannette sat next to him, holding André to her breast, which he clutched with his tiny hand. As we crossed a broad and beautiful plain dotted with trees, Jeannette said, 'I want to show you where my husband Charlie and my baby Edmond are buried.' We turned off the road onto a rough track on each side of which were a series of mounds – you might call them tumuli. Jeannette's smile never left her lips as she told me, 'It was here. The place is called Butelele. My husband and my little boy were bulldozed into the ground along with thousands of other Hutu, about fifty to each grave. Then they pushed the earth on top of them. That's what the mounds are.' She talked of Charlie and Edmond as if they were still with her.

Jeannette had first met Charlie, a Hutu like herself, one day as she walked out of school. 'After a week we were in love,' said Jeannette, and gave a big laugh. A year later they were married. Edmond was born; he was five months old when, in April 1972, the troubles started.

As she fed the child at her breast that evening Charlie came home from work. The curfew fell at six. Just before that, Charlie was sitting happily, his son in his arms, when a knock came at the door. It was a Tutsi friend. 'Come and have a drink,' he invited Charlie, who rose, the baby still in his arms, and walked with his friend to a bar across the road.

An hour went by and they had not returned, so Jeannette walked over to the bar. 'Have you seen my husband?' she asked. 'Why should you want to know,' several people shouted, and came at her, hitting her with sticks – and she showed me, on her pretty face, the marks they had left; her right eye, too, was permanently inflamed.

Jeannette was taken to hospital. There, she enquired about her husband and baby and was told: 'Don't ask, or they will kill you as well.' Discharged two days later, she went to enquire at the prison and again was warned: 'Don't ask for news of your husband. He's gone away, and the baby's gone with him.' 'What do you mean, gone away?' demanded Jeannette, and was told: 'They are both dead.'

You might well wonder how André, the baby, came to be sucking away so contentedly at his mother's breast. Well, one day Jeannette, feeling very lonely, was sitting in a food-shop when a man came in. They got talking; he was a teacher at Bujumbura on holiday. What a holiday, especially for Jeannette! That evening he came round after dark to her house. Jeannette let him in. She longed so much for a man to hold her in his arms, which that teacher did, until the early hours.

Nine months later André was born. The teacher went back to teaching and never returned to see his son and the beautiful girl who is his mother. But Jeannette, there is no doubt, is once more happy. She has her man, very small though he is, and with him lives on happily in that fair and flowery, and now peaceful little city which is Bujumbura.

CHAPTER FIFTEEN

Mumbamba from Kolwezi

When, in June 1960, King Baudouin of the Belgians declared the Belgian Congo independent, Jean-Pierre was seven. A Christian of the Luba tribe, he was one of the hundreds of thousands of Congolese who fled the country when, thanks to tribal and political rivalries, the Democratic Republic of the Congo (now Zaïre) became engulfed in chaos and bloodshed. By the end of 1960 the new republic was divided into various rival regions which in turn refused to acknowledge the central government. Katanga Province, in the south, declared its independence.

Jean-Pierre was a pupil at the Sainte-Thérèse primary school at Bukavu, in the Eastern Congo. One of the most immediate results of independence, he noticed, was that, only a few hundred yards away in the streets, his countrymen began killing each other. He could hear the whistle of bullets and the heavy crunch of artillery and mortar shells. He and all the other little boys of Sainte-Thérèse found themselves in the thick of the battle.

The headmaster addressed the pupils: 'There's no question of your staying here, boys; we must evacuate the school.' The twelve classes, forty boys in each and led by a teacher, were paraded. Then, one after another, each class headed, at the double, into the bush. 'I don't mind telling you,' said Jean-Pierre, 'I was terrified. So were we all.' They ran, and ran – for dear life. Jean-Pierre fell and, although he hurt himself badly – he showed me, on his right leg, an ugly six-inch scar – he picked himself up immediately and somehow kept up with the others. Only after they had put five miles between them and the city did they stop. There they stayed in hiding for the next two days. During that time Jean-Pierre's leg, for lack of treatment, became horribly swollen and septic. There was only manioc and sweet potatoes to eat, so everyone was glad when they began the march back to Bukavu. Jean-Pierre, with his bad leg, only just made it, and a friend had to help him back to his home and his anxiously waiting family.

Jean-Pierre belonged to a large family – eleven children including him. He greatly admired his father, an official in the Katangese provincial government, a fine man full of good advice and the head of a devoted family. The children had a special love for their mother – it was to her that they first told their problems – because she was always there. The family was a happy, united team. Cruel events were to break it up and reduce it to a lot of scattered refugees – like so many thousands of other Zaïrian families.

Things calmed down in Bukavu, but when, in 1966, there was more political trouble, the family moved to Lubumbashi, a town of the Katanga province in the southern region called the Shaba, from where they originally came. Jean-Pierre was now a boarder at a secondary school, the Athénée of Kisangani, in the north. In passing, he explained that President Mobutu comes from a tribe in the north-west – who tend to get favoured treatment. For the people of the Shaba it is another thing: 'When the government forces arrest the heads of families they disappear and are never heard of again,' Jean-Pierre told me; as we shall see, he knew what he was talking about. Katanga was a very troubled province, and at times the Shabia tribe lived in terror of their lives.

All the same it was quiet in Lubumbashi for another ten years or so and the story of Jean-Pierre's troubled childhood would have ended there. But in April 1977, when Jean-Pierre was spending his holidays at home in Lubumbashi, it was rumoured that the 'Katangese gendarmes', militants who had earlier fled the central government's repression in the Shaba, were back. The police began arresting people. Jean-Pierre was afraid for his father – who told him not to worry. He was aware of the danger but now he had retired from his government job and gone into business he felt more or less safe.

One day Jean-Pierre came back to the house to find his mother in great distress. She was in tears and around her were Jean-Pierre's brothers and sisters, trying to console her. Jean-Pierre told me: 'My mother described how the police had come, beaten up my father and led him outside. Then – and the little ones were watching – they picked him up and forced him into the boot of the police car. I realized what that meant. We would never see him again.'

As Jean-Pierre spoke his eyes filled with tears. He looked at the floor, trying to control his feelings. But they were too much for him. He raised his hands to his face, broke down and cried. It was some minutes before he went on with his story: he had wanted, he said, to go straight to the police, but his neighbours advised him: 'Don't, on any account; otherwise they will take you.' So the family waited. The hours passed, then, around midnight, 'a brother of my tribe', as Jean-Pierre called him – he was an ex-soldier – came round. 'Listen,' he said, 'you must leave, all of you, straight away. Otherwise they will get you, too.' So they sent for a taxi – a Peugeot station-wagon belonging to a friend. Then, taking nothing with them but some spare clothing, the whole family piled in. It was just after midnight when they set off in the direction of Zambia, where, luckily, the two older brothers had already arrived a couple of months earlier. During the three-hour journey they were terrified of being stopped by the police. But the driver was an expert; he knew the by-roads used by smugglers and crossed safely into Zambia. Three days after the family's hurried departure, the police came to the house to arrest them. But the birds had flown.

Jean-Pierre showed me on a map the escape route. Once inside Zambia he had left his mother and the younger children with his two brothers at Kitwe. Alone, he continued by lorry the six hundred-odd miles to the southern shore of Lake Tanganyika. Then, helped by fishermen, he sailed north – the whole length of the lake – another four hundred miles until, reaching Bujumbura, smugglers helped him to get ashore. Not that Jean-Pierre is dishonest. He was desperate to set foot, without hindrance, in Burundi, where, he knew, fugitives from persecution were well treated. Soon afterwards he obtained his official refugee papers.

That was in 1977. When, a year later, I met him, he was at the university in Bujumbura studying for a degree in economics: for that at least he feels grateful – especially to the Burundi authorities. But no kindness can restore to him his father, his home and his country – they are lost to him for ever. Which leaves Jean-Pierre, like countless thousands of other refugee boys and girls, with a grieving heart which may never be consoled.

When in April 1977 the avenging 'Katangese gendarmes' returned to the Shaba, they put the town of Kolwezi to sack.

Mumbamba lived in Kolwezi. If, at nineteen, he was not exactly a child, he was not yet a man either. And because he was typical of the young people who fled from Zaïre, I tell the story that I gathered from him at Maheba, in the bush of northern Zambia.

Mumbamba lived with his uncle in Kolwezi, because he was at school there and had great hopes of getting a good job. He had a pleasant room to himself and had covered the white-washed walls with photos – the one of President Mobutu was in the place of honour; then there were others of footballers – Mumbamba was a keen supporter of the Mazembe team

– and a variety of Zaïrian stars. He was a motor-cycle enthusiast, too – there were photos of Yamahas, his favourite make, on the wall. But it was on his flat feet that he was shortly to make the most urgent journey of his life.

One morning – it was about six a.m. – he was awoken by automatic rifle fire. A little while later he and his uncle, looking through the window, saw soldiers in the street – Katangese soldiers, the dreaded 'gendarmes'. 'I was scared to death, knowing what they were capable of,' Mumbamba told me. Without waiting another instant he and his uncle slipped out of the house and ran. 'People were tearing, panic-stricken through the streets, streaming out into the bush, thousands of them, fleeing towards Zambia.' Mumbamba had no clear idea in which direction the Zambian frontier lay; he just followed the stream of fugitives across the bush. Having lost touch with his uncle, he walked on all day until, in the evening, coming to a village, he asked the way to Zambia and was told, 'You're already there.' He asked for food, but it was refused. So he had to sell his shirt, his trousers and shoes; all he got for them was the price of a few yams. He came to Kakoma, where a lorry fetched him and took him to Maheba.

Mumbamba had been there two months when I saw him and, despite his shining white smile, he admitted that he was in the depths of depression. 'I'm sad, anxious, frustrated,' he said. The three months' school holidays he had looked forward to spending with his family in Zaïre had to be whiled away in this refugee camp where conditions were very hard. But what saddened him most – and it was obvious from his expression – was that he had lost home, parents and family. He has no news of them, nor of his uncle.

'Can't you help?' Mumbamba asked me. It was a frequent and exasperating question to which I could only reply, honestly. 'I'm sorry, I can't. I'm not an official and have no influence. I can only hope to help in a small way by telling of your tragedy and your sorrows.'

Money and charity go a long way to alleviate the results of evil, but they do not prevent evil itself. How is it possible to prevent evil to children and to all innocents? That is the question to which no one has yet found an answer. Men find increasingly effective ways of harming people; their invention is sadly lacking when it comes to preventing people, and above all small, defenceless people, from being harmed.

CHAPTER SIXTEEN

Biafra – 'the Children's War'

In 1962, there occurred in Europe two events which caught the world's attention: in March the cease-fire, after seven years of rebellion in Algeria; in August, the hideous death of a young East German at the foot of the Berlin Wall.

Algeria had been declared French territory in 1848, but it was not until 1884 that the French gained full control. For another seventy years no serious challenge came to their authority. In 1954, there began a concerted uprising of Algerian nationalists. From then until the cease-fire signed at Evian in 1962 both open warfare and terrorism inflicted grievous suffering on innocent families of both sides. One of its most disastrous aspects – humanly speaking – was the uprooting of families from their homes. Independence drove some one and a half million Algerian-born French *'pieds noirs'* out of homes which had been theirs for generations. Before that, about the same number of Algerians – that is, Arabs – had been ejected from their homes in the frontier zones by the French Army and settled elsewhere. Another 150,000 fled to Tunis and Morocco. There, in sight of their own country, sometimes even of their own homes, they were scattered about the desolate landscape, sheltering, according to the season, either from bitter cold or torrid heat, in grass-thatched huts, mud hovels or holes in the ground, sharing the dire poverty of the local people.

Medical services were organized in Oujda, the frontier town, by the Red Cross and in the field by voluntary Save-the-Children teams. Listlessly, without the energy to laugh or play, sick children queued up – a baby here, half-starved, hollow-eyed, its little belly grotesquely swollen, its fair skin hanging loosely on its spindly bones; and there, elder children with red, running eyes and ugly sores. The shaven heads of little boys with fabus, a scalp infection, were anointed, not with ointment, which was not available, but with used axle-grease – scrounged, who knows, from the trucks and tanks of their ever-present foes, the French.

Algeria won its well-deserved freedom. But did that add to the freedom of those miserable million-and-a-half Algerians who had borne the brunt of the struggle? The only freedom they had ever known was that of the hills and the desert dunes and open plains. That, the most sublime freedom of all, they had always possessed, French or no French.

With the young East German, Peter Fechter, it was quite another thing. He had never known what freedom was, having been a prisoner all his young life of a system he hated. At seventeen, he felt an overwhelming desire to break out – and over the Berlin Wall.

It was on 17 August 1962, exactly a year since that cursed concrete wall, six feet high and topped with barbed wire, had been put up to stop the stream of refugees from East Germany to West. The wall was very effective; it dammed the stream. But there were still some young people prepared to run the gauntlet. Peter Fechter was one; his friend another. Their chances were practically nil, for the East German guards knew what they were up to and were waiting.

Peter's friend made a dash for it and, miraculously, scrambled over the wall and dropped into West Berlin. Peter was not so lucky. Felled by machine gun bullets, he lay bleeding while the guards closed in on him. He begged for help, but none came. As he lay dying, tear-gas grenades lobbed by the guards to repulse the crowd only added to his agony. Within an hour of his dash for freedom he lay dead.

The following day a girl of twenty got through unscathed. Nearly four years went by, then, one evening as the sun was setting, two small figures were seen by the guards, running towards the 'death-strip' near the S-bahn Plauterwald station. Shots rang out; the two figures crumpled. One was a child of thirteen; the other ten.

Two years later people in the frontier town of Coburg were startled one evening by an explosion, then, a few minutes later, another. In the strip of no-man's-land created by East Germany as a barrier against the West, a sixteen-year-old boy lay dying, his two legs blown off by land-mines. East and West police raced to the spot, trained their searchlights on the mutilated body, listened to the young voice begging – 'Help me, I don't want to die.' No one moved – until, still held in the glare of the searchlights, the body ceased to move, the voice was silent. Then the East German police, after exploding seven more mines, reached the dead body and took it away.

The world had gone stark mad. The hopes were that the sacrifice of fifty million human lives in World War II had redeemed it from the curse of war and persecution. But the sacrifice had evidently been in vain. War and persecution had never ceased. On the contrary, the killing, nearly two decades later, of humans by humans had reached a point so absurd that in Germany communist men were shooting children, and in Indonesia children were clubbing communist men to death.

The time was 1965–6. The extract is from *The Violent Peace* by Carl and Shelley Mydans:

> The smiling young boys who bring flowers to tourists and guide them through the Balinese temple of Besakih bashed in the heads of three local communists one night just outside the temple gates. When I asked their leader last week if he understood the difference between communist aims and the aims of his own party, the nationalist party, he replied: 'No.' ... Did he hate the communists? 'No, I do not hate them,' the boy said. Why *did* he kill them, then? 'Some authorities just came by one day and said to get rid of them,' the boy answered with a shy, pleasant smile. 'And so we did.'

But nowhere were children more involved than in Biafra. Of the many names by which the Biafran war has been called – civil war, tribal war, war of survival, etc. – none fits better than 'Children's War'. Not that Biafran children killed anyone, but it was they who died in the greatest numbers in that tragic conflict.

Biafra, the eastern region of Nigeria, is the land of the Ibos, who, being an ambitious, resourceful and hard-working people, are to be found all over Nigeria. The Ibos, with the Hausa-Fulani in the north and the Yoruba in the west are one of the three largest ethnic groups.

In 1966, political conflicts convulsed Nigeria. The Ibos demanded secession. During May, thousands of them were massacred in the northern cities. Thousands more died in further massacres two months later. As a result, two million Ibos streamed back to their own land of Biafra and, on 30 May 1967, the regional governor, Colonel Ojukwu, declared Biafra an independent republic. The federal government reacted by sending troops into Biafra for what it called 'police action' – which was to last nearly four years and cause the death of two million Biafrans. The Churches, the International Red Cross and voluntary organizations sent food and medical supplies which – Biafra being under rigorous blockade – were flown in to temporary landing strips at such great risk that a number of aircraft crashed and their crews were killed.

Though thousands of Biafrans, especially children, were dying daily, Nigeria's partners in the United Nations were slow to react. When they did they gave priority, as usual, to political and economic, rather than humanitarian considerations.

Arms and equipment were supplied to the federal government by the USSR, Egypt and Britain. 'We have to maintain an influence and protect our economic interests,' said Lord Sheppard in the House of Commons. Who could deny that he spoke, quite frankly, for the rest? Portugal, South Africa and China supplied the Biafrans. The United States sent arms to neither side, but, in the political and economic sphere, rooted for Nigeria. Czechoslovakia and France sent arms to both sides – that, perhaps, was not such a bad idea. Their governments could argue (tongue well in cheek) that they were neutral. And another thing, far from negligible, it would increase profits, possibly even double them, from arms sales – apparently it did not matter that the death and suffering caused by those arms might be increased or even doubled. No arms-producing country, with its balance of payments uppermost in mind, could allow itself to be diverted from possible profits just because of the sufferings of some far-away Africans.

Cosmas was one of those Africans, a very small one, it is true. He has told me what he went through in those days when British, Russian, Chinese, French and every other kind of foreign shells and bombs and bullets were killing his people – normally, like all African people, the happiest, most natural and friendly people in the world. Cosmas is now a student in America. I quote him verbatim because some of his phraseology is beautifully picturesque, bizarre even. It may make you smile. All right, as long as you don't doubt the sincerity of Cosmas. He suffered very much through bereavement and starvation, and has been deeply marked by them.

Before I go on with what Cosmas has told me, I should like to say this: I had appealed to the Nigerian delegate of the International Union for Child Welfare to help me meet children who had survived the Biafran war. When I met him in Geneva he was reticent: 'We never want to hear the word "violence" again in our country,' he told me. That answer impressed me. I did not go to Nigeria; instead I have used written testimonies to relate the sufferings of Biafran children. There is one more thing to say: since the Biafran revolt, an unusual, if not unique thing has happened: there has been no revenge. Instead, the Nigerian government has bent itself to the task of reconciliation.

At the onset of war, says Cosmas, several factors were overlooked 'such as the fate of the aged and the children and students who were forced to stay away from school for about three years'. Not that political or military leaders normally give such matters a thought, but they meant everything to young Cosmas. Other factors were the availability of food and the ignorance of the leaders about war and its consequences. 'As a result,' Cosmas observes, 'things fell apart in Nigeria when war was adopted as the sole means by which to settle the conflict.'

At the approach of the enemy, 'everyone', says Cosmas, 'had to start running, taking with him only what he could carry for the long and indefinite journey, usually on foot'. The aged and children (including Cosmas) had to trek long distances 'which resulted in swollen legs and other uncomfortable situations'. Above all, he says, 'hunger was never at rest and more impact was on children'. As things got worse 'people were forced to revoke their personal resolutions and offered what they ought not to have offered in return for food'. To make his meaning clear he explains, 'God's commandments were by some considered not necessary to be observed. Such situations made unborn babies to have incredible and untold experiences.' Foremost among these was abortion: 'Potential mothers,' says Cosmas, 'preferred to have their babies aborted rather than have them exposed to the pangs of hunger.' Premature births, he says, 'were rampant due to lack of drugs and proper care'. That, added to famine conditions, led to many mothers being so weak that they died during labour, their baby too.

For several reasons 'young babies were exposed to dying before the completion of their life-span'. One was that, due to the famine, nursing mothers had not enough milk in their breasts. In that case the mother might simply abandon the baby; or it would be given solid food which, as Cosmas puts it, 'forced it to move as fast as possible to join its great-grandfathers in the grave'. Desperately, some mothers fed themselves on any kind of edible plant or root in the hope that the flow of milk would be maintained. But this rudimentary diet might affect the babies. Cosmas comments: 'Such babies were usually forced to kick the bucket.' Not all mothers survived the diet. As Cosmas says, 'Such cases were settled amicably in the grave.'

Sometimes children were abandoned by their mother because she had to yield to the demands of the soldiers. Some were taken as concubines or as second wives. 'The worst thing,' Cosmas goes on, 'was that some women willingly abandoned their husbands and children to join the soldiers to unknown destinations only with the intention to feed fat and enjoy themselves in various forms.' However a mother might disappear, the consequence was starvation for the children, since the fathers and grown-up sons could not risk going in search of food for fear of being captured and shot. Women were the breadwinners and, when there was no bread to win, 'both parents and all the children,' says Cosmas, 'were forced to die. The worst of all,' he concludes, 'was when both parents had to die and the children had no one to console them – that was my case' – and of tens of thousands of Biafran children.

This is what happened to a handful of them: Chibiko, though only four at the time, remembered the very beginning of the troubles, before the war: 'Many people in our village were crying because one day my brother had come back from Lagos and told us that many Ibo people had been killed there by the Hausa.'

'We had to stop going to school,' Chibiko went on, 'and hide all day long in the bush, because aircraft kept coming over and dropping bombs on our village. My eldest brother and I were playing when he was killed by a bomb.' Not long after, Chibiko's mother told him that she could buy no more food; the money had run out. Chibiko had always loved the soup his mother made. 'Now,' he said, 'mother had to make soup without fish or crab or salt.'

That meant that the little boy had to go short of protein. He became ill. 'One day I had pains all over my body. I had to go very often to the lavatory because I had terrible diarrhoea and couldn't eat. First I got very thin, but later I became very bloated and pale.' Chibiko was taken to Amachara Hospital, suffering from *kwashiorkor*, an illness caused by lack of protein. The patient begins to waste away, then develops chronic dropsy. His legs, arms and face and especially his abdomen, swell up and his black hair turns a rusty-yellow. The kidneys suffer damage and anaemia sets in.

Chibiko was flown out to Gabon where, in hospital, he recovered. That was something to be grateful for: but since leaving Biafra no word had come from his parents; no one could say whether they were still alive. Yet Chibiko hardly realized what that meant. For the moment, at least, other things kept his thoughts from wandering back to his dead brother, his mother and the good fish soup. In Gabon he was living in a family group – Rose's. 'She often smacked us when we did not go under the shower,' Chibiko said, but apart from that everything was fine. At school, too; his favourite activities were football and singing – they, though not quite the same as the good times with his family, kept Chibiko happy.

A terrifying vision still haunted a little Biafran girl called Ihunuaya. She could not say her exact age but it must have been around eight. Her home was at Eluoma-Uzuakoli. 'One day,' she related, 'we saw something that looked like a huge bird. We ran away because there was so much noise and fire came out of it, killing many people.' The fire spread. 'Everything burned, all the houses burned in our village that day.' Ihunuaya saw and heard worse. 'Several people had their heads blown off, some their hands, and some were burned. People were screaming and crying in every corner of Uzuakoli for a whole week.'

What was Ihunuaya's first wish? She smiled at the thought. 'To return to Biafra.' Incredible, after all that Biafra meant in the way of horror and war (which was still going on)? No. Just a love for home and native soil.

To return to Cosmas, who, his parents dead, had 'no one to console me except my creator'. He had to remain in Biafra and fend for himself. Children like him experienced, as he says, 'indescribable problems, at times beyond human endurance, and death was in most cases the only available solution'. However, he goes on, 'with God several impossibilities were made possible. Despite the fact that hunger and disease helped death to take proper care of such an awful situation, God made it possible for many, like me, to survive.' And Cosmas concludes: 'With the experience encountered especially by innocent children and the young men who were almost wiped out, it is likely that people will learn from their past mistakes and resort to peace-making instead of war.' Which is what the Nigerian government has done.

CHAPTER SEVENTEEN

Prison or Exile: Equatorial Guinea

Revenge, not conciliation, characterized the régime of Francisco Macias Nguema, the first president, in 1968, of independent Equatorial Guinea, formerly a colony of Spain. Independence is a fine thing, but how much, for the inhabitants of a country, it may differ from freedom was proved by the tales I heard at Libreville, Gabon, from children and their parents who had been forced to flee from persecution in Equatorial Guinea.

Pascual (he spoke to me in French) was fifteen at the time of the presidential elections. A Catholic, he had been to the Spanish Mission school and the *lycée*, both mixed schools where, he said, 'I used to play – or fight – both with white boys and with my black brothers – it made no difference.' During the holidays he would go to stay with '*mes petits blancs*', his little white friends. His favourite was Miguel, son of a Spanish sea-captain. By 1968 Pascual had his *brevet* (Certificate of Education). He was happy. 'We were free,' he said. 'But there were many who were not so fortunate as you?' I asked. 'Yes,' he replied, 'I admit that, but even if you were not rich you were still free to do as you pleased.'

Pascual's father had an important post in the Ministry of Finance. Of the three candidates for president – Atanacio, Bonifacio and Macias – he supported Atanacio. Though Macias won the election, Pascual's father was appointed Governor of the province of Rio Muni. Life in the governor's palace, Pascual agreed, was more pleasant than ever. But it did not last, for in 1969 Atanacio attempted a *coup d'état*, which failed. Early the following morning Pascual, his parents and his sister, Isabel, found themselves confronting a squad of rough-tongued soldiers who had broken into the governor's palace and were now covering them with their guns. Pascual was terrified; his sister clung to her weeping mother while the soldiers assaulted Pascual's father, His Excellency the governor, tearing his coat and shirt off his back. Then they took him away in a lorry. Pascual and Isabel and their mother tried to climb in too, but the soldiers swore at them and pushed them back. Pascual did not even know what a *coup d'état* was; when he asked he was merely told: 'It means they tried to kill the president.'

For a week the whole family remained under house arrest. Then they were told to take food to their father. They carried it on a three-layered tray: a plate of mashed banana, another of fish and one more, of salad – a day's ration. At the prison Pascual could get no closer than ten yards from his father, and even then it was only thanks to an old scar above the left eye that he could tell that it was him, for otherwise he was unrecognizable, his face being completely disfigured by ugly wounds, his hair cropped and his body thin and bent. The sight of him made Pascual so sad that he cried; so did his mother and little Isabel. But the soldiers chased them away, shouting rudely, 'Leave the food and get out!' So they returned home, once more to be put under guard.

Pascual's father remained in prison for five months, during which time Pascual sometimes accompanied his mother on her daily visits to bring food – the only food provided. The day his father was freed, he was escorted back to the governor's palace by soldiers. Pascual told me how painful it was to kiss his father, whose face and arms were still covered with wounds and sores. The soldiers ordered them: 'Take what is yours and get out.' That same day, in a hired lorry, they moved themselves and their belongings to their house in Rio Benito. There, Pascual's father told him, 'Listen, my child; I am finished, but you – you must get on with your schooling. Go to Bata [fifty kilometres away] where you can live with your cousin.' So Pascual said goodbye to his father, a spiritless, ruined man. And from Bata, Pascual could not even write to him or his mother because of the government censorship. He was able to get home for the holidays but only to find that his father was still in a very poor state and despairing of his son's future.

In 1971, soldiers came to the house, searched it and again arrested Pascual's father. He was imprisoned temporarily at Rio Benito, then moved to the *parquet* (the Public Prosecutor's gaol) at Bata. 'It was there,' Pascual told me, 'that they liquidated prisoners.' One day in June 1972 Pascual went with his mother to the prison. He saw his father as he returned from his day of forced labour; it was obvious that he was in the last stages of exhaustion. His father told him: 'My child, this cannot go on for much longer. I'm already half-dead. Try to persuade the prison authorities to give us an hour together so that I can pronounce to you my will and give you my blessing.' But when Pascual asked the captain of the guard he just swore at him: 'Fuck-off. I can do nothing.' So Pascual then asked the sergeant, who said, 'Okay, but I can only give you fifteen minutes – and it will cost you five thousand pesetas and a bottle of whisky.'

This was provided, and Pascual and his mother were led to the cell where he found his father, so weak that it was only by propping himself against a piece of furniture that he could remain standing. To his wife and his sixteen-year-old son Pascual, he declared his last will and testament. Then he gave his last instructions: to his wife Monica: 'Never leave your son,' and to his son: 'Never leave your mother.' Finally, as is the custom, he blessed his son. Young Pascual demonstrated this simple ceremony, as if I were his son, he my father. He took my right hand in his and, squeezing it each time he emphasized a word, said: 'All reproach or anger that I may have expressed against you, I renounce this day.' And so saying he turned aside and spat, as a sign that he had rid himself of all bad feelings. Then, blowing on my hand as a preliminary to the good wishes, he went on, 'You must try to lead a good life; make no enemies and you will have none; may you be spared from trouble and from violent death. In the name of the Father, the Son and the Holy Spirit.'

Next day Pascual rose early and took a Thermos of coffee to his father. 'Still dejected and utterly exhausted,' Pascual said, my father told me, 'My son, I believe it will be my turn today. After today we shall see each other no more.' As he repeated the words, Pascual's face was convulsed with anguish. He sat down, his head in hands, and cried bitterly. After a while, he pulled himself together and went on: 'I gave my father the Thermos and watched him as he tried to climb into the lorry. He was so weak that he had to be helped. It was the last time I saw him alive.' Pascual could not free himself of that last, pitiful sight of his father. All the way back to his home, he cried.

The house was quiet, unusually so, as Pascual drank coffee with his mother. Then came a man who said, 'Madame Monica, I have serious news. Your husband died at a quarter to nine this morning. I was there,' and he described how Pascual's father was beaten and bludgeoned till he fell. Cold water was poured on him in an attempt to revive him, but he was already dead. Other prisoners were then ordered to drag the body away. It was left under a bread-fruit tree until a lorry came and took it to the morgue. There Pascual saw his dead father. 'He was no longer as I had seen him a few hours earlier. He seemed to have shrunk; he looked almost like a pygmy.'

'Papa's body,' Pascual said – and he talked of 'Papa' as if, after six years, he was still very near – 'was so covered with mud that it had to be washed.' It was buried that day. 'A Christian burial?' I asked. 'No question of that,' replied Pascual. 'The priests were not allowed to. Papa was buried without any rites.'

Pascual went back to school. He passed his *baccalauréat*. Soldiers kept coming to the house, ransacking and insulting, until one day Pascual could bear it no longer. 'You're a lot of shits,' he yelled at them, 'Get out.' That earned Pascual two weeks in prison, where he was beaten. On his release he told his mother: 'I can't stick it any more. I'm at the point where I risk doing something foolish. Then I shall end up like Papa. I've got to leave.' His mother agreed. When the day came, she woke him early, took his hand, as his father had done, and blessed him.

So, despite his father's last wishes and despite himself, Pascual left his mother. Following jungle tracks, he walked for five days till he reached the sea at Kogo, about eighty kilometres away. There he spent another three days, hidden in the sugar plantations. Sugar-cane was all he could find to eat. Each day he watched for a pirogue whose owner might take him south to Gabon. But it was very risky to approach a fisherman, who might give him away. So he quite simply stole a pirogue and in it rowed all night until he reached Coco Beach, in Gabon.

Did Pascual regret having left his country, I asked him, and his reply was yes and no. He is grateful to Gabon for sheltering him but has no real friends among the Gabonese. He would like to get around more, but every time he goes into a bar or café people ask him, 'And what are you doing here, poor Guinean. Why don't you go back home?' Pascual sadly misses his home, to which he dare not return. 'Quite honestly,' he told me, 'I am desperate.'

It was not in a pirogue but on foot that Jacintha, now seventeen, fled from the persecution of President Macias. The reason for her escape went back some years to the time before independence when there was an *Assemblée* (parliament) in Equatorial Guinea. Her father Martin was a *député* (member), only he was not for Macias.

It was in the late afternoon when I called at their small iron-roofed house in a suburb of Libreville. On the doorstep children were chattering and laughing, blissfully unaware of the terrible events which had exiled them from their country. Inside, in a simple cement-floored living-room, the grown-ups were at table. They ate – meat, rice and banana – in total silence, a sign, perhaps, that they were sad, as they had every reason to be, and preferred not to discuss their troubles among themselves. With a stranger like me it might be easier; they could unburden themselves. And this, after we had exchanged polite, friendly greetings, Jacintha and her father did.

It was 1969, and Jacintha was living with her parents at Bata. She was then eight, and had all she needed in the way of creature comforts to make her happy, including TV, radio and a record player, on which she played pop-music, and danced, as only an African girl can. But having fun did not prevent Jacintha from being very good at her lessons.

On 5 March (the day that Pascual's father was arrested) Jacintha's father, Martin, fetched her from school. Hardly had they arrived home when a lorry pulled up in front of the house. Eight men got out, rushed at Martin and began beating him – before the eyes of Jacintha and her mother – with heavy sticks. 'I cried very much,' said Jacintha. 'My father was knocked out and fell to the ground.' The men then tore off all his clothes and dragged him naked to the lorry.

Two weeks later Jacintha's mother took her to the prison, where they were placed at ten yards' distance from a group of dejected, ill-kempt prisoners, among them her father, whom Jacintha could not pick out among the other prisoners until one of them made a faint sign of the hand – talking was forbidden. At that she recognized her father; his face now covered with two weeks' stubble, was raw with open wounds. At the sight of him Jacintha burst into tears. 'I cried,' she said, 'all through the visit.' Martin was no less affected. Through one of the prison officers, a relative of the family, he sent a message: 'Darling Jacintha, don't come back. I can't bear seeing you so sad.'

Martin broke in here to say that on the day of the visit the Equato-Guinean delegate to the United Nations, Saturnino Ibongo Iyanga, was beaten to death. 'I saw the body,' said Martin, 'it was Saturnino's all right.'

Martin told me what he went through as a prisoner. 'There were five of us in a cell, three metres by two. We had to relieve ourselves into a box, which remained there until full. Despite the smell we somehow managed to eat our one daily meal, which was brought in by the prisoners' families.' At night, two guards would come in, take three prisoners and there, just outside the cell, make them lie down on their stomachs. Then they would lay about each prisoner in turn, beating him unconscious with a rifle butt or a heavy stick on the head and back. Martin took off his shirt and showed me his back, on which were four deep scars.

During the months that followed, Jacintha, knowing that the prisoners were being tortured – often to death – lost all hope of seeing her father again. Then one day – it was in June – he returned home. 'I cried,' she said, 'but this time with joy.'

Martin and his family were ordered back to his village, some 280 kilometres from Bata. He had to report to the local government offices three times a month, but soon he was again imprisoned. Though spared the daily torture, he was condemned to forced labour – fourteen hours a day. As the daughter of a political prisoner, Jacintha told me, life became hard. She had to leave school to help look after her father and with him in prison the money ran out until there remained hardly enough to buy food. Following a visit by Macias, Martin was put on a life sentence. I asked Jacintha what she thought of the president and she replied quietly, 'He is a wicked man.'

Martin, with three other prisoners, planned a break-out. He warned his wife, then, the following day, during the midday meal, slipped away. The frontier was not far. That evening Jacintha's mother told her that, with her baby sister Maria-Theresa (Marité) they were all going to escape next morning. She was so frightened she could not sleep all night. Then, before dawn broke they set off into the jungle, her mother carrying Marité with Jacintha walking in front. Before them were twelve kilometres of jungle paths, which, fortunately, they knew. But many times they had to hide, not from soldiers, but from elephants! Once safely across the frontier, they made for a village. Jacintha's father arrived soon after.

Jacintha's story would have ended there, but for a boy called Gabriel. The romance began one evening when Gabriel was on his way home from a film. It was love at first sight. Gabriel was twenty, Jacintha fifteen. About two years later, their son Emilio was born.

Gabriel was no local boy. His home had once been in Equatorial Guinea, in a village near Rio Benito. The son of a farmer, he told me, 'Before Macias, all was well. Frankly, I did not know what independence meant until it happened. Before it did, things were much better; blacks and whites got on well; you could see whom you liked, get around everywhere, even go on holiday to Malabu island [now called Macias Nguema Island]. There was plenty of food, both African and imported. Since Macias there is nothing.' (I quote Gabriel verbatim.)

Gabriel, who was doing well at the *lycée* at Bata, hesitated long before deciding to leave. He went for two reasons: first, his father had been forced to give up his farm because he could not sell his harvest. When the women took goods to sell at the market, they were attacked by the militia. Second, Gabriel had reached the age for compulsory service in the militia, Macias's *Juventud* (who have made a name for themselves for robbery, pillage and rape and have been accused of violating Human Rights). It was hard for Gabriel to leave. His father allowed him, as the eldest son, to pass before the others. His mother was worried to see him depart into the unknown and told him to keep out of trouble. Gabriel walked the fifty kilometres to Kogo, then, like thousands of his countrymen, continued his flight by pirogue across the estuary to Coco Beach, Gabon. In one way he regrets leaving his country. His ambition was to be a surgeon, now he is unemployed. In Gabon an Equato-Guinean has little chance, despite the common language, *Fang*, of finding a job. So Gabriel, the aspiring surgeon, and Martin, the one-time Member of Parliament, work together on any odd job they can find. The little they earn goes to feeding the family.

Gabriel's great consolations are Jacintha and Emilio. He would love to have more children – after first getting married. But with no money and no future he can do neither. Jacintha is glad that at least Emilio is safe in Gabon, but she fears for his future. And Gabriel agrees. 'My opinion is that he will live in greater poverty than I do.'

It was due to circumstances both strange and terrible that a little girl, Concepción, came to be talking to me. She sat on the knees of a man called Santiago, who had brought her along.

In 1968 Santiago was *Chef de Canton*; during the presidential election he campaigned against Macias. The election over, he was immediately thrown into prison at Bata. His cell, in which he was to spend the next five years, measured ten metres by four and was shared by 150 prisoners. As his cell-companions were executed or simply died of hunger or exhaustion, they were replaced. But in June 1974 a massacre took place. In less than two weeks all 150 occupants of the cell were executed. Santiago alone remained – the reason, he learned, was that there was no more room at the cemetery, or perhaps it was that they could not dig graves quickly enough. Whatever the reason, the massacre was halted and this gave Santiago his chance. He sent for his wife: she brought him money. He gave thirteen thousand pesetas – which was gratefully accepted – to the officer in charge, and Santiago, after five years in prison, was free.

He returned straight away to his village, and there for the first time he set eyes on Concepción, who was in his wife's arms. She had had the child with another man. Santiago had received news of the birth when in prison and did not give a damn that he was not the father. All he wanted now was to see Concepción. He took the baby girl and hugged her. 'It is difficult,' he said, 'to explain how much she meant to me at the moment. I felt she was the symbol of my freedom.'

I asked Santiago, 'Do you feel any resentment towards your wife and the man with whom she deceived you?' 'None at all,' he answered. 'I understood quite well that while I was in prison she could not bear the loneliness. And all children in Africa are considered a grace.' 'Do you love Concepción as much as your other children?' 'As much?' he laughed, 'I love her more.'

CHAPTER EIGHTEEN

The Flight from Idi Amin

Some two thousand miles due east of Equatorial Guinea, Uganda was once a peaceful, happy and prosperous country. I know, because I was there, on my way by car from Cape Town to Algiers, long before anyone had heard of Idi Amin Dada. As I drove out of Entebbe I passed gardens full of flowers, with an occasional wheelbarrow and the garden tools propped against the wall. Children, fat and well-dressed, were on their way to school. Civilization seemed to have taken root firmly in the heart of Central Africa among those stolid, home-loving people. Then, in 1971, the president, Nelson Obote, was ousted by Amin.

1971 was a fatal year for Uganda, Jack, then eleven, told me when we talked together at the Igunga School, near Kisumu in Kenya, where I met several children who had fled from the persecution of Amin, and whose headmistress, a warm-hearted lady, had seen her brother hanged in public on the president's orders.

In 1972 President Amin ordered that non-citizens of Uganda were to leave the country; they might have been Anugandans, as in the case of Jack's father, who was of Kenyan origin, or Europeans or Asians. It was the Asians who suffered most. Things then calmed down until, in August 1974, Amin, pursuing his clean-up of non-Ugandans, sent his soldiers out to the villages. Any Kenyans they found were dragged out of their houses, the children first. 'Then,' said Jack, 'they began their violence on the children and continued on the women and the men, shooting them indiscriminately, like shooting hens.'

Jack was a fine-looking fellow; from his shiny, ebony-black face his eyes looked out very straight at me. He was dressed in a clean, well-pressed boy-scout uniform – a white short-sleeved shirt, its pocket emblazoned with a star and beneath it the legend 'Knowledge is Power', 'Igunga High School'. From the belt around his dark green shorts there hung a coil of rope; Jack explained that one of its uses was to bind up the hands of an enemy. The finishing touches to Jack's smart uniform were his short socks and brown shoes and, on his head, a khaki beret trimmed with pink. Round his neck he wore a red scarf held in place sheriff-fashion by what he called a 'woggol'.

Jack lived in Western Uganda, where his father had built his own home, helped by friends. It was a big house made of cement blocks with a corrugated iron roof – twelve rooms in all, for besides Jack's parents there were nine children. His eldest sister was Jack's favourite. I asked why. 'I liked her best,' he said, 'because it was she who did the cooking; she went out to fetch wood and she washed my clothes.' Jack's father farmed forty acres. It was a well-run, prosperous little farm and Jack was not yet six when he began to help his father. 'It was a lovely time,' Jack said. 'Everybody was happy; the neighbours were at peace and there was no threat from the military or from the police.'

Then Amin took over. A year later, to use Jack's own words, the president was ruling in a harsh way. Later still 'the corruption' began and, with it, came an increase in the killing. Jack was then sixteen. One day he was taken, with forty other scouts, to a bridge upstream from the Karuma Falls, where the river is swift-flowing and full of rocks. The scouts were then made to get out of the lorry and stand on the bridge. Two lorries full of prisoners, bound hand and foot, drove up. Then, one by one, the prisoners were dragged out of the lorry and thrown over the bridge into the raging torrent, which carried them downstream over the falls and on into the calmer water infested with crocodiles. I asked Jack what his feelings were as he watched this appalling spectacle. He replied, 'I felt, and I still do when I think of it, as if I was one of those people being thrown into the water.' When he returned home Jack told his father. 'He listened, shook his head sadly and went to sleep,' said Jack quite simply.

About the same time Amin's soldiers began attacking and massacring Anugandans, and it was rumoured that Anugandans in Jack's town (whose name I shall not mention) were next on the list. At that the whole of Jack's family ran off into the bush, abandoning for ever their house, their flocks and their land, in short, the fruits of years of toil and labour. Jack carried his four-year-old brother on his shoulders; his eldest sister, the one he loved, 'a very strong girl', said Jack, carried another sister of six. For a whole week, walking by night and hiding by day, they journeyed towards Kampala, two hundred miles away. During all that time they ate no food save what they could cull – zimdome berries and leaves of the Misara tree. They knew that wild game roamed the bush, and Jack said that they were all in constant fear of running into lions or elephants, but fortunately luck was very much with them. For Jack's parents hunger and fatigue made the going very hard; often they had to stop and vomit. At last, at the end of a week, they trudged into Kampala one night and, the next day, a relative drove them to the frontier at Busia.

There, at the customs post, the family, mother, father and children, were ordered to strip down, completely naked. Only Jack and his two brothers, twelve and fourteen, who were in their scouts' uniform, were excused and told to stand aside. The men of the customs and police then set about the family, beating the naked father and mother with rifle butts until, crying out, they fell to the ground and were left half-dead. Then the frontier guards turned on the children, naked too, kicking them with their heavy boots. Such bestiality was too much for Jack and his brothers, who turned away, hiding their faces. When it was over Jack looked back and found that his twelve-year-old brother was no longer with him. He had apparently rushed towards his parents and the others, hoping to help them. Jack now saw that the boy lay on the ground, dead. He had been literally kicked to death; on the end of the frontier guards' boots a metal spike, protruding some two to three centimetres, was fixed. The boy had been kicked in the chest and the spike had entered his heart – a patch of blood on his white shirt marked the place. The guards picked up the body and carried it into the building. That was the last that Jack ever saw of his young brother.

This sorry, frightened family was now ejected from Uganda. They walked on into Kenya, were picked up by a European and taken to Kakamega. There the family broke up; Jack and his brother went on to Igunga School, and his parents and the rest of the family went another way – Jack doesn't even know where. He especially misses his father, whom, for so many years, he had helped on the farm. All he knows is that his father, with no land and no money, is completely destitute. Jack cannot find it in him to forgive those brutes at the frontier. 'I think they did bad' – those were the words he used – 'I would like to treat them as they treated my parents and family.' Meanwhile he can think of only one thing, to succeed brilliantly in his studies. Why, I asked him, does he prefer learning to becoming a farmer? 'Because I want to get a good job, earn money, find out where my parents are and help them.' If Jack could not say 'I forgive', his aim in life is perhaps the most effective way of doing so.

David, another Anugandan victim of Amin's tyranny, had no family left to care for. His father had died when David was twelve months old. His three elder sisters married; his favourite brother, four years his senior, died when David was four, leaving him very lonely. The remaining brother was at school. David's life now became centred on his mother, whom he adored.

A promising pupil, his schooling ran foul of 'tribalism'. David's tribe was the Maragoli; the local, most powerful tribe was the Baganda. Though he passed into secondary school, the authorities – Baganda – would not accept him. For two years he remained at home; his elder brother had a job elsewhere, so David was alone, unhappy, kicking his heels. He decided to adopt a Baganda name, passed the exam once more and was admitted to another school. After four months there he was summoned, one day early in 1977, by the Principal, who asked him, 'What is your tribe?' At which David's heart nearly stopped. Before he could answer the Principal went on, 'You are an Anugandan. You are to leave immediately and return home.' David knew he was in danger, like all Anugandans. The military could call any night, take them from their homes. 'And the next day,' said David, 'the neighbours would find an empty home and no more would be heard of its occupants.'

So David fled from the school, leaving behind his books and his mattress for which he had paid. It took him two days' hitch-hiking to reach home. His mother looked surprised, but David told her, 'My life is in danger. I am sorry, I shall have to run away.' His mother, just as anxious, gave him 200 shillings. 'Go away,' she said, 'to somewhere where you will be safe.' David left next day. The parting still hurts him; that was clear from the look in his eyes as he told me, 'I've had no news of her since.'

Taking a little cooked maize with him he set off on the 300-kilometre journey to the Kenyan frontier, first by bus to get quickly clear of his local district. The bus took him to Jinja, and it was there that he was a witness to murder; he watched as a man, bound hand and foot, was carried to the middle of a playground and there, before the crowd, shot dead by soldiers using pistols. David knew that this might easily be his own fate, so he pressed on, barefoot, for the remaining hundred kilometres to the frontier. He lived on bananas; sometimes he came to a halt, his legs swollen and aching. By the fifth day his feet were so sore that, he said, 'It was like walking on glass.' Then at last he saw in the distance the frontier post – and the Askaris on duty. So he made a detour through the bush and, crossing the border unseen into Kenya, came to Kakamega.

Though safe, David's troubles were not over. For three more months he roamed the bush, feeding off guava and other fruits, sleeping under the stars. He kept thinking of his mother, of all she had done for him since his father had died; it was she who had given him a good home, fed him and paid for his education. He reproached himself for leaving her.

Then at last things changed. Through the good offices of the Red Cross he was able at last to pick up his studies at Igunga School. David will never forget the sacrifice his mother made for him; to Igunga School he feels the deepest gratitude, which, he told me, 'I am trying to repay with hard work and good conduct.' David speaks so well and so characteristically for a whole multitude of persecuted children.

How often did the trackless spaces of the bush provide safety and shelter! But Edward, eighteen, and Judy, fifteen, both Tanzanians, and pupils at Igunga school, told me how the bush also has its dangers.

The two children were of the Maraguri tribe and living in Mara province when war broke out between the Wykoma and Wakuria tribes. The Maraguri, though friends of the Wykoma, were living in Wakuria territory. The Wakuria attacked them. Edward's and Judy's houses were burnt down; Edward's sister of ten perished in the flames. Judy's father was killed before the eyes of his wife and six children. With perfect composure and looking very straight at me, as if to help me imagine what was unimaginable, Judy said quietly, 'I had to watch as my father was hacked to death.'

That night, Judy's family fled into the bush and headed for Kenya, walking all night and hiding by day. One day, as dawn broke her eighteen-year-old brother was missing. 'He must have strayed or just been too tired to go on,' said Judy in her calm voice. 'We never saw him again.'

Edward's family fled, too, into the bush. There were his mother and father and nine children. They were camped for the night when, in the pitch dark, a piercing cry awoke them. Very close by a lion roared – at which the family rose up and fled in terror. When they stopped, Edward's little brother was not there. Fearfully, they made their way back to the camp. Of the boy there remained only traces of blood on the ground.

James was still a student when, as he told me, 'I got into hot water.' He was a youth of immense charm – it had certainly helped him during the long odyssey which had brought him all the way from Uganda to Libreville, Gabon, where we met. Though James could not be called a child (except at heart) I tell his story – and those of Adam and Benjamin, which follow – because they depict the tragedy of students whom war and persecution have driven out of school, leaving them only half-educated. Wherever in the world I talked with young people this – the impossibility of completing their education – struck me as being the most unbearable, to them, of all their griefs.

Until he was fifteen, James's best friend was a white boy called John. Though James went to a school for blacks and John to one for whites, the two were inseparable companions and both were ardent sportsmen. 'Cricket was my best game,' said James with an enthusiasm which had not been damped by his sufferings.

At seventeen, he went to high school. That was in 1971, when Amin came to power. Then he went on to university – it was there, in 1976, that he got into trouble. He and four other students published a pamphlet demanding that the military government surrender power to a civilian one. A few days later one of the professors warned them, 'The security people have seized your pamphlet. You had better leave the country, quick.' The five fugitive students managed to reach Kigali in Rwanda. From there two of them went on to Britain, two more to Tanzania. James decided to go to Zaïre. At the border he was arrested and thrown into a dark, filthy cell with some bandits who beat him up, rifled his pockets and stole what little money he possessed.

Released, he was sent on to Kinshasa but, unable to enter the university there, he pushed on to Brazzaville, in the Congo. James's one and only object in continuing this extraordinary odyssey was to complete his studies. He was penniless, but thanks to the generosity of Rwandan students, was able to spend one year at the university of Brazzaville. Then the money ran out and he headed, without a visa, for Gabon. In the frontier village the women, no doubt succumbing to his charm, persuaded the Gabonese immigration people to let him in. 'I really felt that God was with me,' James said, 'and I only hope He continues to be kind to me.'

No sooner across the frontiers than, James bumped into an official, on holiday from Libreville. 'I'm going back there today,' he said, 'I'll drive you!' So James came to Libreville. But, he told me, he was still hoping to go on to Britain and the United States. I wished him luck and, as we walked towards the door of the hotel, the British ambassador, Christopher MacRae, drove up. I introduced James, with a short explanation. Whereupon His Excellency reached for his wallet and from it drew a visiting card which he gave to James. Decidedly, God was still with that young fugitive from Uganda.

Before they fled from Uganda, Adam and Benjamin had both suffered grievously. It was in Bujumbura that they told me their story.

Adam was five when his mother died; he and his elder brother lived with their father, an officer in the Ugandan army, in Kampala: Adam's father knew President Amin well. When I asked him to describe Amin his eyes burned fiercely; and he just said: 'A dictator and a killer.'

There was good reason for Adam's hatred. At school, where he was a boarder, he was waiting one morning with his books under his arm, to go into class, when a day-boy came up to him and said, 'Your father has been murdered.' Adam was so upset that he walked straight out of school and took a taxi home. There, near the garden gate, lay his father, his uniform stained with blood which came from stab wounds. When soldiers came to take his father's body away for burial, Adam asked if he might go with them. They refused – and for this he will never forgive them: he does not even know where his father's grave is.

Adam then went to look for his brother, an officer in the Air Force. At the barracks other officers told him, 'We have just been to the funeral of some airmen. Your brother was among them.' This appalling news decided Adam: fearing that he might be murdered, too, he left Uganda two days later. An adventurous journey by bus and on foot took him secretly across the border into Rwanda. He decided to go on to Burundi and made his way to Bujumbura.

Adam was deeply marked by what he had been through. 'There is no end to my troubles,' he told me. 'With my father and my brother murdered I have no one left. I am very lonely.' Those were the last words that Adam spoke to me.

Adversity had made kindred spirits of Adam and Benjamin. But it had made them mistrustful and suspicious of others. Twice Benjamin shut up completely, glaring at me with his coal-black eyes, his mind in a turmoil. I had taken an immediate liking to him; he had a kind, open face and he was intelligent. He was also physically handicapped and walked with an awkward shuffle.

Benjamin's father was a lecturer in botany at Kampala university. His mother was a midwife. He had an elder brother, Joseph, who was his greatest friend, and a younger sister. Benjamin told me that I might give these details – you will soon understand why.

At his school at Kibuli, in Kampala, the other boys were kind to him about his infirmity. He was doing well and studying for the university.

At the beginning of 1977, he became worried about his father's safety, and after the murder of the Chief Justice, of university teachers and students, Benjamin thought that his father must be a marked man. As the year 1977 continued, students began to disappear from Benjamin's own class – and teachers as well. One day in summer – it was 4 August and Benjamin was at school – something made him ask permission to return home for the day. There he found his mother, very worried. His father, she explained, had gone to market with his brother Joseph the day before and neither had returned. She had checked all the 'lock-ups' (prisons) but without success. Three days later his mother telephoned him at school, asking him to return home immediately. Benjamin knew then that there was something wrong. He found his mother in tears. In the house lay the dead body of his father; it had been found that day. Of Joseph there was no trace. This double tragedy so shocked young Benjamin that now, as he spoke about it, his words faltered and he became completely silent.

Benjamin once more returned to school. A few days later he heard that his mother had disappeared. He went straight home only to find the house empty. His sister had disappeared, too. Benjamin said, 'I then realized that I was the sole surviving member of the family.' For that reason he allowed me to mention the details of his family; they were dead, all of them, and beyond any further harm.

Benjamin was in great danger. With only a little money and no baggage, he travelled by bus to within sight of the Tanzanian frontier. There he left the bus and, handicapped though he was, struck out into the bush, avoiding the Ugandan customs, and entered Tanzania. This was only the start of his prodigious feat of walking or, more exactly, shuffling, a good 130 kilometres to safety. He had fallen in with two companions, Joseph and Sam, and together they decided to make for the nearest country, which was Burundi.

That 130-kilometre march through the bush and over mountains took two days and two nights. Incredibly, Benjamin, hobbling along beside his friends, managed to keep up with them; he told himself, you've got to stick with them, or you'll lose them. They came at last to Bujumbura, but only to find that their main aim – continuing their studies – could not be realized, at least in the immediate future, for none of them spoke French. Benjamin, with characteristic determination, was learning. He was aiming for a standard of education which will at least enable him to serve his country. 'I love Uganda and miss it,' he told me. 'If only things would change I should be happy to go back.'

And, though I have no further news from him, I hope that, with Amin gone, he has already done so.*

---

*In January 1980, Benjamin wrote to me – from England.

CHAPTER NINETEEN

The Cost of Freedom: Bangladesh

On the Indian sub-continent, early in 1971, there occurred a hideous blood-bath and the flight of millions of refugees from East Pakistan. Populated for the most part by Muslim Bengalis, with an addition of Muslim Biharis who had fled there from India at the time of partition (1947), East Pakistan was pressing for secession as a sovereign state, Bangladesh, from West Pakistan. To quell the Bengalis' enthusiasm for independence, West Pakistani forces were sent in on 25 March. Nine months later they were defeated and Bangladesh won its sovereignty.

For Razia, the War of Liberation is an ugly memory. A sweet girl, with a sad expression on her pretty face, I met her with her young sister, Zakiabid, at a sewing-class in an upper room of a dilapidated building in Mahommetpur, the Bihari quarter of Dacca. She described to me the street-fighting she had seen, with the eyes of a twelve-year-old, in front of the house in Dacca's old quarter, where she then lived – people lined up and butchered with knives. Though she tries to forget all that, there is one sight she can never get out of her mind – an old man being pushed and pulled this way and that as he cried in vain, 'Save me, save me!' Razia watched as men of the *Muktibahima*, the Bengali 'freedom fighters', dragged him away towards the riverside, where she saw him stabbed in the stomach and lie there, still crying for help. But nobody came. And all Razia could do was to watch, terrified that the freedom fighters would break into her own home.

They did. They forced their way in and began ransacking the house. For the Bengalis, in their fight for freedom, were hostile to the Biharis, foreigners who spoke a different language, Urdu, and whom they took for allies of Pakistan. The freedom fighters threatened Razia and her sister Zakiabid, then aged nine, and tried to seize their elder brother. Razia pleaded, 'Don't kill him. Take all you want from us, but don't kill my brother.' After looting the house the young Bengalis departed. Razia and her family were later ousted from their home and went to live in

Mahommetpur. At the thought of it, she began to cry. 'The men who drove us out broke up our lives and destroyed our education. For this I can never forgive them.' Razia had set everything on completing her schooling successfully. 'I wanted to help my young brothers and sisters to grow up and stand on their own feet.' She will never be able to do so, for her family can no longer afford to educate her. I left poor Razia at her sewing-machine.

Mirpur Camp, a few kilometres outside Dacca, is not described flatteringly in an official report: '... a slum ... all the members [of one family] live in the same dilapidated hut ... stagnant water surrounds the whole area ... the general hygienic conditions are not good ... most of the children are suffering from various diseases ...' Every word of that is true.

Yet a visit to Mirpur is one of the most uplifting experiences imaginable – because of the children, most of them naked, swimming and splashing in nearby ponds (it was the rainy season), wading in the yellow mud up to the knees so that when they waded out they looked as if they were wearing yellow socks. To Sister Moyra, who was walking ahead, the children cried, 'Sister, *Salaam*', and when I passed it was just the same: they looked up and smiling 'Sister, *Salaam*', reached out and, with their muddy little hands, touched me on my bare arms or my clean white trousers. Among the crowd of naked Muslim boys many were uncircumcised – it is an operation which costs money which their parents do not possess.

As you walk along the raised, narrow and very slippery path, among tiny huts bespangled with a yellow-flowered creeper, among diminutive and very personal plantations, ten feet by ten, of sugar cane and banana trees, you marvel at the instinct of these impoverished Bengalis not only to survive but to survive decently, cheerfully and successfully amidst the mire and the green, oozing slime which surrounds them. Somehow they manage to wash themselves clean. A pretty young mother was pouring water over her infant son, another was washing her daughter's hair, a young girl was drinking water out of a bucket filled with the family washing. They looked up as you passed and out of the sludge smiled at you, a broad, white smile. Nobody looked sad. That was the miracle of Mirpur.

All those destitute Bengalis, from the age of six and up, would spend the coming night at prayer, for tomorrow was the feast of Shabi Bharat – the feast on which people's fate is decided by Allah. I wondered what he would decide for them.

Among those praying would be Saleha Khatoon, praying to Allah to make more bearable her own fate and that of her son, Shiraz. Saleha, as a nineteen-year-old mother, was at home that day the Pakistani army went to war against the people of East Pakistan. She could hear, late into the night, the sound of fighting. During the days that followed Saleha begged her husband, Tasir Maula, a hand-cart puller, to stay at home. But how could he? He earned just enough to feed his family. So, war or no war, he had to go out to look for work. Five days after the war began, Saleha prepared the morning meal as usual and they ate it together. Then Tasir Maula trundled his *thala gari* off down the street. He never returned. That evening his young wife heard that her husband had been bayonetted to death in Chak Bazar by Pakistani soldiers.

The following morning, with little Shiraz, she found his body. The area was guarded by Pakistani soldiers so she could not get near her dead husband. Shiraz, recognizing his father, rushed forward but was immediately driven back by the soldiers. Then they took the body away in a truck; that was the last that Saleha saw of her husband. A teenage widow, she was expecting a second baby.

As I listened to her, so also did Shiraz. He looked so downcast that I asked what he was thinking. 'I would like to avenge my father's death,' he said in a small, low voice.

For the next four years Saleha somehow managed, by begging, to feed her two little boys and herself. Then she was taken to Mirpur camp. Slum though it may be, Shiraz loves living there. He has many friends and they go swimming together in one of the nearby ponds. That, and school, where he learns vocational training, are his great joys — no matter that he has to walk ten miles a day to get to school and back.

What would he like to do, I asked him — pedal a rickshaw, drive a lorry, fly an aeroplane? 'Fly an aeroplane,' answered Shiraz firmly. He did confide to me, however, that he would rather be a bomber pilot than fly an airliner. 'Would you want to bomb the Pakistanis?' I asked him and, in that small voice, he replied, 'No, not if it meant bombing little boys like myself.' That, he thought, would be wrong.

Pakistani soldiers were moved by no such merciful feelings towards the small brothers of Hosneara Begum (nicknamed Buri), when they broke into her parents' home in Shantibag, a residential quarter of Dacca, one day in November 1971.

It was the month of Ramadan. At about 7.30 p.m., after saying the Magib prayer, the family — Buri's father, a Bengali and a lieutenant in the Pakistan Navy, her mother, six brothers and a baby sister — went into the sitting-room for the evening meal. As they sat quietly chatting, the door burst open and four Pakistani soldiers rushed in, guns pointed. 'Hands up,' they shouted, and two of them seized Buri's father and led him outside, while the other two, covering the terrified children and their mother, withdrew, locking the door. Buri, aged ten, was so frightened that she hid under the bed – this probably saved her life. A few agonizing minutes passed, then suddenly there came a burst of machine-gun fire; bullets ripped into the sitting-room, smashing the windows and, curiously enough, Buri remembers, made a noise like heavy rain spattering on the corrugated iron roof. Four of Buri's brothers crumpled up and fell to the floor, dead. The two little ones, Munu, six, and Idu, four, were untouched, but both Buri's mother and the six-month-old girl, Lucky, were wounded. Buri, petrified, remained under the bed long after the soldiers had driven off into the dark with her father. He never returned.

At this point in her story, Buri, a lovely girl, tall and graceful, drew from the folds of her orange and blue sari a colour photograph which she showed to me. It was a close-up of her four dead brothers, their bodies bullet-riddled, their clothes drenched in blood. Quite unmoved, Buri began to explain: her smallest brother, Mitou, who was only three, was hit by six bullets, the next brother, Shah Azgor, by eleven, and the next, Shah Tofazol, by nine. Seven bullets had torn the life out of Shah Mosaref. He was fourteen, and Buri's favourite because, she said, 'He liked me; he was kind and gentle.' To her, but not to the enemy. Young Mosaref had joined the freedom fighters, the *Muktibahima*, and had already been in action armed with a sten gun. He knew, Buri said, how to use dynamite and plastic; only two days earlier he was one of a commando unit which blew up the electric power station – and this, Buri thinks, was what provoked the massacre of almost her entire family. Their neighbours, Pakistanis, had probably informed the army that Mosaref was home.

At the time, Buri simply could not take in the extent of this appalling tragedy. She somehow believed that her four brothers would come back. Looking back, she does not feel all that enthusiastic about independence: all it meant to her was the death of her father and brothers and the destitution of her family. She still feels sad and bitter, and says, 'If armies have to fight, let them fight each other and not kill innocent children like us. We had done nothing wrong.' She agrees that men who commit such wanton murder against children should be punished. 'But that would not give me back my brothers.'

Many freedom fighters, like Mosaref, were in their teens. Johi was another. He told me the story of his short career as a killer; it began when he was fourteen. Seven years have since passed: the slim, well-dressed young man talking to me did not mince his words, which he illustrated with vivid, excited gestures. He told me he liked a Bengali sport called *Iacidudu*, a kind of *karate*. I should imagine it was a good outlet for his aggressive energy.

As, in March 1971, the issue of East Pakistan's independence approached a crisis, no Bengali felt more fired by a desire to defend his country than young Johi, who was then a promising pupil in the 9th grade. Johi was greatly impressed by the young leader of the liberation movement, Sidiki, who hailed from the Tangail District, the hilly area of Bengal famous for its tigers. When 'Tiger' Sidiki called on all young Bengalis to defend their country Johi's young, aggressive spirit was aroused. He was incensed by the bullying attitude of the Pakistan government towards the Bengalis and burned with a desire to strike back. But it was the last speech of the loved and revered Bengali leader, Sheikh Mujibur Rahman, before the crisis broke, that decided Johi. The Sheikh called on Bengalis to defend their rights and fight for freedom. When, on 25 March, West Pakistani forces intervened, Johi, the schoolboy, walked out of the classroom and joined the freedom fighters.

He did a month and a half's intensive training at a camp in the Tangail District. He was by no means the youngest recruit; there were boys ten and twelve years old who were trained as runners. Fourteen was the minimum age for carrying a gun. Johi's first action was when his platoon ambushed a Pakistani army convoy and killed eleven soldiers. He was not sure whether he himself had hit one, but, he told me frankly, the sight of the dead soldiers made him happy; he felt proud of himself and his platoon. He soon, however, discovered that against a well-trained army freedom fighters do not always have the best of it. He got into a very tough spot, as he called it, when, with a force of thirty-five freedom fighters, they were surrounded by the 'Paks'. Johi saw many of his comrades fall; twenty were killed and Johi, with excited gestures of the hands, described to me how, with his Sten gun, he shot his way out. He killed five soldiers, he said, and felt very pleased with himself – despite the losses. 'To be honest,' he went on, 'the more my friends were killed, the more determined was I to revenge them.'

Johi then turned to another aspect of freedom fighting – the pitiless, cold-blooded killing of defenceless and, most often, innocent people, though he was not going to admit that it amounted to that. Among the freedom fighters' victims were village headmen, 'known' supporters of the Pakistanis. They were bayonetted, Johi said, and proceeded to tell me why and how. Bullets, he explained, were scarce and shooting was likely to attract the Pak army to the scene. It was very important to kill silently, and bayonets, he insisted with a big smile as if they were a favour, provided the obvious solution. He told me, with suitable gestures, how he went about bayonetting a village headman. A freedom fighter would take each arm of the victim while Johi drove his bayonet into the man's stomach – he indicated his own navel to show the exact spot. He even described the bayonets used: they were Chinese and about a foot long. Johi, for my edification, then acted the part of a man being bayonetted – his face hideously contorted, he made two or three violent convulsions of the body. Then he let his head loll on to one shoulder. After which, Johi straightened up and said, 'The man then drops down dead.'

Johi, though he told me he could never again do such things, still thought that the atrocities he committed as a teenager were justified. So – and it is the old, eternal process – he would presumably feel able to consent to, if not encourage his own children's doing the same.

He still, moreover, felt no remorse. 'We freedom fighters,' he said to me, 'were fighting against the Pakistanis whose army was behaving as armies do, raping our women, killing them and their children, too. So we did the same thing to them and their friends. It was a rough justice, I know, but there is no real justice in war.'

Innocent victims of that rough justice were the parents of Yassin Sharif and, consequently, Yassin Sharif himself. Biharis, they cared nothing for politics, only for making enough out of their modest business – a general store – to get Yassin educated to university level. But that marvellous dream ended when Yassin's parents were murdered before his eyes.

I found Yassin in the Old Town Camp – adjacent to Mahommetpur – where the Biharis had been settled after their houses had been burnt down by the Bengalis during the War of Liberation. Its sordid squalor made Mirpur seem like the garden of Eden. With my friends of the Save the Children Fund I walked through slime and filth, amongst piles of rotting garbage. Children thronged around us, looking up with bright, inquisitive eyes, smiling, laughing and cheering. It was both terrible and wonderful to find such unbridled joy in these ghastly surroundings.

I entered a building – it had once been a dance hall and the *punkahs*, electric fans, still hung from the ceiling where, for years now, they had remained motionless, unable, through lack of current, to stir the air of that stifling, foetid atmosphere. Not a glimmer of artificial light shone in the gloom, which was only slightly relieved by a few rays of daylight filtering through slits high up in the wall.

Fifty families lived there, on the floor, each in a space barely ten feet by ten demarcated by a line of bricks laid end to end. Within each tiny 'compound' were neatly stacked pots and pans and blankets; washing lines hung with coloured shirts and *saris* helped only a little to embellish the sombre decor. In those cramped surroundings, I was told, you did everything – without the slightest privacy. You made love, you conceived, you gave birth and were born. You lived and finally died – all on that small space of floor, and always in public. Humans had existed there for years. And no one, within Bangladesh or anywhere in the world, has yet done anything to wipe out and demolish this degrading hovel and move these good, clean and patient people out of their squalor into lodgings fit for humans.

It was here, ankle-deep in the mire, that I found Yassin, who told me what happened that evening seven years before when he was nine and lived with his parents in Mahommetpur. Around five p.m. young freedom fighters rounding up Biharis had seized Yassin, his father and his mother. Somehow, in the confusion, Yassin lost touch with his parents, only to join other bewildered children who were running to and fro, crying for theirs. Very frightened, Yassin climbed onto a roof. He could see below that the freedom fighters had herded their victims into a small square. There they began killing them, shooting them, knifing them. Yassin's eyes were riveted on his parents. He saw the men come to his father; they strangled him. Then to his mother; they stabbed her, then cut her throat. All this Yassin saw with his own young eyes, which, as he spoke to me, were full of tears. This is what he saw done in the name of freedom.

After dark, Yassin climbed down from the roof and fled with the streams of Bihari refugees towards open fields.

Since that day Yassin, whose ambition it was to go to the university, has never again been to school. As the years went by he found food and shelter in return for running errands. Then one day he asked a rickshaw-man to teach him how to pedal a rickshaw (it's not as simple as it looks). So young Yassin began to make a few *takka*, not so many as a full-blown rickshaw man, for he was only sixteen and before the day was ended he was too weary to pedal anymore.

Had his parents not been murdered, Yassin would soon be going to the university and on to a well-paid job. Instead, for the rest of his life he will pedal a rickshaw. It is the toughest job in Dacca.

The origins of Yassin and Malik were much the same. Both were sons of tradesmen; both endured a cruel ordeal. But while fate dealt so harshly with poor Yassin she favoured Malik in the most unexpected way.

Malik, a tailor's son, lived in Dinajpur, near the Indian frontier, 112 kilometres from Dacca. He was twelve and beginning to learn the trade in his father's shop when, in December 1971, India, in support of the independence movement in East Pakistan, invaded the country. As the Indian army approached Dinajpur the Bengalis turned on the Biharis. Many people, Biharis and Pakistanis alike, fled to Dacca. Malik's family was among the fugitives. As the train, packed to overflowing, moved slowly out of Dinajpur station, the Bengali passengers began attacking the Biharis.

'I had no idea where we were going,' Malik told me. 'I had never heard of a city called Dacca. The Bengalis were pushing the Biharis off the train; they pushed me off.' Malik tumbled onto the track, fortunately without hurt, and watched the train as it clanked on, carrying his parents he knew not where, and disappeared from sight.

Malik walked back, crying, along the track into Dinajpur. He was wandering the streets when Indian soldiers found him; they took him along with them as they advanced towards Dacca. There they left him. Malik again found himself abandoned. He wandered, begging for food, sometimes receiving a few *pice* (coppers). He went barefoot, clad in a flimsy cotton shirt and grey shorts. The clothes gave him no protection from the cold, and soon were ragged and filthy – like Malik himself. With no blanket to keep off the cold, he slept each night 'on the footpath' – at the roadside. 'I was all the time scared,' Malik told me. Thus, for months, he lived like a vagabond.

He became more and more hungry, cold, tired. 'I was very weak,' said Malik. 'Did you think you were going to die?' I asked him. He answered, 'Yes, that is what I was thinking about. There was nobody to look after me. Dying was the easiest way.' Malik was by now fourteen. At dawn one morning, as he lay on the footpath, he drifted into unconsciousness. His wasted body, inert, was discovered by a government official on his way to the office.

At that moment, Alan Cheyney, a New Zealander in the Under-privileged Children's Educational Programme (UCEP), was driving by. He stopped, picked up the starving, half-dead boy and took him to the Holy Family Hospital. Three days later they informed him that as the boy was merely starving they could not keep him. So Alan took Malik to his own home.

Malik recovered consciousness. 'I didn't know where I was,' he said, 'or who he was. He was kind.'

But Alan's servants told him: 'The boy is a Bihari. They are unwanted people. You should not keep him.' 'We kept him all the same,' Alan told me. He became his official guardian, had him educated, took him travelling to Europe and the United States, bought him a Honda motor-bike.

On his Honda, Malik often used to ride over to Mahommetpur camp, hoping, always hoping, to find someone he knew. One day he spotted one of his cousins. 'I called out to him, but he seemed frightened and moved away.' He had taken Malik for a Bengali student! Malik called again and gave his name. At that the two boys fell into each other's arms. 'He took me to his home,' Malik said, 'to his mother and aunts.' They told him that his parents were still alive and living in Dinajpur.

Before long, Malik was back at home, his real home. 'The moment my parents saw me, they knew it was me, Malik, whom they'd lost two years before.'

But the reunion with his parents put Malik in a turmoil. Should he return to his parents or stay with Alan, who had fathered him with such care and generosity? His parents solved the problems. 'Stay with Alan,' they said. 'He can do more for you than we can.' And, to be close to Malik, they came to live in Dacca.

Dacca, where Yassin, who also lost his parents, pedals a rickshaw instead of riding a Honda, and is one of its poorest citizens.

One, and a very small one, of the millions who fled from the War of Liberation in East Pakistan into India was Kamal. Sheila Dao, the Indian girl who told me about him, has not seen him since the day he disappeared.

It was in November 1971, a sunny day, that Sheila, then seventeen, was revising her history lesson on the verandah of her home. She heard the garden gate creak open, then close. Looking up, she saw a small ragged boy walking timidly towards her. Filthy as he was, Sheila was struck by the beauty of his triangular shaped face and large, limpid black eyes. 'Could you give me something to eat, sister?' he asked her. She led Kamal into the house, where he was washed, fed and clothed.

Kamal's long journey on foot to Sheila's house had started some six months earlier. After soldiers had entered his home and, in front of his eyes, shot his father, a farmer, and raped his sisters, Kamal simply walked away from the place, farther and farther away, sometimes riding in bullock carts and buses and even trains. Then came the day when, very hungry and tired, he walked into Sheila's garden.

He stayed three months and then Sheila and her parents had to go away for a month to the south. Kamal begged to go with them, but they explained kindly that they could not take him. He was to wait and be a good boy and they would soon be back. In due course they returned: of Kamal, however, they found no sign.

Sheila reproaches herself and her family. But her friends ask her, 'Why do you worry so much? There are thousands of brats like him. They are like particles of dust on the roadside.' Sheila said to me, 'If Kamal is indeed a particle of dust it is my constant hope that he will one day get into my eyes again.' Are not we all, who could help, but don't, deserving of Sheila's reproach?

CHAPTER TWENTY

Cypriot Messengers of Death

Ethnic conflicts are not exclusive to the continents of Asia and Africa. One of the most savage in recent times came to a head in 1974 in a small Mediterranean island, Cyprus. For decades Greek Cypriots had dreamed, and their freedom movement, *Eoka*, had fought, for *Enosis*, the annexation of Cyprus to Greece. Turkish Cypriots, the minority community, different in race, religion, language and culture, had, with equal determination, resisted *Enosis*. With the creation, in 1960, of the independent republic of Cyprus an apparent miracle was wrought – reconciliation of the two communities. It was short-lived. At the end of December 1963 and again in 1967 Greek Cypriots made concerted armed attacks against the Turkish community, which they continued to harass until, on 15 July 1974, a *coup d'état* made a Greek Cypriot, Nicos Sampson, president, ready to declare *Enosis*. Five days later Turkey intervened; its army disembarked on the island.

No. 2, Irfan Bey Street, in the Kumsal quarter of the Turkish sector of Nicosia, looks, from the outside, like any of the other pleasant little houses in the row. It is quite different inside where, apart from the addition of photos and other documents, nothing has been changed since, on the evening of 24 December 1963, Murubbet Ilhan, wife of Dr Niat Ilhan, a doctor in the Cyprus Turkish Army Contingent, their three young boys and a woman friend, Feride Hasan, were murdered there by Greek Cypriots. Feride Hasan's husband, Yusuf, described how, all of a sudden, bullets began to riddle the house. Thinking it would be safer, the Ilhan family and their friends shut themselves in the bathroom. A few moments later they heard the front door burst open and Greek voices talking excitedly. Then bullets started flying into the bathroom, instantly killing Murubbet and her three little boys – Murat (seven), Kutsi (three) and Hakan (six months). Feride Hasan was shot dead in an adjoining room; her husband fell wounded. The blood-stains spattering the green walls and the ceiling, and the jagged bullet holes, are still there, in that grey-tiled, macabre bathroom.

In the house next door I met Baidu Temir, who, as a boy of thirteen, trembled with terror that evening of the Greek assault. His family were close friends of the Ilhans.

When the attack started two other families had come over to Baidu's house; together, they felt more secure. Baidu, for all the firing going on around, had heard nothing unusual in the direction of the Ilhans' house. From where he crouched, terrified, in a room at the back of his own house, he could see that the Ilhans' lights were still on.

A few moments later Baidu heard his own front door being forced open – the marks made by boots and bayonets are still there. Then he heard footsteps inside the house. Men were searching; they came to the last room, a cool, shady room when I saw it in the summer heat, where Baidu crouched with the others, 'breathless, my heart beating,' he said, 'and in tremendous fear, waiting for the end.' One of the men outside kicked open the locked door and *Eoka* gunmen entered. 'I thought they were going to kill us on the spot,' Baidu told me. But a baby inside the room started crying and this, he thought, made the gunmen hesitate. What Baidu did not know was that those men had just come from murdering the Ilhans next door.

The officer in charge, a mainland Greek – Baidu could tell from his uniform and his accent – ordered the frightened Turks outside into the street. The men, their hands up, were made to stand against a house. 'We thought the Greeks were going to shoot them before our eyes,' Baidu told me. But they fired above their heads – not all that much, for Baidu's father was hit in the hand. The gunmen then massed the women and children in the street, from the far end of which fire was being directed at the Greeks. Baidu said, 'They forced us to go forward in front of them towards the end of the street. They were hiding behind us.' The human screen was then halted and the gunmen conferred. 'We have come to the Turkish line,' Baidu heard one of them say. Later he heard there was no Turkish line – just two Turkish householders who, in the dark, with a gun apiece, had held up several hundred armed men.

The prisoners, including the men, were then marched off to the Central Prison. Baidu spent a week crammed into a cell with a dozen others. In the December cold he slept, wrapped in a single blanket, on the floor. He particularly remembers a lady of the Red Cross who listed the prisoners and their needs. 'I think this was the reason,' said Baidu, 'why we were not killed or the women raped.'

But it was a near thing. As the prisoners were escorted down the street Baidu saw two bulldozers digging up the ground near the English club.

'We all understood what that meant. We thought it was the very end.' His father came over to him and his mother. 'We all cried and we embraced. There wasn't a thing we could do.' Yet Baidu, noticing his father's wounded hand, tore off a piece of his own shirt and bandaged it.

Tensely, they waited, while the firing squad made ready. Then suddenly Baidu saw that a Greek officer was running towards them, waving – 'you know, like in the movies,' he added. 'Stop, stop!' shouted the officer, 'I have orders from Makarios' (the Greek Cypriot leader and President of the Republic). 'That was at the last minute?' I asked Baidu. 'More like the last second,' he answered.

After December 1963, the Turkish Cypriot community lived through dark days. Both in the towns and the villages they were threatened, sometimes attacked, either openly or, insidiously, by means of booby-traps and mines, with old people and young as priority targets, since they were usually unarmed. However, when the Turkish people in the mixed village of Alaminos, near Larnaca, were threatened that their houses would be burnt down, boys of fourteen and over were given arms, but only at night, when on guard.

In 1967 Dervis Yuceturk, then fourteen, was living in Alaminos, named after a queen of the Venetians – to whom Cyprus once belonged. Alaminos prospered through market gardening, and the villagers, Greeks and Turks, had got on well until 1963, when the first troubles since independence began. Yet that evening in 1967, when Dervis and his young brother Halil, with Hussein, his brother-in-law and an uncle, were working the family plot, they were feeling happy. As they watered the sheep at the well, the three boys were laughing and playing when they noticed on the ground a coloured bag with pictures on it, done up in tinsel. Inside they found what looked like a small radio. Taking it with them, they set off back to the village, their uncle driving the tractor. On the way they picked up two boys, Mehmet and Mustafa. Then they hurried on; there was a film they wanted to see that evening.

They were trundling happily along when, about half a mile from the village, there was a huge explosion; Dervis saw a fiery mass of red about him, and after that – nothing. It was not until four days later, in hospital, that he recovered consciousness. Still, everything before his eyes was black, and has been ever since.

Dervis was the sole survivor. Besides being blind, his face was terribly scarred. Of the other boys on the tractor, Halil, Hussein, Mehmet and Mustafa, 'They were blown to pieces,' Dervis said. His uncle, too: only his two legs were found.

When, after some time, Dervis regained full possession of his senses, only one sensation registered: burning hatred for those who had destroyed the lives of his brother, his friends and half-destroyed his own. Then his hatred cooled. All he wants now is to forget all that evil and sorrow. This brave young man, blinded and bereaved by the Greeks, today only wants to live in peace beside them. And his great ambition is to help found a school for the blind.

Following the Greek *coup d'état* of July 1974, the government of Turkey, on 20 July, despatched to Cyprus a so-called Peace Force whose declared object was to safeguard the independence of the republic (against annexation to Greece) and to save the Turkish Cypriot community.

Fear possessed Marius, then six, when the Turkish Peace Force arrived in his village – or, rather, his grandfather's village, north of Salamis. When the Turkish soldiers came down from the mountain, as Marius said, they first asked another villager 'Where are the Greek Cypriots hidden?' and this man said, 'I don't know. Go and ask him,' and pointed at Marius's grandfather. Marius heard them asking him. 'Where is the hole where they are hidden?' They began threatening his grandfather, and Marius was so frightened that he hid behind a tree. The voices of the Turkish soldiers grew louder. Then a shot rang out. Marius looked out from behind the tree and saw his grandfather lying on the ground, quite still. The Turks were walking away.

Despite all the mysterious things the doctors have given him – psychotherapy and drugs – Marius is still frightened of Turks, even of the United Nations soldiers when they drive by in jeeps – for he takes them for Turks. To him, everybody in uniform is a Turk, like the Turks who killed his grandfather. Marius would like to be a shepherd back in his own village, even though it is on the Turkish side. He would like, he told me, to dig up the bones of his grandfather and give him a proper burial, with a priest and all.

In her funny English a little Greek girl, Flora, told me, 'We did some ill behaviour to them, but we saw many bad things, too.' There were many more bad things that Flora did not see; they are set forth in a United Nations document entitled 'Statements supporting the complaint of Cyprus'. Its 230 pages contain 122 eye-witness accounts of crimes committed by the Turkish Peace Force – among them 51 cases of rape, 56 of inhuman treatment, 67 of murder. Other crimes included robbery, looting, forced labour and forced prostitution. Children, needless to say, were not spared. The mother of one, Sotirou Pantelli Kesme, was murdered. A neighbour said, 'I noticed that on [her] dead body, her thirteen-month-old daughter Maria, was . . . crying and licking the blood from her mother's body.' Another Greek woman, mother of Androulla (five) and Xenia (four) describes how a Turkish soldier 'under the threat of his gun threw me on the bed . . . and in front of the eyes of my children, raped me'. A teenage girl 'was always raped by the same Turk, who fell in love with her'.

The rapings are described *ad nauseam*, but the programme of the Turkish Peace Force did not exclude massacre. A fourteen-year-old girl describes how, at Neo Khorio, 'there were about 150 dead old men, young men, women and children. Some of them I knew.' And at Kythrea 'There were whole families killed.' A Greek Cypriot official, held prisoner by the Peace Force with more than 150 civilians, among them fifty children younger than eighteen, overhead Turkish soldiers complaining to their officer, 'Why do you keep them and don't kill them? During *Eoka* time they killed our children.'

In the same vindictive spirit Greek Cypriots told a twenty-year-old Turkish Cypriot mother, 'As the Turks killed in the north, so we are going to kill you.' Zerrin Mehmet already had three children: Kasif (five), Emir (three) and Tolgay (two), and she was now eight months pregnant. She lived in Taskent, a mixed village in the southern, mainly Greek, part of the island. 'First,' she said, 'there was great joy in the village at news of the Turkish landing, then deep anxiety, for we were in the Greek sector. Some days later Greek soldiers, joined by Greeks from our own village, surrounded Taskent.'

On 14 August, armed Greeks, villagers of Taskent, entered Zerrin's home where some thirty Turkish neighbours had gathered for safety. The men were ordered to give themselves up. 'Otherwise,' said the Greek gunmen, 'we shall kill the women and children.' So the Turks came forth from their hiding places. From Zerrin's immediate family the Greeks took her father-in-law (sixty), his sons, aged twenty-six, twenty-four and the youngest a boy of thirteen. 'My mother-in-law begged the Greek – he was from our own village – to spare the child, but the man just laughed and said, "Are you still suckling him? Is he a baby?" and led the boy away. Zerrin's own little boy, Kasif, threw his arms around his father's neck, clung to him, screaming, and begged him not to leave, but the gunmen forced him to let go. Then, 'like a herd of sheep', as Zerrin said, 'they were driven out of the house.'

In all sixty-nine Turks, aged between thirteen and seventy-four, were taken at Taskent. Next day they and fifteen others, eighty-four in all, were loaded into two buses and driven away. Later they were found dead – all except one, a youth called Suat Hüseyin. He related how, at a deserted spot beyond Limassol, the captives were ordered out of the buses. They were each given a cigarette and told to walk. 'It was at the third puff,' said Suat, 'that the bullets came.' He was hit and fell, pretending to be dead. Then the Greeks went off. Suat heard his wounded brother crying, 'Save me, Suat.' But Suat had barely the strength to save himself. His nerves have never recovered. When asked about his terrible experience he burst out 'How do you think it feels to see your friend's brains spattered over you? Don't ask me any more.'

As for Zerrin Mehmet, she will never find consolation for her sorrow. 'A person dies once, but we die every day – and when our children ask for their fathers, we die once more.' She still remembers, as if it were today, when her husband was being led away, how he kissed her and whispered in her ear, 'This is the end for you and me, but when our children grow up, let them revenge us.' Some days later, resigned perhaps to his fate, he sent a message to Zerrin, 'Look after the children and protect them like the apple of your eye.'

It is that last wish of his, she believes, that he meant her to follow. She and the other villagers were resettled in a new Taskent in the Turkish sector, between which and the Greek sector there still runs a strongly fortified frontier.

CHAPTER TWENTY-ONE

Children at Arms: Bissau

In July 1974 General Spinola, president, for a few fleeting months, of Portugal, made an historic announcement: Portugal (after five centuries of colonialism) recognized the right to independence of her overseas territories. That meant that in Portuguese Guinea (Guinea Bissau), Mozambique and Angola the end of the long fight for freedom was in sight.

Guinea Bissau, though a small country (about the size of Wales), had been the first of Portugal's African colonies to raise the standard of rebellion. *Senhor* Domingo Brito dos Santos, member of the Supreme Council of the War of Liberation (*Luta por la Liberdade*) is today one of the top party members in this Marxist-Leninist country. A charming, elderly gentleman, he greeted my thirteen-year-old son, Pierre, as warmly and naturally as he did me. Protocol, he said, was non-existent in Guinea Bissau.

Comrade Domingo told me that the freedom struggle had cost him fifteen years' absence, away from his family, in the *Maquis*, the resistance. He spoke of the schools set up in the bush where children, though they had to rough it, could continue their schooling. Then he invited Pierre and me to hop into his white Peugeot 204, in which he drove us, through a torrential downpour, to the Commissariat of Veteran freedom fighters. There, he introduced me to the chief secretary of the Veterans, Comrade Teadora Gomez, a jovial and generously-proportioned lady. At the outset, in 1963, of the fight for freedom, Teadora was eighteen, the daughter of a master-carpenter and the eldest of a family of eight brothers and sisters whose home was at Caour in the south. Teadora's father, apart from carpentry, was a militant in the independence movement.

One day Teadora was warned by a young freedom fighter, 'You and your family must get away into the bush.' So they all took to the *Maquis*. Teadora learnt to handle a rifle, but when, a few months later, she was in action for the first time she did not fire a shot. There was not enough ammunition to go round. That day, however, she faced death – a young comrade, Pan, was killed by her side.

Teadora's dream had always been to settle in the capital, Bissau, as a nurse. Now she had her chance, though not in Bissau, but the bush. She told me how, with the most rudimentary means, she, an eighteen-year-old girl without any medical training, often practised amputations: first the tourniquet, then a local injection – it lasted thirty minutes so she had to hurry. Then the scalpel, sterilized, like the other implements, by fire. Finally, the saw: many a time young Teadora had to saw clean through the limb of a wounded man – or child whose body might be shattered by landmines or bomb-splinters.

Many of the freedom fighters were boys and girls in their teens. Armed, they belonged to the Local Army Force (FAL), a kind of Home Guard, for defence only. Others even younger acted as aircraft-spotters – their sense of hearing was sharper. From seventeen onwards, members of the FAL would graduate to the *Maquis* proper, and go off to fight.

When Teadora was not wielding saw and scalpel she busied herself, a pistol always at her belt, looking after the health and feeding of the very young. She fed them propaganda too: what the war of liberation was all about and how, in the end, victory was certain. Teadora was an extremely loquacious lady. Sometimes, when I asked her a simple question in French (which she could speak quite well), she would launch out into a lengthy diatribe in Créole, and I would cut in, 'For heaven's sake, Comrade Teadora, please stop gassing and stick to the question!' At which Teadora would laugh heartily and come back to the point. She and her teaching colleagues had evidently done a good job with their young pupils, for today, among the youth of Guinea Bissau, crime and delinquency are rare.

Despite her apparent flamboyance there was, in Teadora's views on the killing of non-combatants, a cold and terrible logic. The Portuguese, she told me, bombarded civilians, but there were, all the same, among them, combatants, including unarmed ones. 'And what about teenagers, is killing them justifiable?' 'Yes,' she replied, 'in the sense that even from six years upwards, those young ones helped in the fight for freedom, as messengers, scouts and aircraft-spotters. Some even carried arms. They all, then, must be considered fighters.' 'And the really defenceless ones, infants a few years old who do not know the meaning of freedom?' Teadora answered, 'In the bush there was nothing we could do about them. They, the babies, and we, the fighters, were all in the same boat.'

Though he was only fifteen, Bidewer Bola knew very well, he told me, what he was fighting for. He had heard about bombings and massacres and felt incensed. So, encouraged by his father, he joined the freedom fighters.

My son Pierre and I found Bidewer in a suburb – it was more like a village, on the outskirts of Bissau. Before a long, low house, its mud walls and thatch reddened by the setting sun, Bidewer sat chatting with other war-wounded veterans. At the corner of the house a girl pounded millet for the evening meal; around, hens pecked, pigs rootled and goats nibbled voraciously. Night fell suddenly as Bidewer began his story.

He was so small, he said, when he joined up, that he could wear his bandolier neither over his shoulder nor around his waist. So he carried it on his head. He had never fired a rifle until the day when, with some forty other freedom fighters, they were surprised while clearing a minefield by three lorry-loads of 'whites', that is, Portuguese soldiers. In a short, sharp battle, two lorries went up in flames and the other drove off. The boy Bidewer killed a man; he saw him fall. 'I was glad,' he told me, 'and felt impatient for the next battle.' He was filled with hate for the whites, as well as for his 'brothers' who fought at their side against their own black brothers. He despised them one and all.

Bidewer graduated from a rifle to a sub-machine gun, with which he killed more men. Then one day young Bidewer was himself all but killed, worse than killed, he sometimes thinks. With his friends he was advancing warily along a track. At one moment, as he put his foot down, he realized that, underneath it, there was a mine – which would explode the moment he took his weight off it. So, standing there on the mine, he shouted to his friends to get clear. Then – he had to, sooner or later – he jumped. Turning to Pierre, I asked him, 'What would you have done?' To which he solemnly replied, 'I should have remained standing on the mine a bit longer, contemplating my legs for the last time.'

The outcome, either way, was inevitable. Bidewer felt as if a bomb had landed on him. He knew that half his right foot had been torn off, that both legs were burnt and mangled. Somehow, on his elbows, he dragged himself to the side of the track. Later, at the hospital, his left leg was amputated.

Since he was fifteen Bidewer has had to drag himself about on crutches and what is left of one leg. I asked him if he thought his sacrifice was worthwhile. 'Yes,' he said firmly. 'I did it for my country and I'm proud. But I think it was too big a sacrifice to expect of a boy of fifteen.'

Alberto was only nine when, in 1969, he became what he proudly called a symbol of his country's fight for freedom. When Pierre and I talked to him in Bissau he was eighteen. Alberto's most obvious features were his right arm, severed at the elbow, and his badly damaged left hand, from which a finger was missing. His yellow T-shirt was marked JAAC (*Juvendud Africano Amilcar Cabral*). Amilcar Cabral, before his assassination in 1973, was secretary-general of the African Party for the Independence of Guinea and Cape Verde – *Partido Africano da Independencia da Guiné e Cabo Verde* (PAIGC). Cabral, Alberto told me, loved children and called them 'the flowers of our country'.

A simple roof of thatch supported on branches served as a home for Alberto and his family at Banira in the eastern region, near the Sahara, where his father cultivated rice. As a small boy, Alberto's job was to carry water out to his father and mother in the rice-fields. Often, too, he spent hours frightening the birds away from the newly-sown seed. It was a hard life; his parents were poor and the family sometimes went hungry, especially now that the War of Liberation was on.

One day Alberto noticed that his mother was preparing a huge meal – far more than the family needed. 'It's for the freedom fighters,' she told him. Thereafter Alberto's home became a rallying point for the freedom fighters, among them Francisco Mendes, who became the first prime minister after the liberation. Both Alberto's father and his twenty-year-old brother, Faustino, joined up. When Faustino was killed in action, 'I felt completely lost,' Alberto told me. The village was bombed, with far more casualties among civilians than freedom fighters. He accepted that. 'In a guerrilla war like ours,' said Alberto 'you could not separate the two.' 'Did you, as a boy of nine, consider yourself a non-combatant?' I asked him. 'Certainly not,' he answered. 'All of us, young and old, who had taken to the bush, were combatants.' At what age, I asked Alberto, did he think that children should carry arms? 'Fourteen and upwards,' was his reply. 'Do you think that Pierre, whose life, till now, has been easier and more protected than yours ever was, would have it in him to resist an aggressor, as you did?' 'Why not?' Alberto asked. 'I'm certain he would want to.' Pierre agreed. 'It would be only natural.'

That air-raid was Alberto's baptism of fire. He was so frightened that he ran crying to his mother. He had already seen people who had died a natural death. 'But this time,' he said, 'it was as if they were a lot of chickens whose throats had been cut.'

One morning, as he awoke with the dawn, Alberto felt he could not face going to work. However, with an effort, he rose up and took his *coupe-coupe*, a long square-ended knife, for it was his job, with his young companions, that morning to clear the bush for new rice-fields. Once at work he felt better and it was not until three in the afternoon, when the village women brought them food, that the youths stopped work.

Hardly was the meal over when aircraft appeared, flying low. Bombs began bursting around the boys as they scattered, and Alberto, though he felt no pain, saw to his horror that half his right arm was dangling by a few sinews, his left hand a bleeding mess. Farther on he collapsed. He began crying, not, he said, through pain, but because he was frightened by the sight of so much blood. The tourniquet that his friends tried to fashion from a creeper failed to stop the bleeding. Alberto fainted. At the freedom fighters' headquarters, ten kilometres away, whither his friends had carried him, a doctor – he was a Cuban – operated on him. When, next day, Alberto came to, he saw that half his right arm was now completely missing.

Alberto could not yet read or write. Now he learnt to write left-handed and has since learnt much more. He is aiming for a degree in Social Science so that he can help children who have suffered as he has. Never will he forget the words of Amilcar Cabral: 'Children are the flowers of our country.'

Some Bissau-Guineans – particularly those who, in pre-independence days, had worked for the Portuguese in return for special privileges – had fled the country with the coming of independence; others, disapproving of the new Marxist PAIGC regime – which equally disapproved of them – got away later. To find out how the sins (as seen by the PAIGC) of those fathers had been visited upon their children, I spoke to some who had taken refuge in Senegal.

Abdullah was one. He was one of the saddest, most frightened boys I have ever met. He simply could not understand why two of the village notables, both farmers, who were liked and respected, had been arrested and shot. Nor could Abdullah understand why he, a boy of twelve, had been forced, with all the other villagers, to watch their execution. Looking at the ground, he said in a tiny voice, 'I don't understand how they could be criminals.' He was still so shocked by that terrible event that he could hardly speak about it. He kept his eyes fixed on the ground; his lips barely moved and his voice was almost inaudible. Then, silently, Abdullah began crying. Perhaps he took me for an official of the PAIGC – if so, it was not for long, for we gave him some sweets. Thanks to them he cheered up a little. He told me how the villagers went home after the execution, Abdullah with his mother. His father was not there – having already fled. Why, Abdullah could not understand, either. He wondered whether he would ever see him again. Then came good news. A man known to the family came and told him, 'Your father has sent me to bring you and your mother to him in Senegal.'

That is where I met Abdullah, at M'Bour; his father, too. When I asked about his mother, Abdullah looked sad again. He told me that during the march through the bush to the frontier, his mother had had a heart attack. She was taken to a nearby village; Abdullah was with her when, shortly afterwards, she died.

The friend finally brought Abdullah safely to his father, and there he sat, next to him, looking much happier now that all these sad reminiscences were over. Abdullah and his father may soon return to their country, whose government has been singularly tolerant of its dissident citizens.

In Mozambique the fight for freedom began seriously when, in 1964, the Mozambique Liberation Front (FRELIMO) proclaimed a 'general armed insurrection against Portuguese colonialism'. Thereafter, year after year, Lisbon sent more and more troops to fight the guerrillas of FRELIMO until, at the outset of 1969, the government was able to announce that 'apart from three sectors in the north of the country, the situation is perfectly calm'.

Over the years, the Lisbon government's blithe optimism faded. The liberation war intensified – with civilians bearing most of the brunt; steadily FRELIMO gained the upper hand until, in mid 1974, came the cease-fire and in June 1975 Mozambique celebrated its independence.

During those days, in a village called Fombi in the province of Tete, there lived a lady called Lucinda. Hers was a typical African home with mud walls and a thatched roof. There, with her husband and three little girls, she lived happily – until the liberation war hit the village.

When Lucinda and I met it was outside her ramshackle, but by no means charmless, little shanty at Old Kanyama, on the outskirts of Lusaka, in Zambia. Very composed, dressed in a pink blouse and brown skirt, a coloured cloth tied about her head and her feet shoeless, she sat there while her girls, Siria, Rita and Zeripa, clustered around her, nestling one against the other and against her, a very tight little family. At her breast she suckled a tiny boy, Stephen. Then another little boy, Bisalom, joined us.

In a way, Bisalom and Stephen symbolized Lucinda's remarkable feat. First, carrying Bisalom – in her womb – she had walked out of Mozambique into Zambia. She was sent back. Then, this time carrying

Stephen — as she had his brother, in her womb — she walked out once more. Her girls accompanied her, of course, on both these escapades. Siria, a tall, slender fourteen-year-old — dressed, when I met her, with a flair almost Parisian, in a mauve blouse with a bright red scarf across one shoulder — carried, on her back, her three-year-old sister Zeripa. 'And if Siria had become too tired?' I asked Lucinda, who replied, 'Then Zeripa would have had to walk, or die. In the bush it's either one or the other.'

The Portuguese army brought the war to Fombi where Lucinda lived. There were both black and white soldiers. They arrested a number of villagers and burnt down their huts. Lucinda, her daughters clinging to her, watched as the prisoners, among them women, even pregnant ones, were beaten with rifle butts. Being pregnant herself, Lucinda's one thought was to run off into the bush, but she did not dare to, knowing that she risked being shot. To the surprise of Lucinda and her daughters, once the beatings and tortures were over the soldiers began distributing food. 'You remember that?' I asked Zeripa, and the little girl said, 'All I remember is that we were dying of hunger.' Famished as they were, though, the villagers, next time the soldiers approached, fled into the bush.

Things got so bad that Lucinda decided to escape to Zambia. Her husband — without saying a word to her — had already left. So, one evening after dark, Lucinda, with Siria (carrying Zeripa) and Rita, walked out of their home and into the bush. They had brought some rice to eat, but left all their belongings behind. Lucinda had no idea where Zambia was, but she and the girls kept walking — in the wrong direction, eastwards. This seemed to worry Lucinda less than the fear of being picked up by the soldiers. Sometimes she heard them, in their trucks, not far away. Then she and the girls lay low. Zeripa, she said, was very good and never cried. At last, after a week's journeying, they came to a road.

Exhausted and footsore, they sat there hoping for a lift. A truck-driver picked them up and dropped them near the frontier. There she and the girls took once more to their feet, into the bush and over the border into Zambia. They walked on for another day, and were then picked up and brought to Lusaka.

Three months later, along with other Mozambican refugees, they were repatriated. A truck brought them direct to a re-education camp. Siria thought she was going to prison but, except for the shortage of food, it was not as bad as that. They had to beg food from the guards. The 're-education' consisted basically of an incitement to work; they were to take their hoes and grow more food.

Lucinda, frankly, had but one thought – to get back to Zambia. She asked permission to return home for family reasons.

A week or so in Fombi gave her enough time to put her affairs in order and, incidentally, again become pregnant. The escape plans were not complicated – Lucinda already knew the ropes, though this time there was an extra passenger, Bisalom. This time, too, they walked through the bush, but for only one day before hitting the road. A truck came along and the driver agreed to take them all the way to Lusaka.

Lucinda was, of course, an illegal immigrant. So, skipping the formalities, she made straight for her little home at Old Kanyama where the neighbours welcomed her back. But without a refugee's allowance Lucinda had serious money problems. She never really knew where she and the children would find the next meal – and this included the baby, for, on short rations, his mother's flow of milk had diminished.

To help fill the kitty, Lucinda brewed up small quantities of the local gin, made from bananas, sugar and yeast – moonshine, of course, so her clientele was limited and strictly personal. She offered me a nip – it was well below the 70° proof of Gordon's. Lucinda invited me into her house: its walls were of corrugated iron and where gaps occurred they were ingeniously patched with sheets of rusty metal beaten out of odd oil-drums. An assortment of stones, car tyres and an old bicycle on top of the roof held it firmly in place. Much of the floor-space of her little home was taken up by sacks of cement, charcoal and mealie flour belonging to a neighbour, from whom, no doubt, Lucinda exacted a small storage fee. It all helped to make ends meet, as did the old collection of cigarettes and bottles of peanut-oil stored in her bedroom – the stock-in-trade of a modest retail business which enabled her to conjure yet a few more pennies from the pockets of friendly neighbours.

Auprès de Lucinda, the lying was hard; Siria and Rita slept on the concrete floor, the two smaller children on the bare boards of a wooden bed, their mother and the baby on another wooden bed amidst a jumble of crumpled bedclothes. The cooking was done outside on a primitive charcoal stove knocked out of an old oil-drum. Further afield was the privy, a rickety wooden hut shared with half a dozen neighbours, and farther still a well, the public ablution place.

In this arid, dusty slum Lucinda and her family had come to settle – as cheerful, decent and charming a family as you could wish to meet. They have opted for poverty in Zambia rather than for the rigours of citizenship in Marxist Mozambique.

When, on 11 November 1975, Angola became independent of Portugal, the three liberation movements were engaged in civil war. On one side there was the Popular Movement for the Liberation of Angola (MPLA); on the other, the National Front for the Liberation of Angola (FNLA) and the National Union for the Total Independence of Angola (UNITA).

But the conflict went much farther than a lot of confusing names. From the beginning of the struggle for freedom early in 1961 – when the FNLA launched savage guerrilla warfare in the north and the MPLA rose in the capital, Luanda – these two movements differed politically (as well as ethnically), the MPLA being Russian-backed, the FNLA closely supported by neighbouring Zaïre and by certain western powers. UNITA, the most western-oriented of the three, entered the fray in 1966 with a suicidal attack on the garrison at Tuxeira de Souza in the east.

Some two hundred kilometres southwards there is a town called Lumbala, where there lived an African boy, John Bisesi, the son of a carpenter, whose thriving business enabled him to keep twenty head of cattle and six goats. John told me how he now came to be living at Maheba, in northern Zambia, where I met him. His family were Christians; on the white walls of his bedroom in their brick-built, thatched house, John had pasted pictures of Christ, the Virgin Mary and the disciples. 'Happy and united,' was his family, John said. Until he was twelve he was sent not to school, but into the bush, with his father's cattle. He drove them out at sunrise and in the evening herded them back into the kraal.

John might never have gone to school at all, but for a lion, which one day came roaring among the cattle, pouncing on one of the cows. Twelve-year-old John took to his heels and raced back home. Breathless, he told his father, who merely laughed, 'Lucky the lion took the cow and not you, my boy!' John felt grateful to that lion, for from now on he was no longer sent with the cattle into the bush, but to school.

It was after he had been there for two years that, in 1968, there were stirrings of war in Lumbala. One day UNITA people came to the house and, saying that they were the ones who were going to drive out the Portuguese, produced a membership card, red and green with a black cock as emblem. They were threatening to kill anyone who did not join the party. Their threats were wasted on John's father, who happened to be the party's local secretary. Far more disturbing for him, however, were the threats of the Portuguese soldiers – thirty of them – who called a few days later, searched the house and found the cards, which they confiscated, saying, 'We'll be back tomorrow for you.'

Then and there, John's father decided to leave. Well after dark, while the village slept, the family crept out and, under a full moon, headed straight for the bush, the two little boys, Pelela and Kakahu, on their father's shoulders, the baby Mwila bound to his mother's back. They carried no belongings, no food and no water. The Zambian frontier was three nights' march away – they did not dare to move by day, for fear of Portuguese patrols.

After a couple of days, the little boys were in such a bad way that they cried ceaselessly. In the evening, as the family made ready to leave, they heard, above the crying, the sound of voices; then, quite close, a gun was fired and someone shouted, 'Don't move, we are the MPLA.' Then a man appeared, very tall with a great mop of shaggy hair, followed by six others. 'Where are you going?' he asked. 'To Zambia,' replied John's father, 'because of the war.' The MPLA leader swore at him. 'How do you think Angola is going to get independence if men like you run away?' he asked roughly, and the family were led back to the MPLA camp.

A gun was thrust into the hands of John's father, but he refused it, until told, 'If you don't take it, we'll shoot you.' 'Which they would have done anyway,' said John, 'had they known he belonged to UNITA.'

The ceaseless crying of the little boys was now going to be their salvation. The MPLA men, just as anxious lest it might lead to their own discovery by a Portuguese patrol, escorted the family at least a kilometre away, where they left them to camp. 'And don't try to escape,' they warned, 'or we'll shoot you all.' 'But escape we had to,' said John, 'though we were all very frightened.'

Indeed, his two small sisters, Makalu and Mayunda, were so terrified of being shot that they refused to leave. After a terrible scene, said John, 'My father told them angrily, "All right, stay then."' And the family walked off into the dark. Five more nights' marching brought them to Zambia.

The two girls were found next day by the MPLA men, who, to their surprise, treated them well and, though it took them over a year, managed to get them reunited with their family.

John had been at Maheba since 1971. He had learnt English, completed his schooling and was now a carpenter like his father. There had once burned in him a desire for vengeance against the men who robbed his family of their home. But he had forgotten all that. Not so his father; 'Whenever he speaks of the past,' John said, 'there are tears in his eyes.'

As 1975, the year of independence, began, the liberation movements were still not reconciled. While at one extreme MPLA were full-blown communists bent on ousting all whites, UNITA, at the other extreme, counted some Portuguese among its members. One of them was fourteen-year-old Maria Arminda de Jesus da Vinha, who belonged to the JURA, the UNITA youth movement. 'We never called each other by name,' Arminda said, 'but always "brother" or "sister" as the Africans do.'

Arminda's father was a night-watchman and lived in the Cazenga district of Luanda. Times were dangerous, as Arminda's experience proves. One afternoon in January 1975, on her way home from school, she was attacked by four mulattos wearing the MPLA emblem. She managed to run away. Not long afterwards men wearing MPLA uniform broke into Arminda's school. Some of the pupils fled; Arminda hid. A little later her father came and took her home. The family were halfway through lunch when Arminda's mother said, 'Take a look out of the window.' Her father looked and saw that the house was surrounded by the MPLA. He took Arminda and her younger brother, Joel, by the hand, while her mother looked after Agostinho, her elder brother. Her father told them all to jump out of the window. Just as he himself was going to jump, he was hit by a bullet in the right leg and fell backwards. They all went to his help and at that moment the MPLA gunmen entered the house.

What then happened is described in Arminda's words. 'They tied us all with rope – except my father, who was wounded. Him they began to cut to pieces with *machetes*, long knives – first his ears, then his legs; then they cut pieces off his body. They were going to cut off my father's head when he begged them to let him speak to his family. This they allowed him to do, and he told my mother to take good care of all us children, and especially of me. He said goodbye to us, and wept. The men then cut off his head and began to play football with it.'

Pursuing their heroic fight for freedom these members of the Popular Movement for the Liberation of Angola then set about the children, especially Joel and Agostinho, beating them with whips. It so happened that Arminda's mother had been going to bake bread. The oven was lit and this gave the MPLA men an idea. Arminda went on, 'They took little Joel, undressed him and began to rub butter and cooking-oil all over his body. I then saw them take a spade with which they were going to put him in the oven. My brother clung so desperately to Agostinho that they both fell on the floor. My mother shrieked.'

She was heard by UNITA gunmen, who had learned about the school attack and were looking for Arminda. Luckily, the little white girl's black 'brothers', whom she did not know by name, had arrived in the nick of time.

The agony of Angola during the process of liberation can be measured by the half million refugees who fled to neighbouring countries, notably Zaïre. Many of them are still too afraid to return home.

CHAPTER TWENTY-TWO

Bloodshed at Soweto

Spread like a horseshoe between Angola in the west and Mozambique in the east, Southern Africa – that is, Namibia (South-West Africa), South Africa and Rhodesia – still look uncertainly to the future. In October 1974, the South African prime minister, Balthazar Johannes Vorster, who played the leading role in this drama, declared publicly that he would work for peace in Southern Africa. 'The voice of reason,' commented the president of Zambia, Kenneth Kaunda, adding that the time had come to choose between two paths – that of peace or of war. Four years later, children, both black and white, from these countries told me what had befallen them in the meantime. Unfortunately they could speak only of war, terror and persecution – and *apartheid*, the enforced segregation of blacks from whites imposed by the Afrikaner National Party since it came to power in 1948.

Namibia was officially administered by the South African government under United Nations mandate – which was withdrawn in 1965. South Africa, however, refused to budge and *apartheid* was still in force in Namibia when I met Selma, one of the thousands of teenage Namibian refugees in Dar-es-Salaam, at the cramped and rather dingy offices of the South-West African Peoples' Organization (SWAPO), the Namibian independence movement. Selma came from Ovamboland, in the north, where her father owned six head of cattle. That was his allotment; if, at the census made by the veterinary service he was found to have more, they were confiscated by the Boers (as Selma called South African whites of Dutch origin).

At fifteen, Selma went to high school. It meant a long walk through the bush alone – 'rather frightening', she called it, little dreaming that a far longer and more frightening walk was in store for her. It began, really, in December 1973, in her classroom on the first floor – where the girls, as they waited for the teacher, were laughing and chattering. One of them began to sing a SWAPO song, rather a harmless one which went: 'Nujoma [the SWAPO president] will never be beaten by the Vorster regime.' The rest of the girls joined in, and the next thing they knew was that it was they who were to be beaten – literally – by the Vorster regime. The police, called in by the school's principal, loaded them into trucks and drove them off to gaol – where they were to remain for the next three days, with no food, sleeping on the bare floor, forbidden to wash and provided with a single earth closet nearby, which stank to heaven.

A white officer interrogated the girls. 'Where did you learn those songs?' Reply: 'At political meetings.' 'But you know very well,' the officer went on, 'that they are banned. You will all be expelled from school.' On the first and second day the girls were taken one by one, escorted by a black policeman, into a corridor, where they were beaten by a white policeman, using a truncheon. Selma was first made to strip her flowered dress – like the one she was wearing now – down to the waist. She showed me how she was made to stand, bending over, her arms in front of her. Then the blows began to fall. Aloud, the policeman counted them: one – two – three ... For the first ten strokes or so Selma screamed with pain. After ten, she said, 'You don't feel any more.' The policeman continued counting up to thirty, but long before that Selma had collapsed. Then she heard the man shout, 'Now get up, kaffir bitch, and get out.'

On the third day the girls were released. Selma's parents, shocked at her condition, were relieved to see her home. It took two weeks for the wounds to heal, though the marks are still there. Selma showed me some, on her arms and legs. One ugly scar ran for fifteen centimetres down her shin-bone. But this, Selma said, was another story – she had been at an open-air meeting when the police set dogs on the crowd. Selma had fallen badly while running away.

She and all the other girls were duly expelled from school. Early in 1974 she went to stay with a cousin, far away in the south. But there again the police were always in the offing. Sometimes, at night, they would call at the house and say, quite politely, 'Don't mind us; just go on sleeping while we search the house.' Selma told me, 'I had had enough of this harassment by the Boers.' She decided to leave Namibia.

I asked her if she put all whites, including me, in one category. 'Not a bit of it,' she laughed. 'My country has plenty of white friends, so they are my friends, too.'

Selma returned to her village in the north, but avoided her home, fearing that her parents might prevent her leaving. As she walked on she came across a girlfriend; they were still together on reaching the frontier.

There, they slipped off into the bush and slid under the fence – into Angola. Selma and her friend were lucky, for later, as I was shown on a photo, the bush was cleared on each side of the fence, exposing it to the watchful eyes of the frontier guards.

The two girls walked on alone, without food, for three days, when they fell in with a large group of Namibian refugees. With them, they found food and company for the march, which lasted three long weeks, across Angola, until, in a pirogue, they crossed a crocodile-infested river and came to Zambia.

There, at Senanga, on the Zambezi, the over-fifteens, boys and girls, were given a course of weapon-training. SWAPO rules, Selma said, insisted on this. She was sent to the front but met no Boers. She did, however, meet a boy called Simon and the two fell in love. Not long afterwards Selma found she was pregnant. And that, alas, meant separation from Simon, who could not, all at once act both as father and freedom fighter. In March 1976 Selma got a message through to Simon saying that he was the father of a beautiful girl. Selma called her Nangola, in memory of the long march across Angola. Back came a brief reply from Simon, 'Thanks for the baby.' Since then Selma has had no further news. She would like to marry Simon, but, she told me, 'I don't even know if he is alive.'

A year later there came another separation – from her baby. Nangola was sent to the SWAPO settlement in Zambia, her mother to Dar-es-Salaam for secretarial training. When, six months later, she visited her daughter, she called to Nangola. But the baby would not go to her mother. 'She did not know me,' said Selma. 'It must hurt very much, being separated from her?' I asked Selma. 'Well, even if it does,' she answered, 'it is no good minding. I am here helping to fight for my people and that means for my baby's future.' I asked her, 'Who do you love best, your nation or your baby?' Selma's reply was evasive, 'My great love is my nation. My baby belongs to it, so I love her as much.'

Since I spoke to Selma, Vorster has fallen from power, but the regime he once headed has still, despite pressure from the United Nations, not relinquished its hold on Namibia. So Selma's exile continues while she waits to be reunited with her baby, who has forgotten her, and with Simon, if she ever finds him again.

In 1947 the King and Queen of England – and of South Africa – toured that country, then a Dominion of the Commonwealth. Wherever they went Africans, in organized choirs or in little groups at wayside stations, greeted them with the anthem *'N'Kosi Sikelela Afrika'* – God Bless

Africa. Their Majesties, Prime Minister Smuts and other members of the cabinet would listen, entranced, to this haunting air. A year later Smuts was ousted and the Afrikaner National Party, headed by Dr Malan, took over. It is still in power. South Africa's policy of *apartheid* separates its five million whites and its twenty million blacks into two nations – with the whites in the driving seat. In face of criticism of *apartheid* South Africa withdrew, in 1961, from the Commonwealth.

Apartheid is responsible for driving thousands of young blacks to desert their families – often without a goodbye. Jefferson, whom I met in Tanzania, was one. Until he was fifteen, he told me, he had never spoken to a white.

He had never thought deeply about *apartheid*, or 'white domination', until, one evening, his father, who worked in a building firm owned by whites, came home more tired and depressed than usual. He told the children (there were seven of them), 'Here I am, working hard all day long in this country, which is rich and is my country as much as anyone's, yet I still can't earn enough to feed you all and pay for your schooling.'

Jefferson, who had to be lodged with an uncle, eventually passed into the high school – for blacks, of course – at Vereeniging, south of Johannesburg. The teaching facilities were so poor, said Jefferson, that the pupils organized a peaceful protest. The answer to their grievances was swift and unexpected. The police broke into their classrooms and beat them up. Jefferson was hit by a truncheon over the right eye; he showed me the scar, nearly two centimetres long. Another time the police arrived with dogs, which they unleashed on the pupils. The tactic, Jefferson explained, was for the pupils to crowd, one against the other, in a corner of the classroom. The unfortunate few in front got bitten. The school was closed, and Jefferson, sickened and frustrated, decided to leave the country. He went off without saying a word to his family, which only made him miss them more.

Patricia, to whom I talked in Lusaka, was a quiet, charming girl and outstanding pupil, but once down in the street, demonstrating against *apartheid*, she saw red. By the time she was seventeen she had taken part in six demonstrations, singing revolutionary songs and shouting slogans, stoning the police and throwing petrol bombs (which she carried in a plastic bag); she had joined in the smashing, pillaging and burning of government buildings and transport; she had been fired on by the police and once, looking straight down the barrels of their guns, knelt with other girls in the road singing 'Children of Africa'. She had seen the dead bodies of her friends lying in the street. Patricia's name was on the police books. For this reason she, like thousands of other students, had to leave the country.

Soweto ('south-west town'), the African township near Johannesburg, was, on 16 and 17 June 1976, the scene of violent rioting in which scores of students were killed and injured. I spoke separately to several students who marched in the streets at that time; all agreed that the demonstrations were provoked by the compulsory use of Afrikaans in all subjects; that the intention was to demonstrate peacefully; and, finally, that violence broke out the moment the forces of the law used tear-gas and started shooting. The police had their story, the students theirs.

Peter, whom I met in Gaborone, Botswana, was born in Soweto; his parents and their seven children lived in a leaky four-room house, with no electricity or bath and an outside WC. Peter still uses his Christian name, but 'I am no longer a Christian,' he told me. 'After all the terrible things I have been through I came, like many of my friends, to question the existence of God. Another thing, this Christian religion came from the white people who have so maltreated us.' 'Do you feel the same about all white men?' I asked him. Peter replied, 'The black South African has been brought up from his earliest youth to treat the white man as an enemy. Even those whites I know as friends, I treat with a certain reserve.' 'That includes me?' He smiled and said, 'Yes, frankly, it does.'

When a boy Peter was warned by his father always to play within the precincts of the house, never to go out alone on the streets. The danger came from young people in their teens, drop-outs from school who could not get work. They were dangerous criminals, using both guns and knives, preferably the latter, for they killed silently. Then there were the street brawls. Though a Basuto himself, Peter admitted that it was tribal hatred between his own people and the Zulus that led them, armed with knobkerries, to fight savage battles, invariably on a Saturday night when they were all drunk on African beer, brewed from sorghum. 'No one would dare to stand in the street and watch,' commented Peter, who added that he felt a contempt for the police. 'Black and white, they are as bad as each other; they can't even provide protection for the citizens of Soweto.' For that reason he was never late back from school, where he worked hard, loved cricket and, like most of his friends, worshipped Martin Luther King as his greatest hero. Peter, at this time, was happy.

I met Justice at Morogoro, in Tanzania. Events had brought him all the way there from his village in the Transvaal. Because his father, a manual labourer, was too poor to feed his wife and eight children, the family had to break up. Justice was sent to live with an uncle at Soweto, three hundred kilometres away. The uncle, despite a weakness for the bottle, was kind, but Justice, who was deeply attached to his mother, felt homesick. He worked well, however, and at sixteen passed into high school where his comrades elected him class-leader. This gave him responsibilities – for which, young as he was, he was later made to answer to the police.

I also met Gloria at Morogoro. At the time of the Soweto riots, she was only thirteen. She too lived in a typical four-room house with her parents, two sisters and a brother, Godfrey. Her father left every morning around six to go to work with a firm of lawyers – whites – at Johannesburg.

In the small hours of one morning the whole family were awoken by men banging on the door and tapping on the windows, shouting 'Police'! Gloria hid under the bedclothes, which, a few moments later, were pulled off her by a policeman flashing his torch in her face. She heard them go into Godfrey's room, asking roughly, '*Warr is jou pass, kaffir?*' Godfrey did not have a pass, being under the age limit, but this did not save him from being hit on the head. Gloria's father was dragged out of bed, beaten up, then taken off to the police station. Next day he was back with a lump on the head, complaining – for obvious reasons – of pains all over his body. He had to leave for work as usual next morning, or lose his job.

Gloria, in 1976, was in Form I at junior school in Soweto. She wore a uniform but disliked it, she said, 'because it was imposed by the whites'. For the same reason she disliked history because it was put across in a way to make the blacks feel inferior to the whites. She had never heard of the Battle of Isandhlwana where the Zulus defeated the British. Incidentally, Gloria informed me that she preferred the English whites to the Afrikaners.

On the day of the riots – 16 June 1976 – Gloria was walking home from school in the early afternoon. She was always 'basically frightened' – her words – because, as she walked, she had in mind stories of *Muthi*, ritual medicine, of kidnapped children having pieces of their body cut off to mix into the medicine. As she walked she noticed helicopters; they were hovering above the student processions, spraying them with tear-gas, as they made their way from their different schools towards Orlando, the concentration point. After reaching home Gloria heard firing and she wanted to rush off and join the demonstration, only her mother stopped her.

Next day, the streets were full of soldiers and police and before leaving for school Gloria was told by her mother not to get mixed up in the riots. After the shooting of the previous day the students' tempers were up. School had hardly started when the Form I students, including Gloria, were invited to a meeting at the Madibane High School, almost next door. 'A fairly animated meeting,' Gloria called it, with the student-leaders shouting '*Amandia!*' (power!) and the students yelling in response '*Nga Wethu!*' (it's ours!). The meeting over, Gloria formed up with the rest and marched off with them. The procession, wide enough to fill the street, headed for a local government-licensed bottle-store (liquor shop). Gloria was by now completely carried away in the general delirium. When the procession met a 'Putco', one of the green buses belonging to the Public Utility Transport Corporation, Gloria joined furiously in the assault, throwing stones, smashing windows and cheering as the bus went up in flames. Then she marched on, singing as lustily as any of the hundreds of other students as they stamped out on the asphalt road the rhythm of their song. Little Gloria shrilled '*Nantsi Indoda Emnyama Vorster!*' (Look out, Vorster, here comes the black man!), '*Baleka Nantsi Ieya Vorster!*' (Run away, Vorster, here he comes!). As she sang and stamped Gloria's youthful fervour rose. '*Asikhathali Noma Siya Boswa – Sizi Miseli I Nkuleke!*' (We don't care if we are arrested, we are ready to fight for freedom!).

This was Gloria's wild mood as she joined in the attack on the '44', a government building, half offices, half library; she cheered on the leaders as they set fire to the building, which was soon enveloped in the smoke and flames of burning books and files. Then she marched on, this small, frenzied teenager, stamping and singing more deliriously than ever, ignoring the police guarding the bottle-store, which she helped with all her might to put to sack, pulling it to pieces, breaking it up, smashing the windows and the bottles with chairs. Then, with all the others, she screamed and danced wildly with joy as the building went up in flames.

At that moment the police opened fire. Fear quickly cooled Gloria's excitement and she ran into the cover of the shadows and hid until the crackling flames died into silence. Then, in the dark, she crept home to her mother, who had enjoined her so strictly at the start of the day to keep away from the riots.

The following day the police called at the house. But Gloria's father had disappeared, no one knew where. Her brother Godfrey, too – she has not seen him since. Gloria herself kept away. For months she lived in constant dread of the police. Whenever she saw them she ran off and, thanks to her long legs, she always managed to avoid them. But the police were keeping a close watch on all the students. Gloria decided to run away from them for good. Her mother, bidding her goodbye, said, 'Never forget your family and your people in South Africa.'

When I met Gloria in Tanzania she was fifteen. At that age she had paid a heavy price for rebellion: for illegally leaving the country she is classed under the Terrorism Act as a terrorist; worse, for her, she is exiled far from her family and her people in South Africa. But, true to her mother's words, she does not forget them.

Justice, the boy who had been elected class-leader, told me that, on the sixteenth, during the morning break, a lot of students, including him, slipped off and joined a procession. Some of the placards bore the slogan 'Away with Afrikaans'; Justice explained that until recently some subjects had been taught in English, some in Afrikaans; it was against the new law which made Afrikaans compulsory for all subjects that the students were protesting. English, after all, was a universal language, Afrikaans a local one 'and the language of the oppressors', as Justice remarked.

Singing songs like '*N'Kosi Sikelela Afrika*' and '*Azania Ikhayalami E Ngi Li Thandayo*' ('I love my home Azania – Black Man's country' – the name designated by the blacks for South Africa), the procession, with Justice marching about ten ranks from the front, made its way towards the Bantu Department of Education (BDE), where its leaders intended to present a petition. But the police barred the way; before their tear-gas bombs the students in front broke up. Justice found himself leading the advance on the police, who opened fire. Close to him, a fourteen-year-old boy, Hector Peterson, dropped dead.

The students scattered, then re-formed. Justice, a mild, sensitive youth, told me, 'Our tempers were now up', and admitted that it was anger which drove him to join the mob of students, stoning and burning. At the end of the day Justice kept away from home. When, three days later, he returned, his uncle told him that the police were looking for him.

'I had no *a priori* objection to Afrikaans,' Peter told me, 'but I objected to its substitution for English. So I took part in the student demonstrations.' Calmly and with complete frankness, this diffident youth who treated all whites, including myself, with reserve if not as enemies, told me how, armed with stones which he threw at the police, he joined the fray, smashing and burning vehicles and buildings. 'But what hope,' I asked him, 'did you students have with your sticks and stones against the guns of the police?' 'We were driven to sheer desperation,' he said in his quiet way. 'Four of my class-mates were shot dead. I had never seen a dead body before; the first I ever saw belonged to those friends of mine.' Peter thought he was lucky not to be among them. He was facing the police and saw the flashes from their guns as they fired.

At two a.m. next morning the police – two white and two black – banged on the door of Peter's home. His father was away; his mother pushed him into a wardrobe and turned the key. After searching everywhere the police were leaving when one of them said, 'We forgot to look in the wardrobe.' As Peter was dragged out one of the African policemen hit him with the butt of his sub-machine-gun – at which his mother ran screaming out into the dark. Peter was then handcuffed.

He arrived at the police station at 2.30 a.m. From then until six a.m. the police went to work on him. They wanted the answer to one question: where could they find the organizers of the demonstration? That, Peter told them, quite truthfully, was a secret that no one including himself knew; he could not answer. So they tied a plastic bag on his head, keeping it there until he nearly suffocated. They hit him with their fists, made him stand with his hands above his head until he could hold them there no longer. When, exhausted, he collapsed, they kicked him as he lay on the ground. Then they locked him up, keeping him in solitary confinement for four months. During that time he had to face two more interrogations; again, he was hit, punched, kicked. The second time, after he had collapsed on the floor, the interrogation officer, a white and very weighty man, came and sat for half an hour on Peter's chest so that he could hardly breathe.

It was quite obvious that Peter, from the way he spoke and his charming, wistful smile, was a sensitive person. He told me, 'After that terrible time in prison I lost faith in men.' With his closest comrades, even, he felt reserved and insecure. After his release he debated a long time with himself whether to continue his studies, but the fear of the police always prevailed. He decided to escape. Regretfully, he said goodbye to his family, and headed for Botswana, where he was immediately hospitalized. Despite four weeks' treatment for his injuries received in prison he still suffers acutely from pains in the chest. But at least he has picked up his studies and is heading for the university.

After all the violence he has experienced, would he, I asked Peter, be prepared to use it himself? 'As a last resort, I suppose,' he admitted, 'but I should always prefer to negotiate.'

Justice had been home, at his uncle's, only two days when – it was at midnight and he was fast asleep – there came a banging at the door. 'Police!' It was now that Justice had to face up to his responsibilities, modest as they were, as class-leader. The police fired questions at him, but Justice, afraid of being trapped, denied everything. Suddenly, on his head he felt a blow which made him dizzy. Quietly, the officer continued his interrogation. But at each question Justice was slapped by a black policeman on each side of his face. The police left, telling Justice to report next day to the nearest station.

In the event, he reported to his cousin where he lay low for the next nine months. The cousin was a devout man and often spoke to Justice about the evil of violence. I asked Justice, 'Did you repent at having taken part in the riots?' and he replied, 'Yes, I did. I wept in church and asked for forgiveness.' 'Would you, in turn,' I asked him, 'be able to forgive those who did violence to you?' Justice answered, 'Really, no. I can't, for it is because of them that I am here today in a foreign country, far from my home.'

His cousin did manage to organize for Justice a visit to his home. He was shocked by his mother's poor health – doubtless due to worrying about her son. Bitterly he realized how much he had missed her and, worse, how much more he was going to miss her. For Justice's mind was made up; he had decided to leave South Africa. 'I cried a lot during that stay,' Justice said.

He returned to his cousin's, got in touch with 'the right people' and, when the time came, he left without saying a word to anyone. Justice's heart was so full of regrets he did not care to say which was the greatest. What still preyed on his mind was the injustice of being driven from his country, from his brothers and sisters, his father and mother, to whom he was so close. His was the ultimate in *apartheid*; he was completely separated from his family and his country. But still he was haunted (as I am) by that beautiful air, rhythmic and incessant as the sea-waves, '*N'Kosi Sikelela Afrika*', God Bless Africa – the air that so enchanted the King of South Africa before *apartheid* clove that beloved country in two.

CHAPTER TWENTY-THREE*
Good Zimbabweans

Since 1972 a state of war has existed between the multi-racial, white-dominated Rhodesia and the black (though theoretically multi-racial) Zimbabwe of the Patriotic Front, jointly led by two exiles, Joshua N'Komo and Robert Mugabe. Since the elections of May 1979, when the black Bishop Abel Muzorewa replaced Ian Smith as prime minister, the country has been renamed Zimbabwe-Rhodesia.

The men who fight for Rhodesia are called security forces; those who fight for the Patriotic Front are variously termed guerrillas, freedom fighters or terrorists. Your appraisal of the deeds of one side and the other will determine the choice of name you think each best deserves. One thing meanwhile is certain: this is a war in which children are closely and cruelly involved.

Peter (he asked me to call him that), a fugitive from the war in Rhodesia, had an unusual background; he was born in Soweto. His father, in search of better wages, had gone to work in the Johannesburg gold mines. Peter was from the Shangana tribe; he remarked that *apartheid* did not stop at the separation of blacks from whites. Each tribe, Zulu, Basuto, Swazi, Shangana and so on lived in their particular areas; nor at school did the tribes mix.

'In Soweto we were living at the mercy of thieves and criminals. My father wanted better for us,' said Peter, who, when he was thirteen, returned to live in Salisbury, Rhodesia. There he immediately noticed that there was less racialism. 'The whites did not seem to mind,' he said. Though he queued with the blacks, the whites would sometimes say, 'Come and join our queue.'

At fourteen, Peter's schooling ended abruptly because, being born in South Africa, he could not produce a Rhodesian birth certificate. He decided to educate himself — at the township library, essentially 'all-black', as he put it, but like all public institutions in Rhodesia, open to black and white alike. He would often call at the high school to

*This chapter and the ensuing one, Chapter 24, were written in May 1979. Since then there have been a cease-fire and new elections (February 1980). *Author.*

compare notes with his student friends.

In mid-1974, Peter took part in a student demonstration in Salisbury. It was quite a peaceful one and when it broke up he went home and to bed. At four o'clock in the morning there came a knock at the door. Police. Peter was driven off to the station, where he was questioned. 'I grant you,' he told me, 'I lied by omission in refusing to admit that I had organized the demonstration. That was no crime, anyway.' Unfortunately, Peter's denials made the police lose their patience. He was led outside, stripped to the waist and tied by a rope, three metres long, to a motor scooter. A black policeman got on it, started up and proceeded to pull Peter round the building — he reckoned he did eight circuits but in any case was so out of breath that he fell and was dragged another twenty metres over the gravel, finishing up with his arms and torso covered with abrasions. He was allowed a few minutes to regain his breath, then the questioning continued. Still he refused to admit anything. So he was then bound round his bare arms and torso with wet sacking. A wire was connected to it and plugged into the electric mains. A switch was then clicked on and off, very rapidly, three times. The question was repeated: 'Who was the ringleader?' the reply, too: 'I don't know,' and the words were hardly out of his mouth when the current jerked him again. Peter said that the shock was not such that it made him cry out in pain. 'But it made me feel desperate and very exhausted.'

The white officer in charge then said, 'He obviously hasn't had enough. We must give him some more.' Peter gave a surprising description of this man: 'Medium built, about five feet ten inches, good looking. I would almost say his face was charming.' He was less flattering about the black policeman who made him strip naked, sit in a chair and then, with a pair of pliers, began to tweak his genital organs. 'The man was a ferocious-looking brute. His only concern was business — to do it as efficiently as possible. He took real pleasure in his work.' Peter concluded, 'The treatment those men gave me was absolutely inhuman.' It continued, at intervals, from four to eleven a.m. Yet, after the initial, excruciating pain, astonishingly, 'Something happened to my body,' Peter said. 'I couldn't feel any more.' His father had turned up at eight o'clock but was not allowed to see him till eleven. He had always been against the demonstrations. Yet now he came bringing food.

Peter was in a dilemma. His father said, 'I have asked you over and over again not to get mixed up in these demonstrations. You risk spending the rest of your life rotting in gaol.' Peter respected his father's feelings, yet his conscience drove him to continue in the resistance movement. 'Would you ever resort to violence?' I asked him. 'No,' he said. 'If you try to force an idea on people they don't understand it.' As for terrorism, Peter commented, 'If you have got to fight, well, fight the people concerned and don't involve innocent people.' His remark, as the Rhodesian problem deepened, was to have increasing relevance. Indeed, on Rhodesian soil itself, civilians, by far the greatest proportion of them blacks, were being sorely harassed, on the one hand by the freedom fighters in their attempt to terrorize the population, on the other, by the security forces in their efforts to locate the 'terrs', terrorists – that is, the freedom fighters.

Peter, embittered by his experiences, decided to escape. He left without a word to his father and arrived in Gaborone, Botswana, on Christmas Day 1977, which he spent in a police cell. Since then he has been living at the government's refugee settlement at Broadhurst Farm, a collection of ramshackle buildings on the outskirts of Gaborone. It was there that I talked to Peter until long after the sun had set and stars shone out of a dark sky, against which I could discern only his white teeth and the whites of his eyes. Peter is drawn by the sky; his dream is to become a flight engineer. 'If I have to wait another thirty years I shall never give up trying,' he said earnestly.

Another night of waiting and hoping faced Peter and a hundred other young refugees in their cramped, unlit quarters at Broadhurst Farm. Among them, waiting almost without further hope, was Paul – it was by coincidence that he chose that pseudonym. By definition he was a Zimbabwean for, his parents being members of Zimbabwean African Peoples' Union (ZAPU), Joshua N'Komo's organization, Paul, at birth, automatically became a member. Like N'Komo, Paul belonged to the Matabele tribe. His father, a businessman, died when he was thirteen.

Paul was only sixteen when the police arrested him. At that time his home was in Plumtree, south-west of Bulawayo. He had led two young friends through the bush and across the Botswana frontier five kilometres away, and so was accessory to a criminal act – leaving the country without authority. He was imprisoned, beaten on the soles of his feet with a fan-belt, given electric shocks. He went on hunger strike, was hospitalized and finally released. He named two of his white tormentors, one-time pupils at Plumtree High School. Two others, blacks, were of the Shona tribe. Paul, had he been a Shona too, thinks he would have got off more lightly.

While recovering from his prison treatment he played records of Mozart, rock and reggae music. Then he returned to his studies, bent on getting into university. A year later, when the police got news that ZAPU freedom fighters were in the vicinity, they questioned Paul about them, giving him the 'full treatment' followed by nine months at the detention camp at Wha-Wha, where, he said, the conditions 'were not too bad'.

On his release the school authorities refused to take him back; he had taken part, they said, in subversive activities. Paul felt like an outcast. He sank deeper and deeper into depression, listening ceaselessly to his reggae music, with its protest against authority, against life. He felt no more desire to live, indeed tried to end his life with an overdose of sleeping-pills. Finally, despite his mother's entreaties, he decided to escape to Botswana. On the eve of his departure he played reggae. It acted almost like a drug, he told me; you listened, then you took a 'trip' to Botswana. Several of his friends, after a reggae session, had done so. Paul, as he listened that evening in his room, took the decision to leave next day.

Since he has been at Gaborone, he has telephoned his mother but, he said, it takes him days to get over it. Occasionally she has visited him, but each time he takes her to Francistown to catch the train back to Bulawayo, Paul told me, 'she breaks down and cries. I can hardly bear it any more.'

Paul did not believe he would ever return home. 'If I tried I should be arrested. And this time it would probably mean a bullet.' He is listed in Rhodesia as a criminal and – because he left illegally – as a terrorist. After talking to him it was hard to believe that he was capable of being either; about terrorism Paul was explicit: 'It is immoral and inexcusable.' Meanwhile, all he had suffered for the cause of ZAPU had brought him to nothing. He had been stagnating for months; the last words he said to me were, 'I have lost all hope in the future.'

The most obvious thing about ZAPU's president Joshua N'Komo, whom I met at his house in Lusaka, is that there is plenty of him. He is massive but not corpulent. Dressed in a well but loosely cut suit of grey, he could move, like an African elephant, with surprising agility. In one hand he held a black baton, by the other a diminutive boy whom, after greeting me jovially, he introduced. 'This is Geneva. He was found wandering alone in the Botswana bush. When questioned by the police, he said, "I have come from Rhodesia and I am going to Geneva to find Mr N'Komo." He refused to say more, so we called him Geneva.'

Joshua N'Komo is a great showman. Bidding three of my compatriots from the BBC and myself to follow him, he drove a few miles out of Lusaka to the Victoria Camp (how the name sticks, after so long) for girls. On the president's arrival eight thousand of them, at a given signal, downed their books and pencils and converged, running, on the gathering-place, where they danced and sang and swayed in unison before him. A little girl told me, 'I like him and when he visits the camp I am feeling very happy singing songs.' That they were revolutionary songs did not diminish by one whit their haunting, incessant rhythm.

The Victoria Camp was relatively sophisticated, with its permanent buildings and workshops, which N'Komo inspected. He spoke to a group of women and their infant children, then, turning to us, said, 'The only thing these mummies could snatch from a burning house, the only bodies they could pick up, were those of their children.' Three-quarters of them, however, in these two camps, were orphans, or separated from their parents. Every one had a story to tell. Sitting on a log in the sun, I listened to some of them, while a dry, warm wind blew dust into our eyes.

Fikeile's story was typical. She was nine and lived with her parents and five sisters in a round house with mud walls and a thatch on top, in a village near Plumtree. She was in primary school and happy as a little girl can be – until, one evening at dusk, Rhodesian security forces surrounded her village.

Fikeile was playing hopscotch, laughing and having fun, when the soldiers came to her house. There were two truck-loads of them, wearing dark green uniform, 'kind of gumboots', and green caps. She had never seen soldiers before and was frightened. She was frightened, really, she said of all white people, 'because I had heard about their deeds'. I asked if she was afraid of me, and she said, 'Yes,' but with such a cute little smile that I hardly believed she was serious. Was she afraid of the black soldiers? Yes, again 'because of their deeds'. She had heard that soldiers questioned people, asked for their papers and, if these were not forthcoming, shot them. This is what Fikeile had heard. In a few moments she would find out.

The soldiers called roughly to her father to come outside. He appeared, followed by her mother. Both looked so frightened that Fikeile began to cry. She saw her father being questioned. After a few minutes he and her mother, both in tears, disappeared with the soldiers behind the granary. Fikeile and her sisters waited, wondering what would happen. Suddenly, two shots rang out and at that the five girls ran away, two of them into the bush, while Fikeile and her two other sisters, Qiniso and Gloria, hid in oildrums.

There they stayed until the soldiers had gone. Fikeile and her sisters then went to look behind the granary. Fikeile said, 'There was one big pool of blood.' That was all. The bodies had been removed.

Fikeile, Qiniso and Gloria, fearing that the soldiers were still around, did not dare to go off into the bush looking for their other sisters. They waited until it was completely dark then they themselves set off into the bush, taking nothing, not even food, with them. As they walked through the night, Fikeile was frightened that the soldiers would catch them. But they came safely next morning to the frontier at the river Shashi. The water was low and Qiniso and Gloria (with Fikeile on her back) waded across into Botswana. The daily 'Freedom Ferry' plane brought them on to Zambia.

Fikeile told me she could never forgive those men who killed her mother and father, whom she often sees in her dreams. Would she, as a freedom fighter, want to avenge their death? 'No,' said Fikeile firmly, 'I do not want to see any more people killed.'

Leaving the Victoria Camp, the presidential cortège, trailing a cloud of red dust, drove on some miles to a boys' camp, the 'J.Z.', named after a Patriotic Front freedom fighter, Jason Zitsata Moyo. The president stepped from his car and eleven thousand boys, at the shrill of a whistle, packed up their books and, from their 'classrooms' beneath the trees, streamed at the double towards a large clearing where, on the grey, dusty soil, they were formed into a hollow square. The president, jovial as ever, entered the square. Raising his baton, he cried, like a bull-elephant, 'Zi-Zi . . .' and eleven thousand lusty young voices yelled back, 'Zi-mba-bwe'. It was an impressive and moving performance.

With my BBC friends I trapesed behind Joshua N'Komo as he visited the camp, answering questions — mostly theirs. But N'Komo was understanding. He said to me, 'I will arrange for you to talk quietly with the boys.'

Meanwhile we visited the 'classrooms' — groups of twenty or thirty boys gathered here and there in the shade of a tall tree, surrounded by a screen of plaited grass and brushwood, a thatch of the same material over their heads — fine-looking boys, though poorly clad, seated on logs and tree-trunks. Besides geography, the curriculum includes, of course, political education, or rather re-education to the communist way of thinking. Meanwhile, inside Rhodesia, the terror-tactics of the freedom fighters had caused the shut-down of 845 schools, depriving nearly a quarter of a million African children of education.

At the cookhouse, cauldrons were simmering over wood fires. We stood before a mountain of cooked, white, porridgy cereal. 'That is *sadza*,' Joshua N'Komo told me. 'It is the basic food.' 'How do they manage to cook for so many?' 'How they do it I don't know,' he confessed. 'There are a hundred cooks.' He went on to say that these were only the young people. 'When it comes to the bigger boys and girls my wife says it is really a task.' Joshua N'Komo obviously felt quite at home amidst all this *al fresco* domesticity and did not avert his eyes, as I did, when we passed another mountain, a red one this time, of fids of meat, beside which stood a young stalwart, fanning off the swarming flies.

Several thousand boys were at play. Such was the hubbub that I asked the few who had volunteered to talk to me to walk off, with our interpreter, Sikile, some way into the bush. There we sat down to listen to Zambia, a diminutive boy who said he was fifteen but looked no more than ten. On one of his spindly legs a suppurating sore fed a swarm of flies – the best means, in the absence of antiseptics, of keeping it clean.

Zambia had five sisters; he was the only boy and, since his father was away most of the time, Zambia had to assert himself somehow. He poured water on his sisters and beat the smallest ones when they quarrelled. He loved them all the same, he said. He chased the chickens and the goats and, when one of the latter fled into the bush and failed to return, Zambia's mother beat him. She loved him, though, and would always comb his hair before he went to school, where, playing football and hunting (or rather poaching) with his four best friends, he was really happiest. Except when his father, who worked as a gardener in Bulawayo, came home for Christmas. Then Zambia could talk with him as man to man.

Zambia told me he feared the whites, the reason being that they would come into the reserve near Plumtree where he lived, in a mud house, and ask the whereabouts of the guerrillas. The whites had come into his own home, clipped him and his sisters over the face, kicked them and even hit them with rifle butts.

One day the soldiers – a mixture of blacks and whites – came to Zambia's school in two big trucks. He and his classmates were ordered outside to the playground. Asked one by one whether any of them had seen the guerrillas, they all answered NO. One little boy who had been in the lavatory and missed the parade was beaten up. 'The soldiers,' said Zambia, 'took him to hospital.'

Solemnly, Zambia told me, 'Life was more dangerous even for a man of my age than for women.' He and his four young friends decided to escape. It was holiday time and one evening, having first bought some bread in Plumtree, they met just as the sun was setting. Then, in the moonlight, they walked off into the bush – very scared of being picked up by a patrol. All went well, however, and at the first village in Botswana they were given cooked maize.

The first thing that struck Zambia about the J.Z. camp when he finally arrived there was that it was safe — no more soldiers to worry about, at least for the moment. For when he reaches the age of sixteen, he said, 'I want to become a freedom fighter and kill as many of the enemy as possible — black or white, it doesn't matter — and regain my country.' That done, he went on, 'the whites can stay as long as they don't rule us.'

His friends shared the same feelings. Among them was Max, who, though still only sixteen, was dreaming of becoming a teacher. 'A teacher of whites as well?' 'Certainly,' he said, 'as long as they are good Zimbabweans.' Though Max's English was too good to need an interpreter, it was he, Sikile, who cut in to say that ZAPU's fight was not a racial, but an ideological one. 'We have a strong tendency towards communism.' Which explained, no doubt, why Max, on his beige-coloured cloth cap, wore two badges — one a red star with 'Lenin' engraved in its centre, the other a square badge with an impression of Lenin in one corner. 'They were given to me,' he informed me, 'by a comrade at the camp.'

Max, a thoroughly decent, well-spoken boy, told me the familiar story of how, at a village far out in the bush (it was holiday time), the security forces came to his home to question his father about the freedom fighters. When the father protested his ignorance — 'he was telling the truth,' Max affirmed — the soldiers laid into him shouting, 'Go on, you tell us where they are!' They beat him unconscious. 'He was bleeding through his white shirt,' said Max, who, with his brothers and sisters, cringed in a corner.

Max returned to school, a Protestant mission school which was soon to make world headlines. Its name was Manama and it lay near the frontier. Max and his friends, talking among themselves about the situation, raised the question of escape. Among the pupils were members of the ZAPU youth: they were encouraging: it was planned that the entire school should go over to Botswana and on to Zambia to join the ZAPU. And so, one evening at sundown, some four hundred pupils — about half of them boys, half girls — led by five teachers, walked out into the bush towards Botswana. They took with them maize and soft drinks — orange, coke and water, and walked all night. 'We were not abducted,' said Max. 'We decided entirely on our own. There were no armed members of ZAPU with us.' Max's account, it must be said, does not agree with that of the Rhodesian Ministry of Information, which said that the children were 'herded at gunpoint' by terrorists.

Since his arrival at the J.Z. camp Max's initial fervour had been sustained by revolutionary songs, the ones that the girls were singing to

Joshua N'Komo. The one that Max liked best had the theme that the Smith regime was the prey, the Zimbabweans the lion, and the lion would devour the prey.

Yet the truth is that, although Max and his classmates were told at the time of the escape that they were going to be trained as freedom fighters, in the eighteen months since then he has done no military training at all. For this he would have to be transferred to another camp, run by ZIPRA, the military wing of ZAPU – a camp which, shortly after I visited the J.Z. camp, the Rhodesian security forces attacked with devastating losses to the freedom fighters. Which may since have expedited the call-up of Max and his friends and given them their longed-for chance of returning to Zimbabwe as freedom fighters.

CHAPTER TWENTY-FOUR*

The Zimbabwean Coin Reversed

Freedom fighters. The definition all too frequently has no relation to the deed. In our own time, the atrocities perpetrated against children in the name of freedom, at Dresden, Hiroshima and Nagasaki, reached their basest. Or so we thought. Yet there is no lack of atrocities even baser in the Rhodesian guerrilla war. Guerrilla – of which the traditional, the heroic idea is a war of armed partisans fighting regular soldiers, not of one and the other murdering and torturing civilians and their children.

Max is a Christian, educated in a mission school. It is true that Christians, not least among themselves, have fought the most murderous wars, perpetrated some of the most atrocious massacres in history. But I still would like to know if Max, in his fight for freedom, could descend as low as the freedom fighters did when they attacked the Elim Pentecostal Church Mission in eastern Rhodesia. With bayonets, axes and staves of wood they murdered twelve mission members, including three small children: Philip (six), Rebecca (four) and Pamela Grace (three weeks).

Dr Anthony David Owen did the post mortem. He wrote to the London *Daily Mail*, 'I took part in the delivery of Pamela Grace, the three-week-old baby' (who was found beaten to death beside her murdered and sexually assaulted mother). Dr Owen went on, 'How does one describe the "beings" who would attempt to rape a four-year-old girl [Rebecca], kick her in the face with a heavy boot so hard as to leave its imprint, bayonet her in the arms and legs and finally crush her skull ...?'

Until then thirty-four white missionaries or members of their families had been murdered by freedom fighters. Three Red Cross men, too – unarmed, as their code requires – and two Salvation Army women, all of them shot out of hand. And, as a further example among many of the bloody mockery that the freedom fighters are making of freedom, above all for the young, twenty of them set upon a six-month-old white girl, Natasha Glenny, and bayonetted her to death.

*See footnote, p 173.

Other white Rhodesian children, just old enough to defend themselves, have told me how they had to fight for their own freedom – and their lives – against the freedom fighters. In front of me is the story, written in his own hand (spelling mistakes and all), of a boy of eleven. It is prosaically entitled 'A terr. attack' and continues:

> At about 10 past 12 my Dad woke up with the dogs barking. One dog charged the fence ... to where the terrs. were getting ready ... a rocket hit the outside wall of the house ... the rest of the family woke up with fear ... the terrs opened up with small arms and there were flashes on the inside wall. My Mom and Dad then ran out onto the varander and shot from there. I was very scared because I could emadgen my parents being hit because there were hundreds of bullets flying past them every minute.
>
> After about 15 minutes with continuous fire and rockets and mortars, we smelt petrol. This was when me, my brother and sister were very scared because we thought they were going to burn us out.
>
> Then my mother ... gave me the uzy [gun] and told me to reload it. Her leg was full of blood ... I put on a bandige around her leg ... then I put my Mom on a matres and I took the gun and went out and shot back at them. I came back every five minutes to reload. My Mom was still lying down. I thought my Dad was hit because I had not seen him for about 30 minutes. After a while I thought it was only me left to shoot back ... then soon after I saw my father ... My mother took the gun from me and went and shot from the varanda. I reloaded magazines as I never thought I would. I thought we would never come out of there alive. I started praying.
>
> Then the terrs left. I was glad ... When the army got there they found 3 dead terrs ... We found out afterwards there were 36 terrs. I was so glad it was over.

On another farm, one night, thirteen-year-old Sandy Bye suddenly awoke to the sound of automatic gunfire. She said, 'I lay glued to my bed, unable to move.' Then, 'My mind cleared and somehow I escaped from the blankets and pushed myself along the ground.' Pressed to the floor, she slithered towards the passage, the 'safe area'. Sandy went on, 'The continuous volley of bullets increased at a deafening rate. I ducked as a whistling rocket flew over the roof. The flashes had now increased to an unbelievable rate and I felt sure that I would never reach the passage or my parents. All the time I prayed – it worked and eventually I reached the safe area.' In the dark, Sandy crept next to her father.

She then heard the following exchange on the 'Agric-alert' (the radio SOS system): 'Control calling – we can hear shooting.' Sandy's father: 'So can we, we're under attack.' 'Oh?' came the answer, then silence.

Then, said Sandy, 'My mother placed my sleeping brother, Alan, in my arms. My father had to race outside. I grabbed a gun, and clutched the cold steel to me tightly. My brother Ian, aged four, sat beside me and shook. Every limb and joint in his body trembled, even his teeth chattered, not through cold, but fear.' Sandy kept clutching the sleeping baby – and the gun – repeating over and over, 'When will it end, when will it end?'

End it did, in a crescendo of mortar and rocket and machine-gun fire. Then silence. 'Life,' Sandy commented, 'took a new meaning in our household.'

Kathry Sleigh's father was a cotton farmer. It was August 1977; she was fourteen and just back from school. 'My mind was full of having come home for the holidays and I was thinking of waking up in the morning fresh as a daisy.' Kathry went to bed, dozed off, 'listening, all ears, to every sound outside. I told myself not to worry. Why should anything happen to us?' Then she fell asleep.

'Suddenly,' she went on, 'I awoke and sat up in bed. A moment later I heard shots very close to my bedroom. The bullets were hitting the wall.' The siren started to wail, making Kathry's heart race. She sprang out of bed, ducked and ran to her brother's bedroom. 'I told him to be careful and we ran as fast as possible past the french doors.' In the next room she found her mother crawling on hands and knees towards the Agric-alert. 'She told me in a calm, reassuring voice to get under the bed, but instead I clambered onto a shelf in the linen cupboard where my dad kept his spanners. I heard a few more explosions and thought it was the end of our lives.'

Fortunately, the police arrived. They went to investigate in the compound. 'The men came back with their faces drawn,' Kathry said. 'Our labour party [workmen] were having a "beer drink" when the terrorists ordered them to sit in a circle. They then started shooting them. The only survivor,' she told me, 'was an old man who had been working for my dad for sixteen years. He had been drinking too much at the party and fell down, drunk, among the dead. It makes me sad,' she said bitterly, 'to think of all those black men I had known since three years of age who were just mown down by blood-thirsty barbarians.'

Indeed, it is the blacks whom the freedom fighters have terrorized most. In six years they have killed, of the civil population, 120 whites, 2,500 blacks. The burnings of houses and their imprisoned occupants, the tortures and rapings, the massacres and deliberate, ghastly mutilations of the living flesh of their own defenceless brethren are too numerous to count, too tragic and atrocious to dwell upon. I cite briefly but two such 'incidents'.

At the Mazvidza kraal freedom fighters seized Chikombe Mazvidza and, before his wife, his five young children and sixty villagers, cut off his ears, his nose, his lips and his chin. For the rest of his life – for he is still alive and his photo along with others, all unprintable, is beside me – Chikombe's teeth will be bared in a permanent, gaping smile.

Another blow for freedom: at Chikombedzi school in the Matibi area, freedom fighters took the local school inspector, Ferdi Joseph Chauke, bound him with rope, drenched him with paraffin and set him alight. Then, to music from a radiogram, they danced around the burning corpse.

If this is the way that young Zimbabweans are still being taught to fight for freedom then it is a cruel, callous and cynical perversion of the bright ideas and high hopes which stir the young hearts of decent-minded boys like Max and that little rascal Zambia.

CHAPTER TWENTY-FIVE

Ethiopian Refugees

In May 1936 Italy, having invaded Ethiopia with bombs and poison gas and defeated its medieval army, annexed the country; with Eritrea and Italian Somaliland it became Italian East Africa. The Ethiopian emperor, Haile Selassie, fled. He was restored to his throne in 1941, at the beginning of World War II, when the British drove the Italians out of their East African empire.

In Eritrea, however, there was resentment at being a province of Ethiopia. In 1968, Eritreans rose in armed rebellion, and the liberation movement gained increased popular support after the *coup d'état* in Addis Ababa which, in September 1974, deposed Haile Selassie. Overnight, the imperial regime was replaced by a military junta which, during the last days of 1974, launched a programme, '*Ethiopia Tekdem*' (Ethiopia first), committing the ancient empire to the path of socialism. And before the year was out the Eritrean liberation movement, itself communist-oriented, announced that its rebellion had passed from the guerrilla stage to open warfare. Since 1974, a year of political upheaval and disastrous famine, terror has been abroad in both Ethiopia and Eritrea.

It struck at the family of Mohammed, the son of a government official in Addis Ababa. Mohammed, after leaving school, had been apprenticed to a garage and become a qualified mechanic. He loved his job, which enabled him to have his own car and made him quite a young blood, popular with the girls, with one of whom he was going particularly steady. Life was good, home too. Mohammed lived with his parents, two brothers and a sister, in a comfortable but unpretentious house in Addis Ababa. Now, in Eastleigh, a suburb of Nairobi, he was dossing down in a tiny room, sleeping on sheets of cardboard spread out on the concrete floor.

When I first ran into him in the street Mohammed showed not a trace of his suicidal despair. His face was bright, his eyes smiling; shabbily as he was dressed, in jeans with a hole at each knee and a dirty shirt, he looked happy. A friend of the family, Yusuf, a tailor by trade, had taken pity on him. That is how Mohammed came to be sleeping on the floor of Yusuf's tiny room, which afforded just enough space for his own bed and Mohammed's recumbent body on the floor. A few clothes hung from pegs on the door. Bedclothes, and Mohammed's cardboard strips, were stored on a shelf; in a corner a small cooking stove stood beside a tidy stack of pots and pans. Yusuf's sewing-machine and a wicker chair occupied the only remaining space. This tiny, two-man *pied-à-terre* was dimly lit by a window the size of a pocket handkerchief. Outside, the elderly landlady was berating her tenants for strewing refuse before their doors. Little shanties and stores lined the street – Sixth Street – and just opposite men were cooking on charcoal braziers before a tumbledown shack which passed for the local restaurant. Seated on Yusuf's bed, Mohammed told me his story.

One evening – he was already in bed and asleep – a knock came at the door of his home in Addis Ababa. His sister opened it to three green-uniformed *askaris*. One of them showed an official paper, duly signed and stamped, requesting Mohammed's father to report urgently to the office. The father was aroused from sleep. He put a few necessities in his black attaché case and left with the *askaris*, suspecting nothing. Mohammed was asleep when his father left. Since supper that evening he has not seen him.

Mohammed, as he unfolded his story, became more and more listless, staring into the distance, his words tailing away until he lapsed into a long silence. I asked him quietly, 'Do you remember that supper?' He did not answer, but got up off the bed and without another word walked out of the room.

I stayed a few minutes longer talking to Yusuf. He told me how much Mohammed was suffering. So desperate was he that often he would sit on the bed for hours, his head between his hands, speechless. But he was a good boy, said Yusuf. He was certain he would be glad to go on talking with me if only we could find him.

Find him we did, in the street, about two hours later. He was sorry, he said, but that last memory of his father was too much for him. Sitting once more on the bed, Mohammed went on with his story, though he looked very strained and it was clear that he was not going to hold out for long.

A week after the disappearance of his father, Mohammed found his elder brother, a journalist, lying dead in the street near the house. He ran back to tell his mother, whose first words were, 'You must leave, quickly.' That very day he said goodbye to her and his sister and walked out of his home. He had not heard from them since. As Mohammed talked on I saw that he was becoming listless again and a vague, frightened glare came into his eyes. He was calmer as he described his escape from Addis Ababa with an Eritrean friend who drove him in his car towards the Kenyan border. Mohammed then had to go on by lorry, making a detour on foot at every military checkpoint, until he came safely to Kenya.

He had been jobless for over two years, eking out an existence on a £10 a month allowance from the Kenyan Joint Refugee Council. He wants to work, but his unannounced departure to Mombasa to look for a job cost him his allowance. That is why he now sleeps with only a thin strip of cardboard between him and the concrete floor of Yusuf's room. 'Nothing sleep, nothing food,' Mohammed muttered pathetically. Only what Yusuf can spare him. And with that wild look of distress in his eyes, which were full of tears, he added, 'I would be happy if I died.'

I know that the Joint Refugee Council will take care that Mohammed does not die. But that may not make him any happier.

Strolling in the busy streets of Eastleigh with Phoebe Manthi – 'Mamma Phoebe' everyone called her – of the Joint Refugee Council, I ran into a pretty nineteen-year-old Eritrean girl, Elsa, and her daughter Nadsanat, aged three. Elsa was on her way to cook her dinner at the house of a friend, Mebrat; in her own one-roomed home there were no means. So we walked on with her and came to Mebrat's.

They both insisted on my eating with them – *njera*, a kind of bread like a crêpe, baked on charcoal and made of wheat and maize and flour and very light. You tore off a piece and used it to pick up a spicy curry of meat and vegetables. Elsa was a marvellous cook. Her original home, she told me, was near Asmara, in Eritrea, but her parents, like Mebrat and her husband, moved to Addis Ababa. It was there that, when just sixteen, she married – or was 'forced to marry', so Elsa said. It was only after the baby was born that she really fell in love with her young husband. I asked her in what month she was married and, with a disarming smile, she replied, 'I'm sorry, I'm not very well educated. I don't know.' Perhaps it was January, the harvest month when, in Ethiopia, girls and boys often marry. Then I asked her, would she have preferred a baby boy? She made a beautiful answer: 'The firstborn is from God; there's no choice.'

Elsa's husband kept a general merchant's store, which prospered. Their home in Addis Ababa was, to use Elsa's words, 'such as the common people have'; on the blue walls of the sitting-room were pictures of Jesus, the disciples and angels, all capped with the traditional halo. Elsa is a devout Christian. They lived on, fearing nothing, until the 1974 *coup d'état*. One night the *askaris* banged on Elsa's door. They entered and dragged her husband off the bed where he was resting. Elsa could not bear to watch what followed. Terrified, she took her baby and locked herself in another room. Elsa to this day does not know why her husband was arrested. She feels sure that he must be dead.

A few days later, this sixteen-year-old mother, with the baby she was still breast-feeding, fled from her home. One of the lorry drivers who supplied the shop drove her to Moyali, the frontier post, where the guard simply ordered her to get down and, while he inspected the lorry, to walk on with the other passengers, to Moyali 'Kenya-side'.

I asked Elsa if, apart from Mebrat, she had other friends. She replied 'My only friends are cooking and eating.' Attractive as she was, Elsa had no intention of re-marrying. 'This is impossible because I have no confirmation of my husband's death. As long as my little girl is with me, I shall never feel lonely.' All Elsa needs is peace. 'Whether I get it in my own country or here in Kenya,' she said, 'it's all the same to me.'

'Terbe the magnificent' is how I shall always think of that thirty-year-old Eritrean *belle*, with her blazing brown eyes and garrulous tongue and a smile that could kill — with charm, or mischief. Terbe was the mother of four children with another one on the way, but that belongs to the end of the story. She and her husband had once been rich. Today they live in Eastleigh, in a single room on the ground floor of a drab, concrete building which gives onto an area strewn with garbage and scrap-iron.

Next to Terbe, as we talked, sat a boy, Takru (Johnny), who was still in his mother's womb when her misfortunes began. It was before lunch one day in May 1975 that Terbe, with her three boys, aged six, four and two, waited for her husband, a prosperous businessman. Lunchtime passed and he did not return. Nor that evening, nor next day. On the third day the police called. Terbe, five months pregnant (with Johnny), was taken off to prison with her three boys. The four-year-old was already sick with a high fever. They were all locked into a cell, with no ventilation and no light and so packed with people that there was no question of lying down. Once a day, the prisoners were fed. In these vile conditions and the absence of medical care, the sick boy developed complications. By the time the family was released, nine days later, he had become deaf.

They returned to the house — which in their absence had been completely ransacked. Terbe stayed on there — with never a word from her husband — until, three months after Johnny's birth, she decided to flee. They came to Nairobi. The sick boy was put in a home, where he still is. Terbe went down with a nervous depression. 'She really wanted to die,' Mamma Phoebe told me. Nearly three years went by. Slowly she recovered and today, said Phoebe, it is she who wears the pants, not her husband.

Yes, her husband. He had been imprisoned in Addis Ababa. At last he managed to escape. He had heard that Terbe was in Nairobi. Terbe refused to believe it was him; it was Belanaish, her friend, who recognized him and threw her arms round his neck.

That was in March 1978. When I met her in August she was expecting a baby — in December. Rather appropriately they were going to call it by a name suggesting 'reunion' or 'new found happiness'.

Belanaish had known Terbe all her life. Rather reserved, she was a kind, intelligent woman. She invited me into her home — one-roomed, like Terbe's — where I sat on a bed. On another lay a little girl, fast asleep.

Like Terbe, Belanaish had a fine home in Eritrea — a *shamba* (farm) which her husband worked himself — apart from his prosperous trucking business. It was back in 1970 that their *shamba* was attacked — as part, Belanaish said, of Ethiopia's war against Eritrea. *Askaris*, twelve lorry-loads of them, drove up and put the farm to sack. Belanaish and her husband, with her daughter Astera (then five) and her little boy Takle, managed to escape.

With their bank account stopped, they were penniless. Belanaish's husband eventually got a job as a driver with a firm of building contractors at Shindama, near the Kenyan border. The firm, though Ethiopian, employed only Eritrean workers, who lived — in terror of their lives — in a camp; it was often raided, Belanaish explained, by *askaris*. Astera, a beautiful, intelligent child with ebony-black skin, fluffy hair and the thin face and long jawline of her mother, remembered vividly those killings, when the *askaris* used guns, knives and clubs. She was so frightened that her legs seemed to drag as she ran with her mother and father (carrying Takle), slipping between the huts, out into the bush. The *askaris*, Astera said, were like wild animals. What would she have liked to happen to them? 'Well,' said Astera, 'I was too small to kill any. But I would have liked to see them struck down by lightning.'

Her mother Belanaish was then nine months pregnant. She thought she was going to die, but said to herself, 'God will be my help.' With Astera always beside her, she walked on in agony through the bush until at five a.m. one morning she collapsed. Lying there where she had fallen she gave birth to a baby girl, Mary. No sooner was the birth over than Belanaish stood up and, with Mary in her arms, walked on towards the Kenyan frontier. 'The baby was surely blessed by God,' remarked Belanaish, 'for she survived.'

At that moment the little girl who had been fast asleep on the bed stirred, opened her brown eyes and sat up, yawning. Belanaish took her in her arms and kissed her. 'I have a special love for this one,' she said. It was Mary, who had been born beneath the stars, in the midst of the bush.

The name Addis Ababa, New Flower, should, if anything, inspire optimism. But it means despair to students who have fled the city. Nairobi is full of those frustrated young fugitives; Tadesse is one. Though he hid his feelings behind a playful smile, he admitted that he was in despair.

A tall, slim youth with a mop of fuzzy hair and that smile playing incessantly on his lips, he told me how, at the end of the day, discussion groups of students would meet. More and more, one subject kept cropping up – the Haile Selassie regime. While it had brought prosperity to the country, it had neglected the poor. Young Tadesse said that he, for one, was shocked and revolted by the way the royal family and its diverse and numerous branches behaved; while they lived sumptuously and drove around in the best and most expensive cars, they failed to act as defenders of the poor.

On the day of the *coup de état*, which deposed Haile Selassie on 12 September 1974, a huge photo appeared on the front page of a newspaper, the *Herald*, showing the emperor giving choice meat to his dogs, with, juxtaposed, another photo of the starving victims of the famine in the Wallo province.

The *coup d'état* was made by the Dergur group under General Aman Andom, who, said Tadesse, was popular throughout Ethiopia and Eritrea. But two months later Andom, along with fifty-nine members of the old regime, was executed. General Tefere Bante became president. With the new regime, student reaction intensified; the discussion groups were forbidden, though they continued clandestinely, said Tadesse, smiling. The meeting-places were different each time, and students were posted as sentinels; as soon as military trucks were sighted, the students scattered. Tadesse, still smiling at the thought, said, 'It was dangerous.' Even more so was the one demonstration in which he joined; it was broken up when the police fired and pursued the students. Tadesse escaped into one of the many underground passages which he had explored as a small boy when on the way to school.

As the reaction among the students grew, the government closed the schools and, 'no doubt to get rid of us', smiled Tadesse, initiated a 'renouncement' programme for students; they were to be despatched to the country districts, there to put over to the illiterate peasants the government's *Ethiopia Tekdem* socialist policy.

Life in the country was very hard. The students lived in tented camps and cooked their own food, which was poor and inadequate. They were not meant to work on the land, though they did so, in order to keep in with the peasants. Soon Tadesse's hands were covered with blisters and his feet swollen; gradually, however, he got used to the hard labour. The students' main job was to teach the peasants to speak Amharic, the national language, to read and to write and, of course, to learn and inwardly digest the government's policies. The peasants, however, were not all that receptive. In some places they would advance, brandishing sticks, on the students, who had to run for it before being able to explain that they were really against the government and for the peasants. But once, Tadesse said, a group of students was caught; they were shut in a hut and burnt alive.

Tadesse, with another young Ethiopian, decided to escape. They got hold of a compass and one night stole out of the camp and headed for the main road to Addis Ababa. For the first four hours, they groped their way through the forest; when lions roared close by the two boys scared them by flashing their torches. At Addis Ababa Tadesse called on his parents and for one month kept a low profile while planning to escape to Kenya. In the ragged clothes of a peasant, his head shorn, he took a bus southwards with three other students.

Before reaching the Kenyan frontier, they left the bus to begin a four-day march through the bush – a very dangerous one, again because of wild animals. At night the boys slept in trees while lions roared nearby, and by day they met a horrifying number of pythons and other snakes. But worse, they were tortured by thirst, to a point where one of them had to drink his own urine. Once more they were lucky; they met up with a smuggler who brewed them tea and led them on across the frontier into Kenya.

Tadesse admitted that it was difficult, after his comfortable home in Addis Ababa, to adapt himself to the hard living of the Nairobi slum. He lived, in a room ten feet by ten, with half a dozen other students; they might be Ethiopians or Eritreans, or even fugitive Somalis. They slept on a thin mattress on the floor and managed somehow to survive on the refugee allowance of £10 a month. Their day consisted of sitting around in the room discussing their problems. Education was by far the greatest problem. If only they could continue their studies all other problems would vanish. They had tried, unsuccessfully, to get into universities in other African countries, in Nigeria, Ghana, Liberia. The basic problem was money, of which they possessed none. Tesager, Tadesse's friend, had written to an American state university, only to be informed that the fees were $6,000 a year. He wrote again asking if they could help find him a job to pay the fees. Reply: 'We now find we have no vacancy.' Tesager commented bitterly, 'It's just a mockery.'

David's was a similar story, but with overtones of tragedy. He was one of a family of six. On the wall of his room he had hung a large photo of Mao Tse-tung. 'It was not because I was a communist,' he said, 'but because I love the Chinese people.'

David's father managed a big business. One day, after the 1974 *coup d'état*, the family were at lunch, when *askaris* called at the house and asked for him. David's father left the room to talk to them while the family remained at table. As they waited, a shot rang out; David, his mother, brothers and sisters rushed outside. Their father lay dead, shot clean between the eyes. The *askari* officer spoke harshly, 'The rest of you had better be careful or the same will happen to you.'

By now the schools were closed. One morning, David was strolling with three friends in the city, when they were stopped by *askaris*. Shortly afterwards they all found themselves in prison. They were tortured for three days; on the fourth – though, as David said, he could hardly stand on his feet – they were put to work, digging and hoeing, with nothing to sustain them – save blows from rifle butts. On the tenth day they were released. David was warned, 'Be careful. Any word or action from you against the regime and you'll be dealt with like your father.'

He returned home, where he remained for a month, trying vainly to get over the shock and disgust caused by his treatment in prison. Then, on an impulse, he resolved to escape. That night he hardly slept, thinking about it. Next day, as he left, he caught a glimpse of his mother cooking, his young brothers and sisters playing. But without a word to any of them, he walked out of the house and caught a bus to Mega, in the south. During the next seven days, David walked on about another 150 kilometres, with nothing but oranges and bananas to keep him going until he crossed unseen into Kenya.

When I met David in Nairobi, he had not been to school for over two years. He lives, like Tadesse, in a small room with half a dozen friends whose one obsession was to get back to school. Only five days before we met he had received news that his mother had been killed by the military.

All through, David had spoken to me so quietly and dispassionately, even of his father's and mother's deaths that I got the impression that he was now beyond all feeling – except that one burning desire – to go back to school. 'But,' he said, and he spoke for all his friends, 'I see no hope at all.'

CHAPTER TWENTY-SIX

With the Sahraouis

On the other side of the African continent I found children who were victims of another political upheaval. In November 1975 Spain agreed to hand back, to Mauritania* and Morocco, her territory in the western Sahara. Two months later the last Spanish troops had left. Algeria, with designs on the territory and its people, had done her best to embarrass the negotiations and, following the agreement, reacted violently. Almost overnight, thousands of Moroccans, many of whom had been born in Algeria or lived there for generations, were thrown out. Old and young, sick and invalids, they were rounded up, locked up, questioned, maltreated; wives were separated from husbands, children from parents; their savings and belongings were confiscated. Then the unfortunate Moroccans were crammed into trucks and driven to the frontier near the Moroccan town of Oujda. There, penniless and in the piercing cold, they were dumped. In a great wave of sympathy, the Moroccan people, the authorities and the Moroccan Red Crescent rose to the occasion. The '*refoulés*', the 'throw-outs', were warmly welcomed, accommodated and cared for. Most had been absorbed into Moroccan society by mid-1978, but there still lived, in their tented camp at Oujda, some who could tell me of those bad times.

The case of seventeen-year-old Bachir was typical. He lived at Oran. It was midnight when the whole family were awoken by gendarmes banging on the door and shouting. Bachir was pulled out of bed and, in his pyjamas, taken with the family to the *Gendarmerie*. There they were held for two days with no food – only the insults of the gendarmes. Then they were driven, Bachir still in pyjamas, to the frontier. Bachir, who had been smiling looked sad all of a sudden. 'I was thinking of our house – the furniture, the beds, the carpets and the mattress I slept on. To me all that meant home and security. It's all gone.'

* In August 1979 Mauritania ceded its Saharan territory to the *Polisario*.

If the parents were of different nationalities, they often found themselves separated for ever. Five children stood around their father, Ahmed, a sad-faced man, with a wooden leg. Two of them, Ali and his sister, Tisslem, were twins. Ali told me he would never forget the night the police took his father away. Ali's father asked, 'Can I take the children?' But the police said no, get moving, and kicked him. He had been gone for a year when Ali's mother sent all the children to join him in Morocco. She wanted to go herself, but her brother, Ali's uncle, told her 'You must not. You are Algerian, they are Moroccan.' Ali's mother is dead now – probably from chagrin. He began to cry at the thought of her. So did Tisslem; so did their father Ahmed, and the three little ones. Never have I seen so unhappy a family.

At the hospital of Oujda, the *Médecin-Chef*, Dr Mramar, told me, 'During the first three weeks of the influx of Moroccans we admitted 147 patients; six of them, including four children, died.' One was a diabetic boy. Evicted from his home without either clothes or insulin he was already in a coma on reaching Oujda. A little girl, completely infirm, had her wheelchair confiscated before crossing the frontier. 'I call that really vicious,' said the doctor. A number of mothers, nine months pregnant went into labour after being held at the *Gendarmerie* for two or three days. In that state they were despatched to the frontier; two gave birth *en route*, another on the steps of the hospital. Another young mother was thrown out of hospital just after a Caesarean; she had to be stitched up again on arrival at Oujda.

A camp director, a throw-out himself, nearly lost all his children. One of the first to be expelled, he had to leave his family behind. Nine months went by, when a telephone call from an Algerian friend warned him that the children were about to be sent to Tindouf, the desert camp in south-western Algeria. 'That meant that I should never see them again, so I had them brought across here clandestinely.' I asked him, 'Is there no hope of returning from Tindouf?' 'None whatever,' he replied.

Coinciding with Algeria's expulsion of Moroccans in the north, the *Polisario* and other Algerian-backed elements were abducting Sahraouis, the nomad inhabitants of Morocco's newly-acquired Saharan territory in the south, and carrying them off to Tindouf. It was in the *Jefatura* (as the *Préfecture* is still called) at El Ayoune, 'capital' of the Moroccan Sahara, a trim little city lapped by sand dunes, that Sahraoui mothers and fathers told me how this cruel and indiscriminate campaign of kidnapping had hit their children.

Some were immediate victims, like Ali Salem, a boy in his teens, son of Mohammed (those are not their real names). Mohammed was a man of means and influence. He wore a *djellaba* of fine grey-blue cloth, and a white *ltham* wrapped about his lean face. Like all those desert people his speech was quiet and dignified; not once did he raise his voice. He told me that his wife and Ali had gone off in the Land-Rover (which replaces several camels) to tend their flocks while he went about his business in town. After two days he sent a man to enquire whether they needed further supplies or equipment. The man returned. 'I can find no trace of them,' he said. Nor has any trace since been found. Mohammed, though he said, 'It is the will of Allah,' thought that such a base, inhuman act was unworthy of Islam, of a human being, of the offspring of woman. He had remarried and had more children, but still felt his bereavement deeply. 'All we want,' he said, 'is to be left in peace; we lack nothing except our kidnapped wives and husbands and children.'

Selma, a teenage Sahraoui mother, lacked her husband. She was one of a group who had come to the *Jefatura* and waited in silence, some with a baby feeding or sleeping at their breast. Selma had brought along her two children, Nourredine and Habibullah. She herself was only nineteen, a beautiful girl with her proud forehead and soft, steady eyes. One day her young husband went off into the desert to tend his flocks. He never came back and, though Selma has no hope that he ever will, she still waits. 'It is not good for children to live without a father,' she said, yet she has no desire to remarry, only to devote herself, alone, to her children. Selma, despite this catastrophe in her young life, was so calm and I admired her. All she said was, 'I feel much grief in my heart but I am a Moroccan and must not show it.'

Ahmed, a sixteen-year-old Moroccan boy, did come back, a rifle in his hands. He was an exception. Forcibly enlisted in the *Polisario*, he was wounded in a clash with Moroccan troops and brought home to his mother.

Not so fortunate were another sixteen-year-old boy, Lahbib, and his sister, Oum Lakhout, two of ninety-five Sahraouis seized in five days towards the end of 1975. Their father, Haj Rahali Lel Brini, was kidnapped and bound with wire round the forearms, which in turn were bound to his legs; Rahali showed me the ugly scars. After three of his ribs and both arms had been broken Rahali was forced to reveal where his tents and cattle were. His captors drove off, found his tents and stole everything, including Rahali's boy and girl. They and their father, all bound hand and foot, were driven away to Tindouf, on the other side of the frontier – an imaginary line drawn across the desert.

Rahali was separated from his children. He then hit on an idea for escaping. 'I am an old man,' he told his gaolers – his sufferings, I could see, had aged him far beyond his fifty-six years – 'I desire to see Mecca before I die. Grant me this, or kill me here and now.' As he spoke Rahali chuckled. 'I fooled them all,' he said.

As Rahali, discreetly guarded by two Algerians, was strolling in the streets of Mecca, he at last found a Moroccan, Boujemaa, a former dumb-bell champion. To him he hissed, 'I'm the prisoner of these two Algerians, help me.' There was a short decisive scuffle and Rahali was soon on his way back to Morocco, to his wife and his ten remaining children. With them he ceaselessly mourns the other two, who are still among the forlorn thousands of Sahraouis sequestered in the desert at Tindouf.

CHAPTER TWENTY-SEVEN

The Torture of Children: South America

When, in 1957, I was driving round the world in a motor car, I came to Bogotá, Colombia's capital. There I was warned of *la Violencia*, which for a decade had been smearing Colombia's fair name with blood. I was advised above all: on no account travel by night and be careful by day.

The seat of the continuing brigandage and bloodshed was the rivalry between *Conservadores* and *Liberales*. Yet when you enquired into their respective aims you got the confusing answer that they were practically identical. In a local context, the rivals remained friends, in a wider one they murdered each other in the most bestial manner. When, in 1951, two hundred Liberal *bandoleros* led by Tulio Bautista arrived in the remote Andean village of San Pedro de Jagua, the leading Liberal among the population, Carlos Londoño, found himself begging for mercy for his Conservative friends. The three sons of Francisco Luiz stood before Bautista. 'They are young,' pleaded Londoño. 'They are *godos*, Conservatives,' snapped Bautista, 'they will grow up.' And old Francisco Luiz's three boys were shot dead. Another village boy appeared in a doorway holding up his identity card and a five peso note. He was dropped with one shot from a *bandolero* who then bent over the dead boy and, grinning, took the five peso note from his hand.

The inhuman cruelty of those *bandoleros* was confined to the male population. When the village was put to sack, Bautista's girl, Doña Edelmira, took charge — slim, dark and dressed as a man, with two pistols and a knife at her waist, she saw to it that not one girl was raped or even molested in San Pedro — which earned for the village a singular reputation in the annals of Colombian banditry.*

Already, in 1957, you could sense that trouble was coming to Latin America, where serfdom, if not slavery, was widespread. In Peru, for example, I was told that the country's entire wealth was in the hands of

---

*This passage is based on the eye-witness accounts related to Philip Payne and quoted in *The Violent Peace* by C. & S Mydans.

ten per cent of the population. The *criada* system, as it is called in Bolivia, existed under different names in many other countries of the continent: depressed and exploited *Indios* gave their children to white families hoping thereby to assure them a better future. Instead, the child, usually a girl, became an unpaid bond-servant available, outside her household chores, for the sexual needs of the men of the family. In Paraguay, man-hunts against the Aché *Indios* provided a regular crop of orphans who were sold into slavery or prostitution. Still in Paraguay, as recently as 1977, the president, General Alfredo Stroessner, was reported, on sworn evidence, by the *Washington Post*, to have been a frequent visitor to a suburban home, Barrio Sajonia, 'where young peasant girls [among them nine-year-olds], purchased from their impoverished parents, are made available to the top Paraguayan brass.' And in Nicaragua, Anastasio ('Tachito'), ruling scion of the Somoza dynasty, was, in 1957, firmly entrenched at the head of a dictatorship which was not to be overthrown until 1979, after forty-three years in power. In those intervening twenty-two years, Latin America has been torn with violence resulting from the steady upsurge of popular, leftist movements. Reaction, in Chile and Argentina, was particularly ruthless.

In September 1973, the socialist government of President Salvador Allende was overthrown by a military *coup*, the president himself being killed. A junta, headed by General Augusto Pinochet, took over. Thousands of the former president's supporters – their children, too – were interned, thousands more fled the country. There followed a reign of terror; it led the United Nations' Human Rights Commission and the International Commission of Jurists to condemn the junta for violation of human rights. The Human Rights Commission of the Organization of American States reported after investigation that, under the junta, 'extremely serious violations of human rights occurred'.

This bland, bureaucratic statement, when translated into fact, makes appalling reading, particularly in regard to children upon whom the junta secret security force, DINA, practised the most extreme cruelty. Small children were tortured in front of their parents in the hope of inducing the latter to speak; or the children were forced to look on while their parents were being tortured or executed. Ernestina Aiguila, a thirteen-year-old girl, became insane after being imprisoned with her parents in a torture-centre – the latter were called 'discothèques' because of the loud music played to drown the victims' cries.

Early in 1975 *Newsweek* reported that Macarena Aguilo Marchi, the three-year-old daughter of Herman Aguilo Martinez, a wanted leader of MIR, the left-wing revolutionary movement, had been arrested by

DINA with the object of inducing her father to give himself up.

In May 1975, the Stockholm newspaper *Dagens Nyheter* told the story of Tamara, the three-year-old daughter of a Chilean construction worker who, with his family, had found refuge in Sweden. Tamara had been tortured, in July 1974, in the Cerro Chesia camp in Chile, before the eyes of her parents, in an attempt to make them 'confess'. As Tamara's father said, at a press conference organized by Svenska Hyklingsadet (the Swedish Refugee Committee), fathers and mother are more easily broken down when they see their children tortured than when they are tortured themselves. Tamara's mother described what she saw: 'They undressed my little daughter and whipped her with a leather whip. They put her in a barrel with ice-cold water and held her head under the water until she almost drowned.' She had to watch Tamara tortured thus four times a day during four days. The DINA, finding that Tamara's parents had nothing to confess, released them.

Not so Lumi Videla and Sergio Perez Molina, the parents of four-year-old Dagoberto. The beatings and electric shocks they saw being administered to Dago could exact from them the confession that they belonged to the MIR. That was all they had to confess. It meant, for them, death; for Dago, lasting, incurable suffering.

An alternative form of torture was inflicted by the DINA on the three children, all under six, of an unnamed mother, a socialist militant, whose agonies they were forced to watch. In May 1974, after three armed DINA men had broken into her home, they each raped her. A week later, three others returned and, in front of the children, repeated the process. One day in July, more men came. They brought with them a soldering iron, with which they branded, on her thigh, the hammer and sickle. In the words of Mr John Platts-Mills, the distinguished British lawyer, who met her, 'she was lying stripped naked on the bed, again with the kids watching'. President Pinochet, advised by six magistrates of the outrage, interrogated Manuel Contreras, chief of the DINA, by telephone. Contreras vowed on his honour as a soldier that the report was false. That closed the incident.

Children and adolescents were victims of organized coercion and repression. After the International Commission of Jurists had disclosed, in November 1974, the junta's plans to establish internment camps for children – a disclosure described by a spokeswoman of the Children Mission in New York as 'an untrue and obnoxious lie' – the Mexican daily, *Excelsior*, reported, in April 1975, the existence of a *Seminario Permanente* at Osorno, 800 kilometres south of Santiago, where nearly a hundred children whose parents supported the Allende government were being subjected to forced labour and right-wing brainwashing. Other reports stated that relatives of political prisoners (who existed in thousands) were invited to put their children in the care of an organization run by the wives of prominent members of the junta, CEAP, whose ostensible object was to provide government-financed education – influenced, naturally, by right-wing ideology – to poor children and prepare them eventually for military service. A start was made with four school-camps near Santiago, for children from two to twelve years old. CEAP assumed sole authority over every child it accepted.

In October 1974, the International Committee of Jurists reported that military officers had been assigned to every school in Chile. Among the rules they were to enforce were 'sustained denunciations of teachers or auxiliary and administrative personnel'. Pupils were also included. And among the 'crimes' to be denounced there was an exceptionally serious one: 'spreading jokes or stories about the administration of the junta and its members'. Not that they were much to laugh at.

In Argentina, *la Violencia*, it might be said, is cultural. When, in June 1973, after nearly thirty years of exile, ex-president Juan Perón returned with his second wife, Isabel, to Buenos Aires, their arrival at Buenos Aires Ezeiza airport was the occasion for some fifty demonstrators being shot or bludgeoned to death. Six months later, after Perón had reassumed the presidency (with Isabel as vice-president) he told a press conference that he would discourage violence by patience and pacification. He was over-sanguine; government and 'subversive elements', notably the left-wing Montoneros and the ERP (Popular Revolutionary Army) – both subsequently outlawed – vied with each other in a mounting spate of violence, until Perón's death in July 1974 (when Isabel Perón succeeded him). In the twelve months that followed, over five hundred people died as a result of political terrorism; they included fifty-four policemen, twenty-two soldiers and thirteen businessmen. In the first two months of 1976, ninety-six people were assassinated for political reasons. When, on 1 March, Isabel Perón was overthrown by a military *coup d'état*, General Jorge Videla became president at the head of a military junta.

A colonel serving on his staff was reported as saying of Videla that he exemplified in the highest degree the qualities of fairness, honesty and puritanism. The father of six children, he is a convinced anti-communist, a fervent Catholic; he frequently consulted the chaplain-in-chief of the armed forces, Mgr Adolf Tortolo. But Videla was most admired for his qualities as a soldier; he has used them with devastating – it might be truer to say murderous – effect in a pitiless war against left-wing terrorists. And by 'terrorist', he means, as he told British journalists in February 1978, 'not just someone with a gun or a bomb, but also someone who spreads ideas that are contrary to western and Christian civilization.' Though he gave a public undertaking to respect the laws on Human Rights, the conduct of General Videla's security forces against 'terrorists', who include, besides adults, children and babes in arms, has so shocked western and Christian civilization that both the UN Permanent Assembly and the International Federation for Human Rights and the French president, Giscard d'Estaing – among many others – have called upon Videla to account for the persons – estimated in mid-1978 to number 15,000 – who have disappeared without trace in Argentina.

In Buenos Aires, families of the missing formed the *Comité de Familiares des Desaparecidos y Detenidos por Razones Politicos* (The Committee of Relatives of People Who Have Disappeared or Been Detained for Political Reasons). Known as the 'Mad Mothers of the Plaza de Mayo' they demonstrate there in front of the government building every Thursday. In May 1978, thirteen women formed a group called 'Grandmothers of the Plaza de Mayo' – they were still searching for their missing children and grandchildren.

At that time, three-year-old Carla, granddaughter of the Argentinian actress Matilde Artes, and her mother, twenty-six-year-old Graciela (Matilde's daughter) had been missing for over a year and a half. Matilde herself was not one of the grandmothers of the Plaza de Mayo – 'if I returned to Argentina, I should never get out again'. But she volunteered to tell me the story which led to Graciela's and Carla's disappearance.

Graciela, though an Argentinian, had lived since the age of nine in Bolivia. It was there, at Oruro, in the south, that she was arrested, apparently because, as a member of a student organization, she had taken part in a tin-miners' strike. The kind of thing that the celebrated actresses Jane Fonda and Vanessa Redgrave have often done without the terrible consequences that befell Graciela. Throughout that night and part of the next day, she was beaten up in the offices of the Bolivian *Departamento de Orden Político*, while Carla was deprived of food. Mother and daughter were then transferred to the capital, La Paz, where they were separated. Carla was registered in an orphanage, 'Hogar Carlos Villegas', while her young mother suffered further torture at the hands of one Gernio, an agent of the Bolivian Ministry of the Interior. Carla was brought to watch these torture sessions. Fortunately, the International Red Cross succeeded in bringing Graciela and her daughter together again in August. There are strong grounds for believing that in the days that followed, Graciela suffered further tortures, including electric shock, beatings with a leather garrot and the infamous 'Uruguayan submarine' with detergent added to the water — an Argentinian innovation. For it was the Argentinian Federal Police who, in Bolivian territory, tortured Graciela before they took her and her baby across the frontier into Argentina.

When Matilde Artes told me this pathetic story of her daughter and granddaughter in August 1978, no trace had been found of them, nor had her supplications to a score of the foremost international humanitarian organizations and statesmen elicited a scrap of information from the government of Videla, self-styled defender of western and Christian civilization. What, Matilde wondered, had he done with her daughter and granddaughter?

Veronica Handl-Alvarez, aged twenty-four, of dual Argentinian-Austrian nationality, was one of the many young mothers who were pregnant at the time they were abducted. She was studying at Buenos Aires University when, in September 1976, she disappeared. Two months later her parents were informed that she was in Villa Devoto, Argentina's 'model' prison, a place of purgatory designed for 2,500, into which, in 1978, more than 4,000 were crowded in conditions so appalling that they made a mockery of the United Nations 'Minimum Rules for the Treatment of Prisoners . . .' Women from seventeen to fifty were imprisoned there, their babies with them. According to a one-time inmate: 'Once the child is six months old, decree No. 955 says he must abandon his mother and be given to relatives.'

Veronica's baby was not yet born. Before he was, she was tortured by men, who punched and kicked her, beat her on the head, chest and abdomen with an iron rod; they gave her electric shocks, especially on the genitalia; they submerged her in cold water, isolated her, blindfolded in a cell, deprived her of sleep, degraded her with sham intercourse, terrorized her with sham executions. On 11 April 1977, she went into labour which lasted five hours. During that time she was bound hand and foot to a bed, unattended until the last few minutes. Then she gave birth to a son, who was laid on the floor of her rat-infested cell. Veronica, badly damaged in mind and body, was later released. Her son survived, his health unimpaired — another triumph for Videla's notion of western and Christian civilization.

Most of the thousands of Argentinians who have disappeared have done so without leaving any trace. Floreal Avellanada, the fifteen-year-old son of a former trade union leader, was a rare exception.

In the early hours of 15 April 1976, Videla's men machine-gunned the door of his home. They were after his father, who was not there. So they ransacked the house and beat up Floreal and his mother. Both were taken to the police station at Villa Martelli, and in separate cells, separated and tortured by electric shock. Señora Avellanada could hear her boy screaming in his cell. Floreal was reunited briefly with his mother; she was then transferred to another prison and, after further torture, released.

Of young Floreal, there was no trace. Then, in mid-August 1976, several corpses were washed up on the Uruguayan shore of the River Plate. One of them was that of a youth; on it was tattooed a heart with the initials 'F.A.' – the only remaining trace of Floreal Avellanada.

CHAPTER TWENTY-EIGHT

Children of the Boat People

Vietnam, after the defeat of the French colonialist regime in 1954, was, at an international conference at Geneva, divided by the 17th Parallel into two countries, North and South, with their capitals respectively at Hanoi and Saigon. Half a million people fled from the communist North. It was the aim of the North, under President Ho Chi Minh, to unify North and South in a people's democracy allied to the USSR and China.

The United States backed Saigon with equipment and advisers, but in February 1965 the 'Americanization' of the conflict began when President Johnson ordered the aerial bombing of North Vietnam. For the next seven years (during which the conflict spread to Cambodia and Laos) the number of American combat troops in Indo-China rose to nearly half a million. It was not until 1972 that their withdrawal was complete.

Never, the North Vietnamese charge, were the principles of international and moral law more grossly violated than they were, on Vietnamese soil, by the American forces. Undeniably, the latter committed, against Vietnamese children, monstrous, unforgettable crimes. With their napalm bombs, American bombers burnt young bodies and beautiful faces beyond recognition; they killed thousands more children, often ever so slowly, by fragmentation bombs whose splinters, inextricable, creep insidiously, lethally into the circulation and the tissues. And, as if these crimes against humanity were not bad enough, Nature herself was grossly outraged as American bombers, with chemicals and defoliation bombs, devastated forests and the crops of toiling peasants, who themselves often succumbed to the poisonous sprays and powders.

A captured American pilot recalled the briefing of his last mission: 'Go straight in with napalm bombs first, then fragmentation bombs to look after the fugitives.' The briefing officer added, 'And have no fear, gentlemen; the enemy defences are practically nil; there are only women and children.' During an air-raid on the small town of Hiep Hoa, a bomb splinter pierced the womb of a young mother, Le Thi Khuong, while she was in labour and lodged in the left temple of her unborn baby. Miraculously both survived. At the Huong Khe district hospital, one day in April 1967, a baby had just been delivered by a Caesarian. Minutes later both mother and child were killed by American bombs. In the same district, Huong Phuc school suffered forty-three American air-raids. One of them killed thirty-three pupils. Not long afterwards the village school of Ha Phu was hit by fragmentation bombs: sixty-one children were killed or wounded. In the first two years of air-raids American bombs hit 296 schools.

In March 1968 President Johnson ordered the bombardment of limited targets, adding that his enemies could count on his goodwill to spare the lives of women and children. It was during that period that a greater than ever tonnage of explosives was delivered on centres of population, from the air and from the guns of battleships off-shore. Johnson, in October 1968, ordered a halt to the bombing. It was resumed under the presidency of Nixon, who, during the peace talks which began in 1970, ordered bombing on a scale unprecedented in history. Nixon, almost in the same breath, declared his intention to do 'all in our power to ensure that children the world over might live in friendship and peace'.

Since my request for a visa for Vietnam was refused I was unable to talk to the children who had so cruelly suffered. I did, however, listen to the other side of the story – from children who had fled Vietnam after the capture of Saigon by North Vietnamese forces on 30 April 1975 brought an end to the war. All of them had escaped, not by land not by air, but by sea – they were 'boat people'.

They have fetched up in places all over the world, some of them most unlikely. The first I met were a group of children strolling on the quay at Oslo; the Norwegians, being sea people, have saved many boat people on the high seas. Among those Oslo children were the five sons of Phuong, a Vietnamese fisherman. Such were the hardships of his flight from the communists that he had been driven to cannibalism. He had never heard of Norway and, now he had arrived, did not know where in the world he was. All he knew was that it was a different world from his fishing village. His home was now a modern apartment surrounded by pine-forests and, in winter, snow. Surrounded, too, by blond-headed, big-bodied Norwegian neighbours who complained of the new tenants' living habits, which were naturally those of a poor fishing village in Vietnam.

Not all Vietnamese boat people have travelled so far afield. About half of them have never arrived at all, unless it be to rest for ever somewhere on the ocean bed. Of the others, some, under their own steam, others, rescued on the high seas, have arrived at the shores of a free country; in one case and the other they have often, with a lack of compassion characteristic of the rich and the fortunate, been rejected, forbidden to land.

Three little shipwrecked mariners, a boy called Vu and his sisters, Trang and Thao, respectively six, seven and two years old, had been picked up on the high seas and brought to Japan, where I met them in a peaceful suburb of Tamakura, south of Tokyo. They were 'in transit'. Japan, the most affluent of Asian countries, had not, by mid 1978, accepted a single Vietnamese immigrant; although early in 1979 she agreed to take five hundred. It should be added, however, that Japan is in the forefront of nations who contribute funds for the resettlement of the boat people.

Vu, a tiny boy with an adorable face, bright eyes and a beautiful head, told me that he remembered his father was tall and that he loved him very much. Remembered, because Vu is unlikely ever again to see his father, an officer in the South Vietnamese army who had disappeared three years earlier to a 're-education camp' where, I was informed by a doctor who had been imprisoned in one for a year, the theme of one of the lessons – Lesson Six – was: 'The following are offenders, or detrimental ... to the new regime: soldiers and officers of the former army, officials of the former government, the copper Buddha statues in South Vietnam – all the foregoing must be punished or destroyed. Vu, Trang and their baby sister Thao had no hope of seeing their father again. No more had their mother, a beautiful young woman. She had waited without news; then having given up hope, she packed the children into a pick-up and drove towards the coast at Da Nang. She then walked in the darkness ten kilometres over the mountains, carrying Thao.' Vu and Trang walked beside her. I asked Trang (who had her mother's good looks) whether she had become tired? No, she said. 'Mummy kept on telling us, you must keep up or the police will catch you.' At two o'clock in the morning this little family and the eighty other passengers were rowed out to the boat. Soon after leaving they ran into a heavy sea. Trang, like nearly everybody else, was sick. Vu, though he was not sick, felt terrible. Neither could sleep. Next day they felt, not hungry, but parched with thirst. The boat captain told them: half a cup of water each, no more. If they liked, he said, they could try drinking sea water. But Trang could not face it. Vu took a gulp, but spat it out. Below, it was so hot that everyone came up and lay on deck, covered with tarpaulins which protected them both from the sun and from the danger of being spotted by a naval patrol.

Facing me across the table were these two angelic-looking children, who had been joined by two others, a little girl, Diep, and a boy, Ngang. They sat there, elbows on the table, chins cupped in their hands, recounting this perilous voyage on the high seas as if it had been a trip in a water-bus down the Thames, or up the Seine, in a *bateau-mouche*. Vu yawned and looked so bored that I thought he was going to fall asleep. Then we were joined by Thao, so exquisite a morsel that it seemed inconceivable that she had survived, perfectly intact. It was clear from the children's story that they and the rest of the people in that boat would never have made it alone to a friendly shore. Vu and Trang told me how, exhausted and tortured by hunger and thirst, they were lying, quite inert, when suddenly there came a shout 'ship ahoy!' As one man, Vu said, everyone stood up, took off his shirt and waved. 'We small ones waved our hands,' added Trang.

The ship, the *Liwo Venture*, took them on board; its crew were Hong Kong Chinese, its captain British. 'He was a very nice man,' said Trang. 'He played with us children and gave us sweets. He took us down to the engine-room and up on the bridge.' Before putting the boat people ashore at Yokohama, the captain gave a party for the children. 'He danced with us all,' said Trang.

Fortunately there was no lack of boats in Vietnam. Thoan, a grandmother, had hidden hers in the reeds by the riverside at Saigon, from where she planned to escape with her son Tho and his family, and a few friends. When her boat was discovered by a patrol, she bought a new one – this time at a place (whose name I cannot mention) 450 kilometres away to the north.

I met Thoan in Singapore. With her were Tho and his wife with their nine-year-old boy Thai; and also a friend, Ben, and his wife, with their little girl Nga, eight, and her brother Duc, seven.

Thai and Nga had both been at school in Saigon. When the Viet Cong came everything changed. They had to work much harder. Thai and the other boys were put to work cleaning up the school, sweeping the floor, painting the walls and growing flowers and vegetables in the garden. Both Thai and Nga were taught about President Ho Chi Minh and what a good and wonderful man he was. They were also taught what hateful people the French and Americans were. Thai could not understand this, for American soldiers had often come to his school and played with him and his friends. Thai liked them; now he had to hate them. Nga settled for a compromise: she liked the Americans and 'Uncle Ho' too, because the teacher had said he was such a good person.

Thai's father, Tho, had been a sailor. He was driven, he said, to escape in order to give his wife and family a better life. It was the same with Ben, the father of Nga and Duc. He had been in the army, working with the Americans. Because of this the new regime made life difficult for him; he was continually under observation and could not get a job. Escape offered the only hope for his own and his family's future.

All told, grandmother Thoan's boat carried twenty-three, including herself, the Tho and Ben families. An uninhabited island near the coast was chosen as the departure point. Disguised as fisherfolk, the fugitives rowed out there in sampans; then for three days, while Tho returned to the mainland to fetch the boat, they hid in a cave. Every night patrol boats passed close inshore, sweeping the rocky coastline with their searchlights. Those were frightening moments for Thai and Nga, but they lay low with the rest. I asked Nga's little brother, Duc, how he felt. 'Fine,' he said, 'I was asleep.'

The children were all asleep when, at one a.m. on the third night, Tho arrived with the boat, a nine-metre diesel job. Because of a rough sea, he had only been able to load twenty litres of drinking water. That was all – for twenty-three people. In the dead of night, the fugitives embarked. The children were a problem; the youngest were given a dose of 'Binoctol' to make sure they did not cry. All had to be carried over the rocks in the arms of their fathers. Neither to Tho nor to Ben did it occur that they might be carrying their younger sons, Thuam and Nhut, both of them five years old, to their graves.

Avoiding the big ships in the area, they came to the open sea, where they hit bad weather. Thai was so sick he could not sleep, little Duc too – he already felt very tired. Nga, who was not sick, moved away from the people who were, and found a small corner of her own. By the third day the meagre water-supply gave out, with at least four more days' sailing to the Malaysian coast. I asked Thai, a bright little boy, always ready with an answer, how he felt with no water to drink. 'I drank my urine,' he said in a matter-of-fact way, though he admitted, with a face, that it was salty and smelt bad. Was he told to drink it? 'No,' he replied. 'It was my own idea, and a good one, too, for after that I didn't feel thirsty.' Nga had another idea; she leaned over the side of the boat (the free-board was minimal) and scooped up sea-water in a plastic cup. 'The more I drank, the thirstier I felt,' laughed this pretty little girl in a flowered dress, and we all laughed with her – forgetting the torture and the tragedy that these children and their parents had suffered.

Nga's mother made her daughter and her little boy, Duc, drink their urine. 'It's a regular thing,' she said. Her sister and her mother, on giving birth, had both done so. Meanwhile everyone else in the boat was doing the same and douching themselves with sea-water. Just to feel wet gave some relief. But only the younger men had enough strength to sail the boat. The rest of the passengers lay silent, exhausted – and praying. Tho's wife was so ill that she did not realize her younger son, Thuan, was very near death. Ben's wife, however, knew by now that there was no hope of saving her own little boy, Nhut. He lay quite still, his eyes bloodshot and expressionless. There was no doctor, and no one really knew what to do for the boys. Grandmother Thoan, herself tortured with thirst, while she kept praying they would be picked up, was certain that some would be dead before then. I asked little Thai how he felt and, still without a trace of feeling, he said, 'It got worse and worse; I felt very tired and sometimes I lost consciousness; I only dreamed of water. I began to wait for death.' 'Were you afraid of dying?' 'Yes,' he replied. Nga, too, lapsed into unconsciousness and dreamed, not of water, but of beautiful dresses. 'I was wearing Mummy's clothes and they were not pretty,' she said. As for little Duc, he was already in a coma.

It was now, as some were resigned to death, others praying to be saved, that the motor broke down. After five hours Ben, despite his exhaustion, got it going again, and the younger men had just enough strength to raise a faint cheer. It was then one a.m. on the seventh day. Tho was using all the strength that he still possessed to keep a spark of life going in his little boy Thuan. There were no lights in the ship; blindly, he massaged him, used mouth to mouth resuscitation, but to no avail. In his arms he held Thuan; he could not see him in the dark. He just felt the little body stiffening. By five a.m. he knew that it was lifeless. That afternoon, without ceremony, only a silent prayer from himself and the others, he cast Thuan's body into the deep. An hour later a merchant vessel hove in sight.

It was the motor vessel CYS *Hope*, flying the Liberian flag. So exhausted were the boat people, it took two hours to get them aboard. Thai, too weak to climb the companionway, was carried. So were Nga and Duc, the latter still unconscious. But Nhut, their younger brother, was beyond saving. He died a few hours later. His father Ben showed me the simply-worded certificate of burial, signed by himself: 'Died from exhaustion owing to having been exposed to the natural weathers more than seven days since our escape from Vietnam to the open sea on board our small wooden boat . . . I buried my dead child by my own hands at

07.30 this morning ... into the open sea at an approximate position 05-35 N, 107-53 East...'

Neither Tho nor Ben regretted their tragic escapade. Ben summed up: 'We knew the escape would demand sacrifices. Though we have each lost a beloved child, our remaining children have the chance of growing up in a free country.'

I was back from my travels by autumn 1978 when, as the flow of boat people from Vietnam increased, the world press began to give full vent to their indignation at such a terrible fate. So I tell here only what I heard and saw before then.

On a single – and particularly dangerous – theme, escape by sea to freedom, the variations were many. An, a fifteen-year-old Vietnamese boy of Chinese origin, was in a boat which, on the high seas, attacked and boarded a much bigger iron-hulled boat crewed by seven Viet Cong. It had all been carefully planned – with two friendly Vietnamese already aboard the iron boat. While, during a sharp scuffle, the boarding party from An's boat were putting the seven Viet Cong out of action, An himself was sleeping soundly. The first thing he knew was when he was woken up and told to follow everybody else aboard the big boat, in which they sailed on in relative comfort to Malaysia.

An told me that there were two different tariffs for escaping – one for the Chinese, another for the Vietnamese. The latter, being less wealthy, had to put up with a smaller boat and rougher conditions. For an escape operation the price per Vietnamese passenger varied between seven and ten pieces of gold, each worth £100. The highest prices were paid for babies on account of the risk (crying, sickness, etc.). The money all went on the purchase, victualling and fuelling of the boat. The Chinese, however, each paid twenty pieces of gold – twice as much as the Vietnamese. But ten of these went to buying off the security people – police, military, etc. The Chinese, who escaped in bigger boats, carrying, perhaps, three hundred passengers, represented a flourishing export traffic.

Such considerations did not in the least affect Linh, a plump little Chinese girl who came to Malaysia in a Vietnamese boat. No, the facts behind her escape which she related to me in Kuala Lumpur were extremely personal. Every time Linh smiled, it made dimples in her chubby face, and she smiled a lot at the bizarre situation in which she and her two older sisters became involved.

It was Linh's own idea to escape. She was afraid that the Viet Cong would harm her or pursue her or hurt her in some way. Her parents, at first, would not listen. She was only thirteen and that was much too young for her to venture off on her own. Besides, Linh's two older sisters also wanted to escape and that is where the rub came; there was only one place vacant in the boat. Priority was given to the eldest sister, who was seventeen, and here Linh laughed and said, 'But she didn't like the boat.' 'Why?' I asked naïvely, and Linh smiled coyly. 'Well, it wasn't exactly that, but she had a boyfriend and she would not leave without him.' So that put that sister out of the running. The second sister's problem was quite insoluble. She was born under the sign of the Rabbit. And the boat-leader, who had consulted his own horoscope, flatly refused to take anyone who was a 'Rabbit'. So that put paid to the second sister's chances. Linh, who was born under the sign of the Dragon, got the place so coveted by her two sisters. Which left her torn between the joy she felt for herself and sorrow at leaving them.

As the boat cast off there were some frightening moments when the young children aboard began to cry. In the absence of sedatives, they were silenced, if not tranquillized, by their mothers, who half smothered them with blankets. Linh's boat, after a brush with Thai pirates, brought her safely to Malaysia, where she had spent some weeks looked after by the Malaysian Red Crescent. She was leaving, the day after our meeting, for Hong Kong – where I was due myself in a few days. I promised to get in touch and it was in Hong Kong, where she now lives with her grandmother, that I finally said goodbye to that funny little daughter of the Dragon whom fate had so strangely favoured, yet tormented. Because, for all her smiles and dimples, Linh felt bitter that it was fate, too, that had separated her from her family. She firmly believes she will see them again. And with that hope I left her.

It was in a building in Des Voeux Road, Hong Kong, that two Vietnamese, Qung and Da, both fugitives from communism, told me how they first met in one of communist China's outlying provinces, the island of Hainan. As we talked, in a large but stuffy upper-floor room, other boat people, fathers, mothers and their children, gathered round. On bunks, splayed out, haphazard, some of them in each other's arms, the tiniest children slept.

Qung was one of a group of nine college boys who, running the gauntlet of naval patrols, loaded up their light nine-metre wooden boat with supplies and fuel (including wood, to cook on) and slipped off one night from a northern village. Steering a course for Hong Kong, a thousand kilometres away, they ran into foul weather. For two more days and nights they had to bale for dear life. 'We didn't dare stop,' said

Qung, 'or our boat would have filled and sunk.' None of the boys had been to sea before. 'We were all absolutely terrified,' said Qung, smiling broadly – he could afford to now. 'We never imagined how tiny and helpless our boat would seem in those huge seas.' While all the time their boat was in danger of sinking the motor never faltered. It brought them safely to within sight of the island of Hainan, where, in a heavy surf, they managed to beach. Hainan. That was Chinese territory. So the boys, having jumped out of the Vietnamese communist frying pan had landed, apparently, in the Chinese communist fire. They found, however, that it was a fire which glowed with warmth. The fishermen, said Qung, were exceptionally hospitable, helped them ashore and gave them food. The local authorities, too, were helpful and six days later those nine adventurous college boys re-embarked on their perilous journey. Alas, for but one day, at the end of which the motor, so faithful until now, broke down. In a heavy sea the boys rowed back to Hainan, but this time the surf was too much. Their boat overturned. 'We were so exhausted,' said Qung, 'that we just staggered to the shore and threw ourselves on the sand.' Again the fishermen helped, the local authorities too. They informed the boys, 'Thirteen other refugees have arrived. You are going to meet them.'

They were Da's lot – his wife, his ten children and a niece, thirteen in all. Da, a son of the sea and superstitious, tried not to think of that number. Although he did not take a chart with him, he had previously studied and memorized it thoroughly. In his own nine-metre, ten horsepower diesel fishing-boat he reckoned he would make it to Hong Kong in about five days. But when Da first sighted land it was Hainan, and with a heavy sea running he thought it wiser to make for the shore; but beaching the small boat, half-full of young children, nearly cost them all their lives. As with Qung's outfit, Chinese fishermen were there and helped to get the children through the surf to shore. The boat, his own dear boat, was wrecked.

The Da family and the Qung boys decided to club together and buy another boat. Each group put up 3,800 Chinese piastres – that is, they signed a debit note for that amount. The Chinese fisherman merely told them 'If you find the money, pay us back; if not, forget it.' 'They were poor in money,' was Qung's comment, 'but rich in their hearts.'

The rest of the voyage, with the nine students to help keep watch, went smoothly. At the approach to Hong Kong a police-boat intercepted them. 'What a difference,' exclaimed Da. 'They were kind and gave us some badly needed water. Then they escorted us into the harbour.' And, at last, to safety.

Qung's friends had gathered round him, chipping in every now and again with their own comments. More than anything, more even than their obvious pleasure at spinning a good yarn, they seemed grateful that someone had come to listen to them. Too often, they felt, the boat people had been taken for flotsam and jetsam thrown up on the seashore. Since then the plight of the boat people has become an international issue, leading to a UN conference at Geneva in July 1979.

In a cove at Laemsing, on the east coast of the Gulf of Siam in southern Thailand, there was no end to the tales you could hear of the sea. In that cove was a camp of boat people; their boats were drawn up on the shore. Some were rotting hulks; in others, people were living, in a permanent stoop beneath the low bamboo awnings. Ashore, narrow, rocky paths strewn with garbage rambled among the huts of a little bamboo township. In one of those huts lived Lan, with his wife and three of his children. Sitting on the floor with them and three young neighbours, I listened to their own variations on this theme of the boat people.

It would be hard to find a story so sad as Lan's. He was a fisherman and lived in a village in the south-west. He was also a Catholic and wanted his ten children to be raised in Catholic schools. But after the Viet Cong took over they decreed that all children must go to state schools where communism was taught and Christianism excluded. For the simple, believing fisherman that Lan was, it was unthinkable that his children should grow up not as Christians, but as communists. He decided to quit Vietnam, in order, as he told me, 'To find a good and a Christian education for my children.' There were ten of them, their ages ranging from one to twenty-two.

Lan and his brother, also a fisherman, planned an escape using three boats – his own, only six and a half metres long with a ten horsepower diesel, and the two, bigger and more powerful boats belonging to his brother. They agreed that the women and children should be divided among the two big boats. Lan would take his wife, three children and a few other people. A rendezvous at sea was arranged. But the brothers missed each other. Lan's small boat got into difficulties and he and his party were taken aboard another boat. They reached Laemsing safely. But of his brother's two boats there was no sign and Lan, when I met him, still had no news of his seven other children. Ever since, he said, the saddest moments of the day were sunrise and sunset. Sunrise, because it was then that his sons and daughters used to come to him for their day's pocket money: 'I have lost them and all my money too,' he said. Sunset was the time when the family would gather to talk of their day. Sunrise and sunset, those were the times when Lan thought most of his lost children.

The two others of Lan's neighbours who sat with us in that airy hut, while the sea-breeze wafted the pungent smell of charcoal smoke to our nostrils, were a young couple — Son, a frail-looking eighteen-year-old youth, and Laon, his bride, a comely and enchanting girl of seventeen. Theirs was a case of love triumphing over adversity.

Before he fell in love with Laon, Son, a jeweller's apprentice, had already made up his mind to escape. No such idea had ever occurred to Laon, one of a family of thirteen children. So when Son proposed — both marriage and escape — Laon asked her parents. Their attitude was, 'You want to marry Son, he wants to escape, so you must go along too. And may the future smile on you both.' As Laon talked about her family she looked away, and I could see that she was crying — like that she looked even more beautiful. Then, half-apologetically, she said, 'This is the first time I have ever been away from home.'

Son lived near the sea, moved among the fisherfolk and was well aware of the dangers of the voyage ahead. 'Did you warn Laon?' I asked him, and he shook his head. 'Why?' I asked, and he replied, 'Because I was afraid she would change her mind.'

Though they saw nothing romantic about their perilous trip, the moon did shine down on the two lovers as they made their way through the forest to a point on the coast, from where they had to swim 450 metres to the waiting boat. Once away, all trace of romance vanished. They both suffered cruelly from seasickness, from sunburn and thirst. Then they fell among pirates, Thais, who stopped the boat and came aboard, armed with revolvers. All forty-six passengers were frisked. Son admitted that he was scared out of his wits. Laon was laughing now. 'I was even more frightened and clung to him,' she said. Meanwhile the pirates made off with their booty, gold bars, jewels and rings which the boat people had brought to get them started in a new life. From Laon they stole, among other things, her wedding-ring.

This charming, love-smitten, teenage couple were intending to settle in Australia, whose immigration policy was, until quite recently, for a 'white Australia', but which now, after the United States, has accepted more Vietnamese than any of the many countries all over the world where this dispersed people have come to rest. Although the pirates had left them destitute, Son and Laon were overjoyed at their new-found freedom. 'And you think,' I asked them, 'that love will still find a way over all the obstacles ahead?' They both laughed, and Laon said, 'After all we've been through, we're sure of it.'

CHAPTER TWENTY-NINE

The Agony of Cambodia/Kampuchea

On 18 March 1970 a *coup d'état*, engineered by the Americans (as part of their effort to beat the neighbouring North Vietnamese) deposed the chief-of-state of Cambodia (Kampuchea), Prince Sihounak; General Lon Nol was installed in his stead as president of the new 'republic'.

Descendant of the kings of Ankor, ancient capital of the mighty Khmer empire, Sihounak, for all that, was a communist. From Peking, on the morrow of his dismissal, the 'Red Prince' rallied the Cambodian resistance groups, giving them (with his French background) the name Khmers Rouges – Red Khmers. Five years later, in April 1975, they entered the modern capital, Phnom Penh, on the heels of the retreating Americans. Henceforth the Khmers Rouges (having dropped their leader, the Red Prince) were to impose a bloody, totalitarian rule on the fair land of Cambodia – now the Democratic Republic of Kampuchea.

It was said that in 1970 the entire Cambodian peasantry rose as one man to the appeal of the Red Prince. But against the Khmers Rouges, now in power, the peasants were hostile. A resistance movement was created; one of its youngest recruits was a boy of fourteen, Chan Chiep. I met him in southern Thailand, at Kamput, the Khmer refugee camp – more like a modern village, really, with its broad alleys lined with solid, iron-roofed buildings, its market, shops and school.

Chan Chiep's job in the resistance was to mix with the peasants and collect information on the whereabouts of the Khmers Rouges forces – a highly dangerous job, for, as he said, 'If I was caught, the Khmers Rouges would have killed me on the spot.'

One of those peasants who could talk about the Khmers Rouges was a boy of twelve, Sam Nang. The son of a farmer, he told me how, one day, he was wading in the paddy fields with his father's buffaloes, when along the path came a group of about fifteen children led by a woman. Behind them walked a Khmer Rouge soldier carrying an automatic rifle. Sam Nang heard the man shout to the others, 'Keep going. I'm stopping to rest a bit.' A moment later, he raised his gun and fired, mowing down everyone in the group.

Sam Nang crouched, quite still, in the paddy. He said that, had the man seen him, he could have run away, but I reminded him that bullets go faster than boys can run, and he agreed – his chances would have been small. When the soldier had moved off Sam Nang drove his buffaloes to the edge of the forest; he knew that they represented the family fortune. That was why he herded them every night into a place his father believed to be safe. But the Khmers Rouges found out and stole them. That very night the family heard that the Khmers Rouges were coming to massacre them. His father swore, before fleeing, to get the two who guarded the village. He and a few neighbours crept up on them and killed them with axes. Then they all fled into the forest, and across the Thai frontier.

It was in the schoolroom at Kamput that I listened to two of the most lucid eye-witnesses I have ever questioned. They were Khmer girls – twelve-year-old San Sina and her ten-year-old sister San Sinuol. Nonchalantly, and in the smallest detail, they described to me a scene of utter horror. I describe it exactly as they told it to me, to show the indifference with which these two girls, who at the time (1975) were respectively nine and seven, could regard the cruelty, the bloodshed and butchery going on around them. Their classmates came and sat with us, listening intently, and without the least show of emotion, to every word.

Sina and Sinuol lived in Pailin, a town in the west. After the take-over by the Khmers Rouges, their father, a farmer, was arrested. They never saw him again. They and their mother, leaving all they possessed, were transferred to a village, Sala Krao. There, as Sinuol said, for want of farm implements, 'We had to work with our bare hands.' One day the little girls went fishing. 'We were hoping to catch a few fish and some crabs too,' Sinuol told me, 'but we weren't having much luck.' As they paddled, knee-deep in the river, a squad of ten soldiers, some teenage boys among them, wearing the Khmer Rouge uniform, black blouse and trousers with a red scarf around the neck, came marching down the river bank. In front of them shuffled a forlorn group of about a dozen men, their hands bound behind their backs. As Sina spoke Sinuol nudged her. 'You remember,' she said, 'some of them were crying?' 'That's right,' said Sina, 'and others were just looking straight ahead.'

Sina and Sinuol were curious to see what happened when people were executed. Leaving their nets behind, they followed at a discreet distance until, in the forest, the Khmers Rouges and their prisoners came to a halt. Sina and Sinuol hid behind a tree. 'How far off were you?' I asked, and Sina pointed to a tree outside. 'About twenty metres away,' she said. 'But we were not afraid. The Khmers Rouges could not see us.' Sina went on, 'Each of the victims was tied to a tree by a rope round his waist. Half of them were shot . . .' and Sinuol cut in, 'And the other half had their throats cut.' The girls told how they begged the Khmers Rouges to spare them. Sinuol said, 'They cried out, "Have pity on us".' And Sina added, 'And then the soldiers beat them with their rifle butts.' They began by shooting the first half-dozen prisoners. 'The moment a man was shot,' said Sina with a macabre eye for detail, 'being tied to the tree, only the top half of his body fell forward, and the head touched the ground.'

After the shooting, the Khmers Rouges, seeing the blood flowing, shouted at the top of their voices, 'Traitors, traitors! It's your blood, not ours!' And the girls, when they saw the blood, were very afraid. Sina, with her hands, showed me on her own grubby blouse where the victims' shirts were blood-stained. Then she said, 'If a victim was not quite dead the Khmers Rouges cut off his head.' As she spoke, she was smiling, so was her sister. 'But was it not terrible,' I asked them, 'to see somebody's head cut off?' And both replied at once, 'No, it was not all that bad.' They kept watching (from behind their tree), they said, out of pure curiosity, because they wanted to see what would happen next.

Quite calmly they described to me what did happen. The remaining half-dozen victims were tied, as before, each to a tree. 'Then,' said Sina, 'a soldier would take the victim by the hair,' and with her own little hand, the left one, she took hold, by the hair, of her own head and jerked it backwards. Then, with her right hand she made a sawing motion across her throat. 'They took a knife,' she went on, 'and drew it several times across the victim's throat. Sometimes they kept on until the head came off, sometimes they just left the throat cut.' The cries of the dying victim, she added, were imitated by the soldiers, who were shouting, 'Down with the traitors. Long live the Khmers Rouges!' Then they unfastened the ropes around each victim's waist. Sina remarked, 'It was to save rope.' For the next butchery.

Sina and Sinuol, by now terrified out of their wits, ran home. And Sina was crying, 'Out of pity,' she said, 'for those poor people.' Their mother warned them, 'Not a word to anyone, or we shall all be killed.' And so, in fear of their lives, they waited another three months until the villagers left *en masse* for Thailand. With their mother, Sina and Sinuol walked barefoot for three days, their feet swollen and torn by stones and thorns.

Nightmares still trouble the sleep of those two over-inquisitive little girls. Sina told me, 'Sometimes in the night I see a ball of fire turning and turning. Then it vanishes into the forest; but later it is back again.' Both told me that they longed to go back to their country, 'But never, never, NEVER,' they insisted, as long as the Khmers Rouges are there.

In Laos, immediately after the fall of Saigon and Phnom Penh, in 1975, the communist Patriotic Front, Pathet Lao (led by another 'Red Prince' of the blood, Souphanouvong), provoked demonstrations against the American 'occupants' and the powerful feudal clique. By July 1975 the Americans had all but quit; in August Luang Prabang, the royal capital, and Vientiane, the seat of government, were 'liberated'. The Pathet Lao take-over was complete: they abolished the 600-year-old monarchy and proclaimed a republic. The revolution was widely hailed as 'democratic'. Laotians light-heartedly called it the 'Song and Dance' revolution. I listened to some for whom it was neither.

One was Lien, who told me his story at the Lao camp at Ubon, in eastern Thailand, which houses 27,000 of his compatriots, fugitives from the 'democratic' revolution. That huge camp is more an important township, complete with markets, restaurants, shops and schools, with carpenters sawing and planing, gardeners hoeing and weeding their flower patches, and pecking hens and waddling ducks. All that rich decor reflects the Laotian character – easy-going, fun-loving and attached to the earth.

Lien was a simple country boy, who, through love of the land – his father's – laboured gladly from dawn till dusk. When the land was seized for a communal farm scheme Lien revolted; he downed tools and marched off into the mountains to join the resistance movement, composed largely of peasants. After three days he reached their headquarters. It was three months before he received an M16 sub-machine-gun, captured from the Pathet Lao army. For his first combat he was allowed eight bullets. Lien said bitterly that such was his hatred for the Pathet Lao regime that it was all the same to him if he killed his countrymen who fought for it. Kill them he did, this sixteen-year-old boy, and with pleasure. During his first combat he used up all his eight bullets and felt better. Lien's next fight was against government troops at a village near the Cambodian frontier. One of his friends was killed and Lien himself was badly wounded in the leg by a mortar-shell splinter. With his wound bound up in rags, Lien and the corpse of his friend, were carried over the mountains for three days to the guerrillas' camp. Then, with the festering wound swathed in more rags, he was carried by his friends on a stretcher for another ten days over the Thai frontier. Lien showed me his wound, an ugly one not yet completely healed, which had made a mess of his well-muscled right leg. Now he is convalescing. Can he get around and have fun? I asked 'I'm not interested in having fun,' he replied curtly. 'I'm only interested in getting back to my country and killing more Pathet Lao.' 'How many do you expect to kill?' I asked him. 'I'd like to kill the whole lot,' answered Lien, the farmer's boy whose only desire was to avenge his one love, the land, which had been stolen from him.

Loyal and respectable citizens of Laos, Souvannamacho and his wife Sanga had every intention of raising their children to their own standards. And it was just this that worried Souvannamacho when the Pathet Lao took over. The educational system was basically changed; foreign languages were eliminated, and Lao only was taught. Then of course there was the political indoctrination. Souvannamacho, a Christian, very soon made up his mind to leave, but for family reasons could not do so for another two years. Then he walked out of his job — he was an accountant and comfortably off — and went back to his village on the banks of the Mekong, that mighty river which rises in the Tibetan highlands and flows south through Laos, forming part of the frontier with Thailand, and on through Cambodia and Vietnam to the sea west of Saigon.

I talked with Souvannamacho in his small but pleasant wooden house in the Ubon camp. He showed me photos of his wife, Sanga, a beautiful girl, and her pretty sixteen-year-old sister, Hue, and of his three children, Malivan (four), Duong Chay (three) and little Pierre (six months). He introduced me, too, to Sanga's eighteen-year-old brother, Vixay, who shared his home. Then he went on with his story.

When the night came to leave, the family set off, just after sunset, on foot, to the rendezvous. Sanga carried Pierre, and Duong Chay was in the arms of her father. Malivan walked, holding Hue's hand, and Vixay carried a sack containing the children's clothes and a quantity of gold bars and banknotes.

The crossing of the Mekong was extremely dangerous. At that point, a mile and a half of water, swept by a strong current, separated the Lao and Thai shores. Armed naval vessels were anchored at strategic points, while others patrolled, sweeping the river with searchlights. But the family walked on, confident that within a few hours they would be in Thailand. They reached the riverside; as they waited for their boat another was already crossing. Suddenly the guns of the river patrol opened up on it. At the sound of the firing Souvannamacho asked Sanga (a rather timid girl, he said), 'Are you still sure you want to go ahead?' 'Yes,' Sanga replied. 'I'm ready to risk anything for the children.'

At last their boat, rowed by two young men, arrived, and the family embarked. Towards midstream was an island, uninhabited as far as anyone knew, where the boat had to turn downstream for some way before re-setting course for the far side. As they rowed past the island they were surprised to see men silhouetted on the shore, less than a hundred metres away. That night, for the very first time, a battery had been stationed there. With machine-guns and B-40 anti-tank guns, it opened fire. Miraculously, in the hail of projectiles, none of the passengers in the boat was hit, but the boat itself was overturned by a near-miss. Everyone was thrown into the water, which was shallow at that point. As the shooting continued Sanga clutched Pierre to her and Souvannamacho held Malivan and Duong Chay in his arms. The others succeeded in righting the boat, but in the confusion the sack containing the clothes and the money was lost: worse, an oar disappeared. After everyone had clambered back into the boat, Souvannamacho and the two oarsmen propelled it, swimming. In vain. The shore battery kept up its murderous, point-blank fire on this little party – on that lovely young mother and her infant children, on her teenage brother and sister and her husband and the two young men in the water.

It was a mortar shell which overturned the boat once more – this time in deep water. Souvannamacho saw Sanga, still clutching Pierre, thrown into the water. He heard her cry out so loud that he thought she must have been hit, but he distinguished her words 'Don't worry about me, look after yourselves.' After that no further sound came from her or his little boy. Meanwhile Souvannamacho swam towards Vixay, who, still under a hail of fire, was struggling to keep the two little girls above water. Hearing his sister Hue's cries for help Vixay made towards her, but too late. Hue had disappeared. Souvannamacho was beside him now, but not in time to save Malivan as she slipped from Vixay's grasp. Souvannamacho grabbed the other girl. Gasping for breath, he asked Vixay, 'Can you still make it to the other side?' But Vixay was all-in. Somehow he and Souvannamacho, holding Duong Chay, managed to swim the 450 metres back to the Lao shore. They were immediately arrested.

Souvannamacho and Vixay spent six weeks in gaol before being released on bail. Two weeks later Vixay, clinging to an inflated inner-tube, swam the Mekong to Thailand. Souvannamacho, alone with his three-year-old daughter, rowed across in a small boat.

As Souvannamacho and I talked there lay beside us, fast asleep, a tiny, lissom girl dressed in baggy green trousers and a funny Donald Duck T-shirt, a blue teat between her lips, her arms and legs splayed wide. It was, of course, Duong Chay, upon whom the Pathet Lao democrats, with their machine-guns, mortars and anti-tank guns, had fired point blank. But there she lay — an immaculate little creature, and her father's one remaining consolation.

CHAPTER THIRTY

The Muslim Orphans from Burma

The story of the griefs of the Muslim minority in Burma is a long one. It began, the Muslims say, with the first British incursions into Burma in the 1820s. Since 1947, when Burma, a predominantly Buddhist country, won independence, the blame has been shifted to the Burmese government. In 1958 some thirty thousand Muslims were driven out across the River Naf into neighbouring East Pakistan (now Bangladesh). Twenty years later, in April 1978, there began an exodus of Muslims over five times more massive. Its cause, official Burmese sources say, was the announcement of a census in the frontier province of Arakan; the news sent illegal Muslim immigrants fleeing in panic. The refugees, some 200,000 of them, exhausted and half-starved, found refuge in hastily erected camps in Muslim Bangladesh.

Kutupalong No. 2 was one of them; I got to it by driving through the vivid green rice-fields south of the little seaside town of Cox's Bazaar, in south-eastern Bangladesh. At Kutupalong No. 2 over 15,000 Burmese Muslims lived in communal huts knocked up by themselves out of leafy branches and brushwood – nothing else save a strip of black plastic on the roof, held down by more brushwood. The plastic, if it absorbed the midday sun, at least kept out the monsoon rain. You had to enter a hut on all fours and were immediately greeted and motioned to sit on a mat – there was no choice, so low was the roof. In a small hut lived fifty people; that is, up to ten families, each with its tiny allotted area. Saiful Alam, the camp director – the Magistrate they called him – led me to his courtroom, a small but airy bamboo hut. Alam, a congenial, intelligent Bengali, interpreted with great tact and fidelity the pathetic, atrocious stories of some of his protégés. First, he showed me on a blackboard a few figures: 15,242 camp inmates; births to date 22, deaths 169; cases of rape 160. Half a dozen or so of those unfortunate girls now squatted on the earth floor of the courtroom.

The first to come forward was Hazara, who said she was sixteen, but looked much younger. Small and very thin, Hazara, as she spoke, turned her head aside and with one hand held her head-cloth across her face so that only her two brown eyes were visible. Calmly she described how she was raped by two men of the local tribe, the Mogs. She was already pregnant, she said, by her husband (who was now with her); at the time he was away at work. The Mogs seized her, threw her on the ground and tore off her *longyi* (sarong), their own as well. At this stage of the story, Hazara, to hide her shyness, squatted down beside the table at which the magistrate and I sat. Then, drawing her head-cloth more tightly over her face, she went on, very quietly. 'I did not resist. I could not. Both men carried a short knife and would have killed me.' Hazara said her friends were not ashamed of her. 'Why should they be?' I asked her. 'You are not ashamed of yourself?' 'Yes, I am ashamed,' the girl said and hid her face with her head-cloth.

As may be expected the stories varied only in their details. Abdul Quedus, who was only eight, told me he would have liked to kill the men who assaulted his sister. Though a very small boy, in stature as well as age, he did try, with his father, to defend her, but the rapists turned on him and bayonnetted him; he showed me the wound in his back and a much deeper one behind his right thigh. His sister was crying, 'Brother, save me; father, come and save me,' but neither of them dared. The attackers would have killed them, as they did the girl. Only her they raped to death.

Frequent victims of the Mogs' vicious attacks were the little goatherds who kept their fathers' flocks. One was Young Rahamat Ullah, who tried to defend himself against a gang of Mogs as they made off with two of his father's cows. They stabbed him in the right arm – the scar is there – and pursued him as he ran home, where, after a short fight, they overpowered his father. While eight of those bloodthirsty ruffians seized him and marched him off, two others grabbed the boy; he was stabbed again, this time in the right leg. He showed me the wound, then went on in a listless voice, 'They dragged us both into the jungle. While they held me they forced my father to lie on his back. They spread out his arms and legs. One Mog stood on each. A fifth one shot him, first in the stomach, then he forced the muzzle into his mouth and fired again.' The murderers, he said, were laughing and dancing round the body; then they let him go. He ran off home, told his mother and with her cried, as he put it, 'very much and very long'. Rahamat Ullah, who had spoken so calmly, was suddenly, at the mention of his mother, upset. After a short silence he said fiercely, 'I would like to eat the flesh of the Mogs.'

The children living at nearby Marichyapalong, the newest of the camps, told me some harrowing stories. They were the most pathetic children I ever saw. On arrival at the camp at seven a.m., when the mist was still rising off the rice-fields and the doves cooing, I noticed a group of about thirty of them squatting together on one side of a small square. They were talking quietly among themselves when two or three of them began crying, followed, one by one, by the others until they were all wailing dismally in unison. It was the saddest sound imaginable; when I asked what was the matter I was told, 'They are all orphans; they have come to talk to you.'

One of them came, crying, and sat with me. His name was Fuzal Ahmed and he was dressed in a grubby *longyi* and T-shirt. Fuzal Ahmed was seven and very small and had once been happy back in his village of Sindipran – until that morning, before the first meal, when the family were gathered and suddenly a group of armed men were there, shouting and assaulting the terrified villagers. Fuzal Ahmed was standing beside his parents when the bandits killed them – with a gesture he showed how they were shot. As he spoke, Fuzal Ahmed sobbed and wrung his small hands. He went on, 'I just abandoned my parents where they had fallen and ran, holding my four-year-old brother's hand.' Others were running, too, while the men fired after them. For days Fuzal and his small brother walked with the refugees towards Bangladesh; sometimes he carried the little boy. Since his arrival, life in the camp, he said, still crying, might have been hard, but he never wanted to go back to Sindipran.

The road to Bangladesh had become dangerous. The first flood of refugees had got by unmolested, but groups of bandits were lying in wait for those who followed later. A little girl called Mahmoudia, trying, behind her head-cloth, to hide her tears, told me how while walking with her parents and sister through the jungle they were surprised by armed men. They seized Mahmoudia's sister and, as her father pleaded for her, shot him dead. Mahmoudia and her mother escaped into the jungle; but, to judge by her distress, she was still haunted by the vision of her murdered father. Never did she want to return to Burma, for, said Mahmoudia, 'They will probably kill me too.'

A pretty-faced boy of twelve got up and walked across from the group of whimpering children. Barefooted, with a dirty *longyi* round his thin waist, Sayed Alem's thoughts were far away, his speech vague. With gestures he recounted how bandits, armed with dahs, had hacked his father and mother to death on the road. Flattening his arms and the palms of his hands together, he imitated, with chopping motions, what he had seen the men do. Then he cocked his head slightly, slanting his eyes to the ground, and wept.

Syda, who had drawn the hem of her head-cloth to her eyes, and was crying behind it, told a similar story, only she had seen her father clubbed, her mother bayonnetted. Syda was twelve. Barefoot she had walked on to Bangladesh, leading her two younger sisters. They were somewhere in that little gathering of orphans of whom my lasting impression was one of utter, desolate sorrow.

In September 1978 some Burmese Muslims, encouraged by guarantees from the Burmese government and help from the United Nations, began to trickle back. In time most of them had returned home but it is hard to believe that any of these terrorized orphans were among them.

CHAPTER THIRTY-ONE

Children at Arms: Belfast

My travels took me, naturally, to Northern Ireland, for, even in Europe, the slaughter caused by two world wars has not yet convinced men that it is a better thing to create and preserve life than to destroy it.

The 'Irish Question' goes back to King Henry II's invasion of Ireland at the end of the twelfth century. In recent times it has become a struggle by the Protestant majority of Northern Ireland (Ulster) to resist union with the Catholic south. On 14 August 1969 a protest movement by Catholic civil rights marchers provoked violent riots in the capital, Belfast, and in Londonderry, and plunged Northern Ireland into murderous civil strife which still persists today. The situation in Belfast, where I spent some days in mid-1978, was sensitive, charged with fear and suspicion – and, fortunately, with much kindness and good humour as well. I am bound – to avoid bringing more trouble to good people who have already had enough – to alter or omit certain names and references.

A lady, call her Pat, recalled that 'beautiful sunny day' in 1969. A Protestant, she lived in a predominantly Catholic district and worked in a nursery school. A friend called early and told her the school had been burned down and the streets closed. Pat, despite her husband's warning, 'The area's not safe for Protestants', immediately set off for the school, walking through streets strewn with broken bottles, sticks and stones. The school was still standing! A small one, it was crammed with nearly a hundred children and their mothers, red-eyed and weary, who had fled there for safety after a sleepless night of shooting and street-fighting. Pat and the rest of the staff fed and comforted the wailing, frightened children. The day, nearly a decade later, that she told me all this, she had taken a bus to down-town Belfast: it was full of schoolchildren whose spiritual chief was the Pope. They spent most of the journey breaking up the inside of the bus and shouting obscene words. Pat's remark was significant. 'I thought of that night back in 1969: some of those little vandals were probably among the frightened children we had cared for in the school.' During these ten years of strife, verging at times on civil war, children have played a major part, trapped, without hope of escape, in a ceaseless current of violence.

It is the poorer, 'hard working-class' districts of Belfast which are the battleground; there you see the hated 'Brits', the disciplined, patient men of the British army, and those of the Royal Ulster Constabulary, patrolling on foot or in dark-green armoured vehicles. It is their dangerous and unenviable job to keep apart two sworn and bitter enemies, protecting one from the other and themselves from both. On the Catholic ('Taigs' or 'Micks') side are the Official IRA ('Stickies', named after their adhesive badges) and the Provisional IRA ('Provos'); on the side of the Protestants ('Orangies' or 'Prods') are three groups: the Ulster Volunteer Force (UVF), the Ulster Freedom Fighters (UFF) and the Ulster Defence Association (UDA). The conflict, basically a political one, has become a religious war between Catholic 'Republicans' and Protestant 'Loyalists'. Apart from them there is the vast majority of the population who want to live in peace.

A scary, uncertain atmosphere pervades the 'trouble spots'. The 'fringe-area' of the 'peace-line' which separates Catholic from Protestant districts is utter desolation; garbage-littered streets, rows of abandoned, derelict, red-brick houses, their roofs partly or entirely missing, their windows either shattered and gaping or else blocked up with cement. The grey slate tiles missing from the roofs have been stolen by children; they sell them for five pence apiece and the money, as often as not, goes on drink.

Byron Street, in a Protestant district of North Belfast, is surrounded by houses like that. It lies in the area of the Shankill, Crumlin, Ardoyne and Antrim roads, the 'murder triangle' where some three hundred people have been done to death. In a house in Byron Street I met seventeen-year-old Paddy, his sister Moyra, nineteen, and their father, Patrick. Patrick worked on a night shift. Paddy told me he himself was always home before dark, otherwise he might get shot in the street. Moyra said that she was so frightened at night, she could not sleep. 'How come, then, that there are no shutters on the windows?' I asked, and Moyra simply said, 'Because I don't like being shut in.' Patrick said, 'I'm fed up with the fighting; I'm afraid for the children.'

Paddy then told me a bit about himself. He hated Catholics, not because they were Catholics – 'We're all Catholics, only they're Roman,' he said – but because they beat him up on his way to work. Paddy's two passions were football and swimming – he proudly insisted on wearing the 'Prod' club scarf, even though, for the 'Micks', it was like a red rag to a bull. As for swimming, he was afraid to go to the pool; though his passion remained, he had not been swimming for a year. Paddy, though, was tough. That you could see by his aggressive manner and the way he folded his arms, which were tattooed up to the elbow. Hardship had made him like that; underneath, he was very soft. He had been very happy up to the age of thirteen, then he had got into trouble with the police. He was riding in a bus with a 'wee girl', Lalan, when another wee girl, a Catholic, hit her. Paddy hit the wee Catholic. Then all the wee girls started hitting him. The police took Paddy to court and he was sent to Rathgael Reformatory. ''Twas terrible,' said Paddy. 'Everybody looked at ye.' A week later he escaped. 'Daddy was angry, he shouted at me.' He sent Paddy back. When they let him out he got a job delivering newspapers.

It was better than nothing but was not enough for Paddy. He longed to get right away from Ulster, to another country across the sea. He remembered the happy days when 'you could walk around' after dark without fear of getting shot. He was in a trap, at the mercy of the 'Godfathers', the leaders of the paramilitary groups of each side, who kept the war going. Now and again, it is true, Paddy had a break, thanks to the 'Brits', to the army, who ran a camp at Ballykinler with the object of giving the little ones, both Protestants and Catholics, a change. The army called it a 'Community Relations Weekend'. Paddy and all the rest just called it great fun. There was swimming, sailing and rock-climbing. Sergeant Bryan, in his twenties and a keen fisherman, was in charge. He told me how surprised he was at the 'maturity' of those boys and girls, aged from twelve upwards. They smoked and talked about sex and among themselves were completely relaxed. Sergeant Bryan thought that if left to themselves they would drop 'the Catholic-Protestant animosity' and get together. Paddy agreed. The wee Micks and the wee Prods forgot about fighting and just laughed. Paddy was delighted to find that the Micks were as keen on football as the Prods.

The 'Community Relations Weekend' and all the other numerous attempts to bring the two warring communities together is violently – in its literal sense – opposed by the Godfathers. The war must be kept going – until it is won. Paddy thought that ten years hence nothing would be changed. He even said, 'I can't leave because if there's a civil war I shall have to fight.' And so, after Ballykinler, back to Belfast and Byron Street, and Paddy and the 'wee lads' would go back to fighting the 'Micks' – though he did admit, 'I haven't fought for three weeks,' adding, 'Life would be fine were it not for the war.'

Down Albert Bridge Road, where a young Tommy, hugging his

sub-machine-gun, was laughing with two small children, and where, in the early days, Protestants with bows and arrows had fought Catholics, I came to a house near Short Strand; now that its gutter-pipes had been transformed into a cache for arms and ammunition, water flowed straight down the walls. More arms were hidden in the sewers, which were consequently useless. The houses adjoining on each side were roofless and, of course, empty. Birds had nested in the rafters; mice and rats had followed; they had penetrated the roof space of the house sandwiched between and died there. You could see where birds had tried to peck their way through the ceiling of the two rooms in which slept the nine children of Mr and Mrs Maguire – they themselves slept downstairs in the living-room.

It was in that narrow, low-ceilinged room that I met Maguire, a stocky man, and obviously unwell. His bad health had cost him his job. It was his wife who kept the home fires burning. The Maguires were Catholics, good people, trying to keep their two boys, Jim and Jack, out of trouble – out, that is to say, of the IRA. It was not easy; Jim had already been in trouble with the police, for stone-throwing and insulting language. One night, as an army vehicle passed, the boys threw bottles at it. The soldiers caught them, searched them, stood them hands against the wall, legs apart – made it awkward for the boys. Fifteen minutes later they let them go. Why did the boys act like that? 'We always do,' said Jim, 'otherwise we don't feel we're fighting a war.' A war against Protestants, but Irishmen all the same. 'How do you think you are going to win?' I asked. 'Starve 'em out – let's have a civil war,' they answered, more or less in unison.

It is at Ardmonagh, on the Turf Lodge estate, that you really get that scary feeling – silent, deserted streets lined with empty houses, their windows broken or bricked up. Yet all the time you feel that there are people watching you. Ardmonagh is an IRA stronghold, ruled by the Provos – 'hard-liners'. You have to be a hard-liner to live there. Garbage and rubble litter its streets and the waste ground sloping towards the cemetery, on which stands a derelict house whose nearest wall is used as a target for rifle practice. Ardmonagh has been the scene of battles between the Provos and the Brits. A pretty, but tight-lipped girl of twelve, Sheelagh, told me how she had fought in some of these battles. She disdained to stay in the rear with the 'wee lads' but joined the big lads up front, throwing stones at the Brits. She will never forget the one she hit full in the face; 'I saw him bleeding,' said Sheelagh, without emotion. The soldier was unlucky. Sergeant Bryan, the soldier who took little Catholics off to the seaside at Ballykinler and had himself often been stoned by other little Catholics, told me, 'The kids who stone are between ten and fifteen.' When the stoning starts the soldiers withdraw and wait till the stone-throwers tire, or run out of stones. Then the soldiers move forward. He said that children like Sheelagh have hatred sown in their hearts from the age of five. Sheelagh said as much. 'I hate the Brits,' she told me. 'They took my Dad away.' Sheelagh's Dad had been 'inside' for over two years. She missed him badly.

Sheelagh was frightened of the Brits' armoured cars. 'And if they were painted in pretty colours, blue or pink or red, would that be better?' 'No,' said Sheelagh, more tight-lipped than ever. 'I hate the Brits and their armoured cars.' 'And the Protestants?' 'I hate the Protestants,' snarled Sheelagh. 'You know, Sheelagh, I'm a Protestant, though my wife and children are Catholic. They don't hate me. Do you?' That did it for little Sheelagh. She just looked at me, dumbfounded.

I did not mean to snub Sheelagh. I felt sorry for her because her Dad was locked up. Longkesh, the prison better known as the Maze, is outside Belfast, a kind of military camp with grey walls, a high fence with plenty of barbed wire around it and a watch-tower on the right as you drive in. Once inside, the impression, strangely enough, was less forbidding. Prisoners like Sheelagh's Dad are allowed to see their families for half an hour every week – under surveillance of course, but it is sometimes lax. To the point where one prisoner and his wife managed to have intercourse. The lady was expecting; by now she must be the mother of a child conceived in prison. It will first get to know its father in prison, which will be easier than it is for Sheelagh, who, for nine years, saw her father every day and not just once a week.

Annie, a teenager, was once playing with her friends when they got caught in the Brits' and Provos' crossfire. She told me that the housewives and children always give warning of the Brits' approach by banging on biscuit tins and dustbin lids and blowing whistles; their dogs are trained to bark – but only at soldiers. When bullets began zipping past them Annie threw herself flat. So did all the others, who were terrified – except one little boy who wanted to go and throw stones at the Brits. Annie told me that she and her family thought the IRA were 'a load of rubbish'. She said, 'I refuse to go with it,' but when she was dating a Protestant boy she was threatened. She would like to talk to soldiers, she said, but does not dare. Annie lives in the Springfield Road – a 'hard' area – not far from the police station which is caged within a wire grille over four metres high; outside, concrete blocks prevent the parking of a car which might be booby-trapped. One day some time ago a mother had called at the station, leaving her infant in its pram outside.

Some minutes later a group of paratroopers were leaving the station when they spotted a time bomb – meant for them – lying outside the entrance within feet of the pram. In a second one of the paras had flung himself over the pram. The para, but not the baby, died.

Moyard, another hard area, is an Official IRA stronghold. The district is without street-lighting, which makes it less dangerous at night for the patrolling army and police as they can't be seen, but creates a 'frightening situation' for the residents, as one of them told me, and is one of the reasons why, in the hard areas, there is no social life for the young people – apart from the 'bully-boys', teenagers who frequent the shebeens, illegal drinking clubs, which are run and sponsored by the para-military organizations. Those youths have won their spurs – they have been out in front of the fight – for freedom if they are republican or, if they are loyalist, for the British connection. At the behest of the Godfathers (who are far too careful to get involved themselves) these youthful 'freedom fighters' have committed, in the eyes of the law, crimes and atrocities; they have done manly things and, like the rest of the boys, earned their noggin. (Recently the police and the army have cracked down on the illegal drinking clubs.)

On the Prod side, the Newtownards Road is a key area. The headquarters of the Ulster Defence Association is there, a shabby building displaying all the paraphernalia of loyalty to the British Crown. Should anything important be going on inside, a teenage sentry might be seen lolling against the wall – as with every pub and shebeen in the district, only the latter's youthful watchdogs are employed on a permanent basis and rewarded, at the end of their shift, with a couple of pints of beer on the house. A haven for the UDA was the pub on the corner of Templemore Avenue, notorious for brawling, prostitution and drinking after hours. It gave teenagers of the local 'corner groups' an introduction to adult life. But the greatest excitement to be had was in the junior section of the UDA, the 'Young Newtons', which 'commanded' most of the district. The boys' arms were tattooed with their Christian name, and the legend 'Young Newton – UDA'. They talked excitedly of the killings in the area. Most of them had handled guns, a few possessed the know-how for making bombs. Working in the para-military organizations gave the corner boys, and all that despised, rejected youth the chance of gaining self-esteem, importance even, and popularity. The girls were proud to know them, the Godfathers only too pleased to have such willing, fanatic fighters up front.

'They're not daft; they're watched every minute by the police, but never put a foot wrong,' was how Sergeant Bob (let's call him) summed up the Godfathers. I can't think how, but Bob, a 'bastard Brit', had got to know one of the Godfathers, a married man with children – but not for anything would he have them join the IRA. A Brigade commander himself, he admitted only to the title of 'adviser'.

I also got to know a Godfather, at least for an hour. Call him Rory. A top man in one of the most militant groups, and a really hard militant himself, he appeared as gentle as a lamb, receiving me in a quiet but friendly manner – though I got some dirty looks from those about him. He told me of the Young Fianna, the IRA youngsters who, wee lads as young as eight, may be in the front line, performing lesser, but vital scout duties, running messages and signalling with whistles or, in the dark, with torches, the approach of the Brits. (As Sergeant Bryan had told me previously: 'They're quite good.') Rory said that the IRA needed the young people because so many of their old-timers were in gaol. The young IRA were indoctrinated earlier – it began on the knees of their mother, even more so of their grandmother. Teenagers and younger do the stone-throwing, then, in their later teens, carry guns. The 'big lads' of the IRA would become 'captains' at eighteen.

On the Protestant side there is the Orange Order; the junior order takes boys from nine onwards and teaches them about their religion and how to fight for it. More militant are the Young Citizens Volunteers (YCV), the junior wing of the strongly militant Ulster Volunteer Force. They may be in the front line at the age of twelve, stone-throwing as cover for snipers.

Discipline, Rory told me, was severe and punishments harsh, especially for giving information, for larceny and drug-taking – a very rare offence among the youth of Northern Ireland. Under-fourteens are 'treated' in the 'romper-room', where for half an hour they are kicked, punched and beaten with nailed sticks. For offenders over sixteen, both boys and girls, there was the 'knee job'. It was invented, Rory said, by the IRA but the Prods adopted it. Since the troubles began 650 knee-jobs have been performed. (The vast majority of the resulting injuries have been operated on at the Royal Victoria Hospital, which is entirely non-partisan where religion and politics are concerned.) The victim is shot with a revolver across the knee, causing temporary crippling, or from the front, causing more permanent injury, or from behind the knee, which destroys the joint for ever. More sophisticated 'knee-jobs' are executed with an electric drill – a 'Black and Decker job'. The capital penalty – for seventeen-year-olds and up – is called a 'head job'.

Rory kindly offered me a drink. I needed it. On our way to the door the Queen of England, from her photo on the wall, smiled down on Rory, her loyal subject.

CHAPTER THIRTY-TWO

In the Palestinian Camps

The last lap of my journey took me to the Middle East and, in a way, back to the beginning of this book. Palestine, now Israel, and neighbouring Lebanon form, as they always have done, one of the most troubled areas of the world.

Eighty-five per cent — three million souls — of the total population of Palestinian Arabs (Muslims and Christians) live outside Palestine, which today comprises parts of Israel, Jordan and Egypt. Of this Palestinian *diaspora,* the great majority is dispersed among neighbouring Arab countries, parts of which, like the Gaza Strip and the Jordan West Bank, have been occupied by Israel since the Arab-Israeli Six Day War of 1967.

On 7 June of that year Sami Hadawi, the well-known Palestinian author and Director of the Institute of Palestinian Studies, Beirut, stood on the east bank of the Jordan. He was 'appalled by the scene that met his eyes. A mass of humanity in thousands wading from the West Bank through the waters of the river ... with still others being hurriedly pushed — sometimes by a volley of overhead shots — to speed them on their way ... babies and little children were being passed overhead from one person to another like bundles.' Among the victims of Israeli napalm bombs, 'the saddest sight of all was ... two innocent children between the ages of six and seven lying helpless in bed with burns all over their faces and bodies. The look of disbelief in their eyes, as if to enquire: what was all this about? was pathetic.'

Mohammed and Mahmoud, whom I met at El Aida, on the West Bank, in the hilly country near Bethlehem, were five and six years old respectively during the Six Day War. Mahmoud said, 'When we all saw the Israeli soldiers coming there was nothing we could do except raise the white flag.' Since then he and Mohammed have been living in the refugee camp at El Aida. Intelligent and lively boys, they had finished at the United Nations school. Without money to finish their studies, they now faced the utterly frustrating prospect of spending the rest of their days in the El Aida camp. 'Will you,' I asked, 'eventually marry a girl from the camp?' 'I hope not,' replied Mohammed, 'because that would mean living too near the in-laws!'

Both boys dreamed of a life far beyond the limits of the camp. Mahmoud longed to go back to Palestine, that is, Israel, to his father's village, which, though he had never seen it, he felt was his home. Mohammed wanted to get right away from the troubled land of Palestine and start a new life in America. But not until he had first seen the farm near the Gaza strip, which, until 1967, was his father's. If it could be restored to its original owner – 'Well,' he said, 'I might change my mind about going to America.'

When, during the Six Day War, Israeli soldiers overran the Shati (Beach) camp at Gaza, fifteen-year-old Halil heard them shooting – 'in the sky, to frighten people,' he said; but he could not see them. Halil was totally blind. He sat in front of his shack and, when the soldiers asked him his identity, the people told them, 'He is blind.' But Halil rose up, walked over to the soldiers and handed them his papers. 'Who said he was blind?' the soldiers shouted and became aggressive. So Halil quickly took off his black glasses and said, 'See for yourselves.' Then the soldiers admired Halil.

So did I, from the moment I came upon this young man in black, steel-rimmed glasses, walking at quite a brisk pace, tapping with his white stick the stony path which led down to the Shati (Beach) Camp. I got talking with him, telling him first that there were three Israeli officials with me. They did not, in the event, raise any objection as Halil gave vent to his resentment against the Israeli government. 'I am a Palestinian and have been driven away from my land,' he began. 'Do you remember it?' 'No,' said Halil, 'but from my father's description it is as if I really lived there. We grew vegetables and olives and lived a simple life.' The question, said Halil, that he was always asking himself was, 'Why does the Israeli government ask Jews who are living peacefully in other countries to come and live in my land, when they don't allow me to live there?' He sympathized with the Palestinian Liberation Organization (PLO) and its freedom fighters – the *Fedayin,* whose name is taken from the Arabic *fida'i,* one who offers himself for his native land. But still, Halil had strong reservations: 'We are also human; we don't want any more wars and disasters. I don't like murders – even murders of Israelis. But they have murdered us in our camps, with their bombs and their guns. They have killed our children so we in return kill theirs. I don't like this exchange of killing.'

Halil's blindness barred him from becoming a *Feda*. Instead, he decided to get himself properly educated. He won a university scholarship; he worked, during vacations, in a factory, to get money to support himself and his aged parents. 'My family,' he said, 'is one of the poorest in the camp.'

Halil took me to his home on the beach among a sprawling agglomeration of shacks and shanties intersected by narrow, straggling streets, strewn with garbage and oozing with slime.

Above this scene of desolation rose a forest of television aerials. At the approach to Halil's home was a protective fence: strands of rusted barbed wire vaguely connecting an array of bedsteads, an oildrum or two and a few old saucepans, with here and there the twisted remains of a bicycle; finally, after the household washing, came Halil's home, a low, iron-roofed shack giving on a cramped, but clean-swept courtyard. Halil slept there, on the ground, opposite the privy, a hole in the ground which the user flushed with a small jug of water.

Few university students can be so brave as Halil, with his blindness and his humble diggings. He was reading for a degree in sociology, his sole purpose being to help improve the unhappy lot of his fellow-Palestinians, who, in the congested squalor of a refugee camp, ceaselessly cherish the dream of returning to their holy land, Palestine.

Not all Palestinians live in camps. Some reside in pavilions and palaces, like those overlooking the Shati camp; others in lesser homes or hovels. Some, like thirteen-year-old Lamiel, hardly have a home at all. But before the Arab-Israeli war of 1948, when her father, Mohammed, was a boy, he lived happily near Gaza with his own father, who owned cattle, camels and a vineyard. Today Mohammed was in prison; it was his mother, Lamiel's grandmother, a Bedouin lady in black veil and robes festooned with beads and coins, who told me what had happened as we sat there, with the *Moukhta* (the village headsman) and a small crowd of little girls and boys, in the 'guest-house', a ramshackle hut surrounded on three sides by tattered sheets of plastic and rusted iron and thatched with grass. The miserable décor entirely belied the old lady's warm hospitality.

During the fighting round Gaza, in the war of 1948, the home was shelled. The family fled, their flocks stampeded in terror. The old lady said, 'As Allah is my witness, I put a saucepan on my head for protection and ran for dear life.' Leaving their cattle and belongings, they came, after a two-day march, to Gaza, where, in the direst poverty, they have been living ever since. Lamiel's grandmother said that she could only praise Allah for persuading the United Nations to feed them. Mohammed did well at school and got a job in the Israeli government. Then, following the Six Day War, he was arrested, allegedly for helping the *Fedayin,* and imprisoned.

The old lady, in tears, described the humiliating conditions in which the family had lived since they lost the bread winner, Mohammed. Despite the help of the International Red Cross, they were always short of both food and water and lived, as I saw with my own eyes, in abject misery. 'Our life is like mud,' the aged *Moukhta* blurted out, adding, unexpectedly, 'we were much better off under the British.'

Lamiel is allowed to see her father − but not touch him − for fifteen minutes each month. What were her feelings? Lamiel, a shy girl who kept twisting a lock of her hair, answered: 'May the curse of Allah be on all Israelis,' including, presumably, the two who were present. She went on, 'I wish I could slaughter them all.' Did that, I asked her, include Israeli children? 'To hell with them,' said Lamiel.

I turned to speak to Khalid, a bright-looking boy of fifteen, slightly built and wearing T-shirt and jeans. But it was he who spoke first − in excellent English: 'My father was killed.' He was killed, Khalid told me, fighting with the *Fedayin.* On a chain round his neck Khalid wore a pendant inscribed LOVE. 'I wear it,' he smiled, 'to show my love for my country.' What was his ambition? I asked him. And he replied without hesitation, 'To join the *Fedayin.*' 'Do you think it right to kill children?' I asked this quietly-spoken, intelligent boy; but before he could answer the *Moukhta* cut in, 'You must say no.' Khalid ignored him: 'I would cut off their heads whether they are young or old.'

In an orange grove not far from Gaza is a heap of stones which had once been the house of Khalil Taha. Khalil's two elder sons were *Fedayin* − outlaws in the land of Israel. Khalil and his family were to pay dearly for harbouring them. They were in the house one evening in 1971 with their parents, their three sisters and their younger brother, finishing their Ramadan meal. Suddenly there came a banging on the door and it was kicked open. Israeli soldiers were there; after a few brief questions, they opened fire on the family and threw two hand grenades, then quickly withdrew, slamming the door. Hayat, the younger daugher − she was eleven − heard a soldier shout *'Beseder'* − everything's okay. On the floor lay Hayat's mother, a brother and a sister, all dead, and beside them, both wounded, her father and her fifteen-year-old sister, Farida.

Not far from there, in another orange grove, I listened to the survivors of the massacre: Khalil, the father, Farida, Khamis, the youngest brother, and Hayat. Hayat, a handsome girl with straight, clear eyes, told me. 'When I saw my mother dead I lay beside her and went almost crazy.' Khamis, who was then only seven, recalled, 'It was like being in a slaughterhouse full of flesh and blood.'

Farida was a girl whom fate had not favoured, either in appearance or in the cruel experiences which had befallen her. During the Six Day War, when she was twelve, she was out fetching water when the curfew fell. On the way home she was fired at. Farida showed me where a bullet had pierced the back of her head, coming out of her forehead; another hit her arm. She has been partially paralysed ever since. The night that the Israeli soldiers broke into her home, splinters from the bursting grenades hit her in the leg, the abdomen and near her left eye. As she lay on the floor she cried out, 'Israelis, *khawaja!* Help us, Israelis! You cannot leave us children lying among the dead. Please take us to hospital... please!' The soldiers replied, 'It's the fault of the *Fedayin* that you've been shot, not ours.' But Farida's pleadings prevailed and the soldiers took her and her father away in an ambulance.

Khalil, Farida's father, lamented, 'I wish she were dead! She is only half a human being and not fit to be anyone's wife. What am I going to do with her?' And Farida, listening, said, 'Yes, I wish I were dead. It would be better than this half-living existence.' Hayat said more, 'I wish we were all dead. When I see an Israeli I would rather see death.' Khalil agreed. An Israeli present cut in, 'But when you go to the Israeli Welfare Office to get your relief?' Khalil was not deterred. 'I still don't want to see them.'

He sighed deeply, staring at the ground. Then he put his head in his hands and wept – for an Arab, more than for any man, the most humiliating emotion. As we tried to comfort him he went on crying aloud in his anguish. Farida and Hayat cried too. Then Khalil pointed to the sky and said, 'It is the will of Allah. But Allah will judge.'

CHAPTER THIRTY-THREE

Revenge or Forgiveness?

There lived, in 1975, well over a quarter of a million Palestinians in Lebanon, with its mainly Arab population, about half of whom are Muslims, half Christians. In the Palestinian camps around Beirut, at Tyre, Saïda (Sidon) and Nabatieh, the *Fedayin* are trained. Their revolutionary indoctrination begins at an early age, both within and beyond the family circle.

Ab initio military training takes place around the age of nine, when boys and girls join a unit and, wearing a kind of battledress, learn to handle light weapons – light for the obvious reason that the recruits are too small to carry heavier ones. Some of the guns are wooden dummies, others are real but unserviceable; finally, there are the guns that really shoot – these are confined to the 'older' children of ten years and more. The young *Fedayin* are led and instructed by others not much older, in individual and collective weapon-training. Discipline is rigorous, but mainly self-imposed, thanks to the children's bursting enthusiasm for their training as fighters. For that they have but one incitement: a burning conviction for the Palestinian cause.

Fedayin attacks on Israeli soil set off a chain reaction. Israel riposted fiercely against the Palestinians, in their camps and elsewhere, in Lebanon. In time the Lebanese, notably the right-wing Christians – the 'Chamounists', followers of Camille Chamoun, and the 'Phalangists' of Pierre Gemayel, weary of their trouble-making Palestinian 'guests', turned against them. In April 1975, in the Aîn-Remmaneh district of Beirut, Phalangist militiamen fired on a busload of Palestinians, killing twenty-six. The massacre of Aîn-Remmaneh sparked off a civil war which, for its savage, indiscriminate and pitiless killing, has few equals. It was not a war of soldiers, but of people – grown-ups and children. In the streets of Beirut and on the barricades, Christian children, 'militiamen' of fourteen, twelve, of nine even, could be seen armed with guns and grenades. Both sides exploited the youthful contempt for danger of their children which enabled them to slip through strongly defended positions in order to snipe, to dynamite and, at point blank range, to kill – and usually get killed themselves. A Christian mother, at her fourteen-year-old son's funeral, read a poem exalting his glorious death in battle, of which, she declared, no one could be more proud than she. Religious belief and love for their *doux Liban* were the inspiration of these youthful crusaders.

But not all. If, on the Christian side, conviction was not lacking, neither were drugs. They were practically unknown to Lebanese youth before the war. It needed the war to convert them. In a long talk, of which I can give only the bare details, a Lebanese youth enlightened me. He told me of the traffic which grew up during the civil war, of the hashish grown in Turkey, brought into Lebanon through a secret airfield near Baalbek and distributed the length and breadth of the country.

In the ranks of the Christian militia, he said, were boys who had joined out of loyalty to their cause. But the militia was not only a fountainhead of virtue, but of vice – in the form of drugs; they used drugs as an inducement to recruit youths, from fifteen upwards. Nabir, a boy he knew, had joined, 'Not to fight for any cause', except his own – more drugs. 'The sole aim of boys like Nabir,' pursued my friend, 'is through hashish, to become a hero, a new man, stronger than a bull.' Another boy had told him that, under drugs, 'I feel strong and happy when I am fighting – and especially when I see blood, for the more blood there is, the more hashish there is for me.' My friend commented, 'They don't give them medals for bravery, they give them more hashish.'

My friend told me of yet another boy, Ali, whose father was killed in the war. Ali, inconsolable, began taking hashish. Then, determined to avenge his father, he contacted the militia. They gave him a gun and told him, 'All you have to do is to use it.' Ali was very scared, but he was given a cigarette and told, 'That will make you feel better.' It did. Ali felt very relaxed and happy; his world had changed. 'After that everything was easy,' he told my friend. 'I felt ready to fight ten men.' And the infernal process began. The more he killed, the braver he felt and the more hashish he smoked. Drug-besotted, blood-crazy, Ali was killing anybody he saw, old people, women and children, innocent victims – killing them for the sheer, drunken joy it gave him. Then in a lucid moment Ali realized what he had done and was beside himself with remorse and sorrow. 'He was crying and begging me to help him get a cure,' my friend said. But that was not possible. Ali, as a killer, had served the militia well; they had confided to him some of their secrets. So they would not let him go; if he quit, he was told, they would kill him. So

Ali was stuck, a prisoner of the militia and of its hashish-filled cigarettes. A prisoner, too, of a savage, uncontrollable lust for killing.

Among the victims of the militia's fury were the father and mother of a Lebanese Muslim family whom I met on the outskirts of Beirut. There was Sabah, a girl of fourteen, her three younger brothers, Abed, Ali and Jafat, and two sisters younger still, Wafa and Sana. The eldest brother, Ahmed, was away at work. The family were living in Maslakh, a poor district of northern Beirut, in January 1976 when the militia wiped it out. The family joined the headlong flight, but the militiamen overtook them. One drew his revolver and fired, hitting Sana. More bullets hit her father, who, still holding Sana by the hand, staggered on for a few paces then fell dead at the children's feet. A moment later their mother was shot and killed instantly. Huddled about the corpses of their parents, the children waited and watched as the massacre proceeded. Abed, with his own eyes, saw a militiaman plant one foot on a child's corpse while he held a champagne bottle to his lips and drank. Another Christian soldier, his foot on a corpse, strummed on a guitar. Wherever Abed looked he saw horror; in some detail he described to me how the militiamen took people, alive, fixed a butcher's hook beneath their chin and hoisted them on an iron bar.

The massacre over, the militia withdrew. The children, not knowing where to go, camped for the night beside the corpses of their parents. In the morning they tried to drag the bodies off the street, but they were too heavy. The militia then returned and from the children's father one of them snatched a gold medallion. When he read 'Palestine' on it the Christian took his gun and fired point-blank into the corpse, lengthways and from one side to the other, making the sign of the Cross.

Ahmed, Sabah, Abed and Ali were led off to a building and locked in. Sabah's head was shaved. Abed's hands were bound with wire. From Ahmed's thigh the militiamen cut a strip of skin. Then they lined him up with the others who were to be selected for execution. When Ahmed began praying aloud to Allah a Lebanese whispered to him, 'Don't! They will take you for a Palestinian. Come and stand with us. We are going to be spared.' Ahmed did as he was told and that is how he came to be at work that afternoon while his brothers and sisters were talking to me.

In the same month, January 1976, the *Fedayin* wreaked revenge on the Christians at Damour, a village in the hills south of Beirut. It was midnight and Toufic Eid, a boy of nine, and his younger brother and sister, Tony and Soumia, were fast asleep. It was Toufic who told me the story as I sat with the three children in their grandmother's house near

Saïda. 'We were all woken up by a knocking on the windows. We were very afraid,' Toufic said. Moments later all inside, grown-ups and children, were confronting two *Fedayin*. They beat Toufic's father over the head and on the back as they led him outside. Then they asked roughly, 'Where's his wife?' and Toufic's mother was led outside. With others, in all two men, three women and four youths, they were lined up against the wall of the church. 'We were not forced to watch,' said Toufic, 'but we were so afraid for Mummy and Daddy that we wanted to see what was happening to them.' What did happen was quickly over. Toufic saw it. He saw his father and mother and all the others shot to pieces by the *Fedayin*.

I asked Toufic what his feelings were towards those men who had killed his father and mother and his friends. To my astonishment, he beamed at me and answered, 'I forgive them, in the name of Jesus, with joy.' Toufic's answer was quite spontaneous, as was that of the villagers of Damour when the *curé*, the night before the massacre, having assembled his flock to prepare them for death, asked them, 'Are you willing to forgive those who seek to kill you?' After a short silence the congregation replied as one, 'Yes, we forgive them.' Père Mansour Labaki, who lived, with his parishioners, the tragedy of Damour, later founded, with the blessing of the Bishop of Beirut, a *foyer* (home) for orphans, Notre Dame de la Joie, at Aîn Saade. Musician, composer and lyricist, Père Labaki formed a choir of these orphans. He told me, 'They are children who once were divided by hate and whom love has brought together. In their turn, they will go out and sing of love, even to those who have done them such harm.' In Lebanon, their songs have been adopted by both Christians and Muslims and have even spread to Arab countries.

No such charitable feelings existed between the Christian militia and their Christian brothers living in the Jisr al-Basha camp in a north-eastern suburb of Beirut – the reason being that the latter, if Christian, were Palestinians. The militia, on 29 June 1976, made their final assault on Jisr al-Basha. Among the many children under shell and mortar fire that day were three small Christian Palestinians, Boutros, a boy then eleven, his young brother Elias and Eugénie, the baby. Beautiful, laughing children when I met them in the peaceful surroundings of Beit Atfal Alsomoud, the Palestinian children's home near Beirut; two years had passed since that day when they had crouched, petrified, in a shelter at Jisr al-Basha.

It was Boutros, being the eldest, who did the talking. He said, 'We never wanted to fight but we had to – it was life or death.' After a siege lasting months the defenders were almost out of food, water and ammunition. The camp defence force included teenage boys and girls – and the father of those three children. During the militia assault he was badly wounded. Two days later he died.

I asked Boutros about the militia. 'They are very bad men,' he said. 'But they are Christians?' 'Yes, but very bad Christians,' was the opinion of Boutros. His dream, after finishing school, was to join the *Fedayin*.

Little Eli, who had been so smiling, now looked glum. He had been listening to Boutros and me and began to cry; all this talk, he said, made him very sad, and he added, 'I would like to join the *Fedayin* and avenge my father.'

Half a mile north-east of Jisr al-Basha was another Palestinian camp, Tal-al-Zaatar. Within its seven acres there lived, in flimsy tin huts, some 30,000 people, 17,000 of them Palestinian, the rest mostly Lebanese. The ground, provided by the Lebanese government, was under United Nations (UNRWA) administration. There were eight schools and a hospital, run by the Palestine Red Cross. From the start of the civil war in April 1975 the camp was blockaded. The siege proper began on 22 June 1976. On that day alone the Christians shot 8,000 shells into Tal-al-Zaatar. By 1 July hardly a tin hut remained standing. The only provisions available, *hadas* (lentils), *boghrol* (crushed wheat) and tinned food were running short. On their meagre rations, mothers breast-feeding their children found they could not give enough milk, and, with reserves of powdered milk exhausted, infant children just died.

Water was the most dramatic problem of all. Every day ten to fifteen children died of thirst. With the main supply cut, water had to be fetched at the well – under the deadly fire of Christian snipers, who, like big-game hunters, waited for their quarry to come to 'water'. It was said that every drop of water cost a drop of blood, and it was mainly to the women and girls that fell the perilous 'water-fatigue' (*corvée de l'eau*). Over two hundred people, nearly all of them women and girls, were shot dead by the wellside.

Claude was one of those Christian hunters keeping watch on the well. Pushing a piece of chewing-gum between his teeth, he told Robert Pfeffer, a reporter of *Der Stern*, who sat beside him, 'That is the water-place where I am hunting. I have only to wait here until the sun is high enough in the sky to drive the rats out of their holes.' One of those 'rats' was fourteen-year-old Zainad, who, in Beirut, told me that the women and children would go to the well six or seven at a time.

Sometimes only two returned. Zainad could not understand how she was always among those who did.

It was one day towards the end of July, when the mother of Fadi, a three-year-old boy, set off alone on the perilous walk to the well. As she reached it shots rang out – from the United Nations school where the militia were entrenched. Ignoring the firing, Fadi ran towards his mother. He had nearly reached her when he saw her fall. In an almost inaudible voice, he told me, 'She was lying on the ground and the blood was running.' Since that day, two years before, the sight had preyed incessantly on Fadi's mind. He kept painting pictures of it, which he showed to me. Invariably, they depicted a crude kind of water-pump, a grotesque figure lying on the ground, toes and fingers splayed, and, around it, dabs of red paint.

On 12 August, early in the morning, the Christian militia overwhelmed the last defenders of Tal-al-Zaatar. Previously, they had agreed that the Red Cross should evacuate the wounded and the non-combatants. But as the evacuation proceeded, male Palestinians between sixteen and forty caught by the militia were murdered. A Red Cross worker told me of a mother, fleeing with her four young sons, who was ordered: 'Choose one of them. We're shooting the other three.'

Hassan and Issan, eight-year-old cousins, made surprisingly light of their headlong flight from Tal-al-Zaatar. Yet the experience had left unmistakable traces. Hassan's eye twitched ceaselessly and his thin, squeaky voice was like that of an old man; he fidgeted and teased Issan, who began by giggling and finished up in a fit of hysterical laughter as he described how, when a rocket landed nearby, he was hit by a splinter while Hassan's father was crushed under a door. To my question, 'Why, do you think, did those men try to kill you?' Issan gave an ingenious answer. 'Because,' he said, 'before the war, there was a film on TV called *The Ten Little Nigger Boys* – I saw it myself.' Issan went on, 'There were men armed with revolvers who killed others. So, you see, there were men in Lebanon who were jealous of those men in the film and they bought revolvers so that they could kill us. And that's the reason why my father and Hassan's were killed.'

Zainad, the teenager who could not understand how she had survived the water-fatigue, could find no explanation either for the war, the butchery or the swollen corpses she passed each time she went to the well. 'I simply don't know what the war was all about. All I know is that it is the people who have to pay. I know that at Damour [now a Palestinian camp] most of the women are widows with half a dozen or so children on their hands.'

This was the case of Samira, though she was not yet a woman, but a teenage girl, olive skinned, with dark glistening eyes. When I met her among the ruins of Damour she was sewing, a picture of innocent girlhood, at an embroidery class. About her neck she wore a medallion of the Virgin Mary. 'She belongs to us too,' she said.

Samira was fourteen at the time of the siege of Tal-al-Zaatar. When her mother was killed at the well by a sniper's bullet, she replaced her as a drawer of water and 'mother' to her five younger brothers. But one thing Samira could not do for her mother was to breast-feed the baby; he died. During the final assault on the camp, while the shells rained down, Samira, with everyone else, was in the shelter. She had learned to fire a gun and had one handy in case she found herself face to face with the militia. A lull came in the bombardment and the loudspeakers of the besiegers called to the Palestinians: 'Come out of your shelters and give yourselves up. You won't be hurt.' The men, including Samira's father and elder brother, had only just left the shelter when Samira heard an explosion. She rushed outside straight into a scene of carnage. 'There were bodies shattered, limbs severed,' she said. Samira joined in helping the victims and dressing their wounds. Ten people, including her father, were dead. Samira helped to carry her wounded brother to the clinic, where he died two hours later.

All these frightful things Samira related in a quiet voice, smiling. I asked her, 'How is it possible that you can smile?' and she replied, 'I may be smiling, but you don't know how fast my heart is beating.' At that she suddenly put her face in her hands and burst into tears.

She was soon herself again and led me up the street, amidst heaps of shattered masonry, to her home, of which the approaches were filthy, the interior spotlessly clean. There she introduced her young brothers, who obviously adored her. I asked Samira, 'Do you often think of your home in Palestine?' (which, of course, she has never seen). Her face suddenly lit up and she answered, laughing, 'I never stop thinking of it.' Had she yet thought of marriage? 'No,' she replied. 'First I must raise my brothers.' 'Then what is your greatest wish?' Again Samira's face – a very pretty one – brightened into a smile. 'I should like to be like Dalal,' said this quiet, charming girl. Now Dalal was a terrorist; she had died in a recent *Fedayin* attack in Israel. It took place on the sabbath, 11 March 1978, on the Haifa-Tel Aviv road.

A few days after Samira told me of her admiration for Dalal I talked, in their house on a hillside outside Jerusalem, to victims of Dalal and her companions: Sharona, an Israeli mother of seven, Adiel her sixteen-year-old boy, and Reviva and Coroneth, twin girls of thirteen. Sharona gave me the broad details: she, her husband, Adiel, his brother Imri, soon to be fifteen, and the twins were on their way to Haifa, in their Peugeot 404 station-wagon, to visit their elder married daughter. Between Haifa and Hadera, to the south, they saw, ahead, a big traffic jam; a red bus was blocking the road. Slowing down, they passed a dead body lying by the roadside. An accident, they all thought. Adiel took up the story. 'Suddenly we saw a man in soldier's uniform; he was running towards us. First we thought it was one of our boys; then he raised his gun.' Adiel went on, 'I shouted, "Duck, duck everyone!" Then the man started shooting at us and there was a smell of gunpowder and all the windows were shattering.' Adiel's father, at the wheel, was crying, 'My arm, my arm', as the car slithered to a standstill.

It was then that Sharona, in the middle seat, turned round towards Imri, on the back seat. 'I asked him, "Are you okay?" and there was no answer. He was dead.' Imri was fourteen and, from his photo, a fine-looking boy. Very musical, like the rest of his family, he was a gifted clarinettist. Sharona told me, 'He received a beautiful new clarinet – three days before he died. It was the joy of his life. When I got home and found it in the hall, I just sat on the stairs and cried.' Sharona thought for a moment. Then she said, 'I don't think that the pain of losing a child is one that you can ever overcome.' Despite her grief, Sharona had it in her to say of those young men who had killed her son: 'I feel sorry for them because they are boys who, from Imri's age and younger, have all humanity taken out of them. They are hardened to murder innocent people.'

Adiel said, 'I would just not let them live, because they are dangerous; their only aim is to kill people. It makes them heroes' – not that Adiel thought so himself. ' "Cowards" is the right word. With their machine-guns and grenades they attack unarmed civilians. But when captured by soldiers – two of them were caught in this hold-up – they kiss the soldiers' feet and beg for mercy. It's disgusting. Then when they see they won't be harmed they come to the TV and talk as if they were heroes. That's even more disgusting.' The only way to deal with them, thought Adiel, was to attack their camps. Which made Sharona remark, 'Their camps are in civilian areas; everybody is sorry when those civilians are killed accidentally. Imri was not killed by accident; he was the deliberate target.'

No civilized human being could fail to sympathize with Sharona. But is it true to say that in an air-raid civilians are killed 'accidentally'? When a target is bombed (or bombarded) it is hardly true to say that civilians and their children living in the area are killed unintentionally. Rather, they are killed inevitably, it may be deliberately. So, if the children of one side are foully, deliberately murdered by the other, do the latter's children deserve to be slain and maimed in return? As long as military targets are sited in civilian areas this will happen. It did when, in reprisal for the attack in which Imri and some forty other innocent people were killed, Israeli forces struck at Palestinian camps and villages, Damour among them, in Lebanon.

In the Rambam Hospital, in Haifa, Israel, I found two very small people who were grievously harmed — by the Israelis, who were now caring for them. In a ward overlooking the sea stood a little boy, Ibrahim. He was five. Out of one leg of his blue pyjamas protruded a small bare foot; out of the other a metal contraption twice the size. That leg had been amputated above the knee. Ibrahim's face was permanently lit by a smile. He stood there, his arms round the leg of another boy, short and thick-set — his ten-year-old brother Hussein. There was nothing wrong with Hussein — far from it. He ordered Ibrahim this way and that, then, with a big laugh, picked him up and set him in a deck-chair. Hussein, said the doctor, was like a father to Ibrahim (their real father was dead). Since the day when their house was hit by Israeli bombs Hussein had stoutly refused to leave Ibrahim's side. So the Israelis had brought him along, too, to Haifa.

The boys were fast asleep when, in the early hours, the attack on their village, Randourieh, in south Lebanon started, with the terrifying scream and swoosh of low-flying aircraft and the blast of bombs. One of them demolished their house, knocking Ibrahim unconscious; he soon recovered though his leg was hurting him terribly. It was not until evening that he and Hussein were pulled out from under the debris by Israeli soldiers who had occupied the village. Their mother and seventeen-year-old sister were pulled out too. Both were dead.

Ibrahim was flown to Haifa, accompanied by Hussein, who told me, 'I'm older and stronger than him so I have to look after him.' Hussein was full of youthful praise for the Israelis. He felt so thankful to them that he was still alive that he would even like to become an Israeli. That done, and Ibrahim's recovery complete, he would like to return to Randourieh and work on the land. Ibrahim interrupted him. 'I want to stay here.' 'Even if I go back?' asked Hussein, hurt. 'I don't care,' Ibrahim insisted, 'I want to stay here and' — he raised a small finger and smiled mischievously — 'don't you try and stop me!' Ibrahim had decided views: if all those people wanted to kill each other, well let them.

There are them — and us. 'They can die,' he said, 'but I want to live and it's thanks to the Israelis that I can do so.'

Ibrahim, with the wisdom of his five years, had put his finger on the absurdity of war. Thanks to the Israelis his mother and sister were dead and he himself had lost a leg. Yet, also thanks to the Israelis, he was still alive; they had shown him every kindness. It was a pity that they had first to hurt him so much.

EPILOGUE

Nothing Has Changed

Since the Israeli strikes against the *Fedayin* in the south and their occupation of the area, an uneasy situation had prevailed in Lebanon. On 2 July, 1978, as I left Paris for Beirut, I was told, 'They're at war again.' The day before, the Syrian 'Peace Force', stationed in Beirut to help the Lebanese army keep order, had bombarded Beirut-east, the Christian quarter east of the Damascus road, where the militia were resisting. The Hôtel Dieu, the French hospital, took in twenty-four wounded that day. The day of my arrival it was fifty-four, and, as the exchange of blind, devastating fire between the Syrian Peace Force and the Christian militia grew more furious, the carnage spread. During the week I was there it ran into several hundred.

Nine out of ten of them were civilians and their children. On 3 July I read in *L'Orient-Le Jour,* the Beirut daily, 'Deluge of Fire on Achrafieh' (east Beirut), 'Monster Blaze at the Port' and, in an adjoining column, '130 shells on the Hôtel Dieu', with a stirring and dignified statement by the Mother Superior. I felt compelled to visit this brave lady. But how? Crossing over to the eastern district meant a suicidal dash by way of the 'Ring' or the *Passage du Musée*. Both routes were at the mercy of snipers, and they were pitiless. One sniper was reputed to have killed, in his time, over a hundred people; he 'preferred' women and children and worked for both sides. Corpses, irretrievable because of the snipers, lay by the roadside.

Next day there was a lull in the firing. Driving with my French friend, Bernard Lion, delegate of the International Union for Child Welfare, we came in sight of the *Passage du Musée*. 'What about it, Bernard?' I asked him. *'D'accord, allons-y,'* he replied, and put his foot down. Down the deserted road we went, across the Damascus road, and arrived after a few tense minutes at the hospital.

An hour later we left, but in rather more dramatic circumstances. The firing – heavy artillery and, close by, machine-guns – had started again.

Young mothers, their babies in their arms, were gathering in the corridor, fear and uncertainty in their faces. How much longer, their wondering eyes were asking, before a shell falls on us? To Bernard and me the Mother Superior, calm as ever, said, 'If you are going, you'd better go now – and run.' We ran while, uncomfortably close, a machine-gun chattered.

In the previous hour, within the battered walls of the Hôtel Dieu, I had witnessed the direct confrontation between the forces of good and evil. Sitting at her writing-table – which had been torn by a shell splinter – the Mother Superior told me, 'The hospital is open to all comers. We have received Palestinians and Syrians, Muslims and Christians, communists and so-called fascists. We are neutral, but that has not saved us from wanton, savage bombardment.' She then walked me round, showing me the damage: shells which had pierced the walls, wards devastated, debris scattered in the upper-floor corridors. Maternity cases and children had been moved into cloakrooms and corridors on the lower floors. Defying the thunderous cannonade, the Mother Superior and her devoted staff worked on, regardless of danger, to save life.

As we walked she told me, 'The battle-front is in the streets and houses. They have brought us children and babes in arms, at times entire families, at other times a single child picked up in the street, the sole survivor of a family. Nearly all our casualties are civilians; since things have flared up again, we've only had three combatants.'

One, with a bullet in his head, had been dragged, the night before, to the hospital doors by a boy of fourteen. The same evening two young teenage boys were brought in. I stood by the bedside of one of them, Elic, still bewildered by his frightful experience. In a tiny voice he told me how, with his mother and uncle, he had been going down to the shelter when a shell – fired by the Syrian 'Peace Force' – exploded, killing outright the uncle, wounding Elic in the stomach and almost severing his leg. It was amputated at the hospital. What evil, inhuman cynicism, I thought, as I looked at Elic's wan face, his frail, maimed body with its blunt, bandaged stump.

I came to another ward. There lay the other boy, an Arab Christian – he was thirteen, the age of my own son. Joseph Assad was his name, a marvellously handsome boy, his fine head crowned with thick, black hair; in his dark brown eyes was a look, bold but tender. Speaking in Arabic, which the Mother Superior interpreted, Joseph told me how, the evening before, during a lull, the family had decided to leave the shelter and go back to their upper-floor apartment to watch the news. While in front of the TV a shell exploded among them, killing Joseph's cousin.

Joseph, who was standing, suddenly found himself on the ground. His left leg had been shorn clean off above the knee. As he spoke, he drew back the sheet and showed me the handiwork of the Syrian Peace Force: the grotesque and stunted remains of what, the day before, had been a lithe and youthful limb.

Nothing, indeed, had changed, in the persecution of the innocent (unless it be for the worse) since that other child, two thousand years ago, fled the violence of Herod and the massacre, in Bethlehem, not far to the south from where Joseph lay, a victim of the Beirut massacre. I asked Joseph what he could say of the men who had hurt him so. He hesitated a moment then looked up at the Mother Superior and asked, 'Must I say ill of the Syrians?' Joseph's words echoed those of that child of long ago when, later, nailed to a cross, he pleaded for his tormentors: 'Forgive them, they know not what they do' — words which are stronger, in the ultimate reckoning, than the evil of the cruellest tyrant.

Acknowledgements

I have said elsewhere that if, in our time, men are doing more harm to children than ever before, they – and women, too, of course – are doing infinitely more good. I contacted, during my travels, all the people mentioned below (save those marked with an asterisk). All were moved by a desire to help children and most were actually doing so, caring, directly or indirectly for the ones to whom I talked, among thousands of others. They were an inspiration to me and gave me every encouragement. I name them with no particular regard to precedence or protocol, thanking them with all my heart for their ready help and warm hospitality and asking them to believe in my profound admiration for their selfless and devoted work.

Switzerland
Mrs Tara Baig, President, International Union for Child Welfare (IUCW), Geneva
Pierre Zumbach, Secretary-General, IUCW
Jean Brémond, Deputy Secretary-General, IUCW
Audrey Moser, Consultant, IUCW
Margareta Linnander, Consultant, IUCW
   I am particularly grateful for the close support of Audrey, Margareta and Jean.
Mrs Eve Underhill, Legal Officer, IUCW
Raymond Courvoisier, late of the International Red Cross (IRC), Geneva, with his long experience of children in distress
P. Vibert, Chef, Service de Documentation, IRC, Geneva
Gordon Carter, Director for Europe, United Nations Children's Fund (UNICEF), Geneva
Christa Roth, his assistant
Jim McDougall, Director, International Year of the Child, UNICEF, Europe

Don Allan, Head of the Information Division, UNICEF
Dale S. de Haan, Deputy High Commissioner, United Nations High Commissariat for Refugees (UNHCR), Geneva
John Woodward, Liaison Officer with non-governmental organizations, UNHCR
Nicole Spuhler, his assistant
    Thanks to John's executive action and Nicole's tireless efforts I was able to meet children the world over.
Fritz Pijnacker Hordijk, Head of the Asia Regional Section, UNHCR
Philippe Labreveux, Public Information Service, UNHCR
Henryka Veillard-Cybulska who, despite the pain it caused her, shared her first-hand knowledge of Poland under the Nazis

France
Gérard Orizet, Directeur de l'Aviation Générale, Air France, Paris
Renaud de Failly, Directeur, Relations Extérieures, Air France
Mmes Bozot, Bataille et Bouchet, Air France, Agence Rue Scribe, Paris, thanks to whose expertise I was able to complete, without a hitch, a highly complicated journey around the world, and another round Africa.
To Air France I owe a special debt. Responding to the humanitarian character of my mission, they granted me exceptional facilities for its organization and execution.
*J. Jousselin, Secrétaire-Général, Centre Français de Protection de l'Enfance, Paris
*Joyce Blau, for her information about the Kurds
Françoise Renaudot, for her help with press research

England
John Cumber, Director-General, Save the Children Fund (SCF), London
Rachel Jenkins, Director of Child Care, SCF
Mrs N. V. Morley-Fletcher, General Secretary, British Council for Aid to Refugees, London
Miss Rice-Jones, of the Standing Conference for Refugees, London
Joyce Pierce, of the Ockenden Venture, Surrey
Joan Poole, of Amnesty International, London
Tom Lawlor, General Secretary, Anglo-Rhodesian Society, London
Mrs Jan Humphreys, his assistant

Northern Ireland
Jim Mitchell, Chairman, SCF, Belfast, and his colleagues

Norway
Sigmund Groven, Secretary-General, Redd Barnen (Norwegian SCF), Oslo
Tore Schjoth, Det Norske Flyktninggerad (Norwegian Council for Refugees), Oslo

Sweden
Judge Gunnar Linnander
Häkan Landelius, Secretary-General, Rädda Barnens Riksförbund (Swedish SCF)
Professor Aage Edfeldt, of Stockholm University
Dr Marion Attems

Canada
Kenric Marshall, Consultant, Cansave (Canadian SCF)

USA
*Bette Ambrosio, Information Co-ordinator, Holt International Children's Service Inc.

Morocco
Mme Fatima Hassar, Présidente, Ligue Marocaine de Protection de L'Enfance, Rabat
Dr Rahle Rahhali, Minister of Health
Mme Zohr Laaziri, Ministry of Health
Ghazi Bennani, Ministry of Health
M. Kadiri, Minister of Youth and Sport
M. Belkohra, Under-Secretary, Ministry of Foreign Affairs
H. E. Ali Assou, Governor of El Ayoun Province
M. Ouchen, Secretary-General
Dr Benmimoun el Ghouti, Médecin Chef
H. E. Mohamed Doulbi Kadmiri, Governor of Oujda Province
Dr Mramar, Médecin Chef

Portugal
*Elvira Mil-Homens, Commisariado Para os Desolofados, Lisbon
Jeanne Franco, Ministerio da Justica, Lisbon

Soviet Union
*Mme X. Proskournikova, Vice-President, Committee of Soviet Women, Moscow
*Mikhail Privezentsev, Deputy-Director, USSR Copyright Agency (VAAP), Moscow
Jean Schnitzer, Representative in France for VAAP

Lebanon
Bernard Lion, Delegate, IUCW, Beirut
A. M. Kohl, Regional Representative, UNHCR, Beirut
Dr François Rémy, Regional Director, UNICEF, Beirut
Bernard Mossar, Chef de Mission, UNWRA, Beirut
Gerda Kernström Head of the Nursing Division, UNWRA
Mme Jamila, UNWRA, who took me to the Palestinian Orphanage of Beit Atfal Alsomoud and interpreted
Nabila Brair, of the UN Economic Council for Western Asia and of the Union of Palestinian Women
Michel Cagneux, Chef de Mission, International Red Cross (IRC), Beirut
Mlle Viviane, IRC
Jean-Michel Monod, IRC, who, by VHF from the Christian Quarter, persuaded me not to attempt a second time the perilous *Passage de Musée*
The ladies, operating under fire, of the Lebanese Red Cross
The Mère Supérieure, a very courageous and admirable lady, of the Hôtel Dieu, Beirut
Père Labaki, founder-director of the Foyer Notre Dame de la Joie, Beirut
Père Georges of the Orphanage of Dat el Alanya and Père Issam, who took me to see Toufic and interpreted
Sister Adèle, who took me to Damour and interpreted
Alain Garachon, physiotherapist of the hospital of Beit Chabab
Mlle Najad, who took me to south Lebanese villages and interpreted

Cyprus
Prince Alfred zur Lippe Weinssenfeld, Chief of Mission, UNHCR, Nicosia
Ray Fell, Assistant Chief of Mission, UNHCR
José Osuna, Assistant Chief of Mission, UNHCR
Mlle Özel, UNHCR
Mme Soulioti, President, Cyprus Red Cross

Dr Z. Hakki, Vice-President, Cyprus Red Crescent
Michael Kazazois, District Welfare Officer, Larnaca

Israel
Dr Shraga Adiel, Director-General, Youth Aliyah, Jerusalem
Shimon Schmidt, Youth Aliyah
Yusef, the Jew who drove me to Muslim Gaza
Issa, the Muslim who drove me to Christian Bethlehem and the West Bank
Lieutenant David Tserlin, Israeli Army
Harald Schmid de Gruneck, Chief of Mission, International Red Cross (IRC), Tel Aviv
Peter Kung, IRC, who greatly helped me in diverse ways
John Grinling, IRC, who took me among Palestinian families in the Gaza Strip
Magnus Ehrenström, Director, UNWRA, Gaza
Jaffa Perez, who interpreted at the Rambam Hospital, Haifa
Mr Harb, Director of Air France, Jerusalem, and Leila, his assistant, who rescued me, and on the Sabbath too, from the caprice of the computer which had cancelled my entire, meticulously planned journey round the rest of the world

India
Mrs Vidyaben Shah, President, Indian Council for Child Welfare, Delhi
Mrs Pramila Pandit Barooah, Secretary-General, Indian Council for Child Welfare
Dr P. C. Chunder, Minister of Education and Social Welfare
B. Chatterjee, Director, National Institute of Public Co-operation and Child Development, Delhi
Sir Robert ffolkes, Bt, Field Director, SCF, Delhi

Bangladesh
Dr Mizanur Rahman Shelley, Director, Department of Social Welfare
Roman Kohaut, Delegate, UNHCR
Dick de Jong, Assistant Information Officer, UNICEF
Peter Amacher, Chief of Mission, IUCW
Bob Kay, SCF
Dr W. Burgess, Senior Medical Officer, SCF
A. Mannan, Manager, Service and Administration, SCF
Mrs Jobeda Khanam, Director, Bangladesh Shishu (Children's) Academy

Mrs Hosne Ara Begum, Assistant Director, Bangladesh Shishu Academy

Thailand
Leslie Goodyear, Regional Representative, UNHCR
Major 'Spots' Leaphard, Field Director, SCF
Vuthichai Saisongcroh, SCF
Lunthin Chanou, who interpreted at the Cambodian refugee camp, Kamput
Nguyen Van Muoi, who interpreted at the Vietnamese boat people's camp, Laemsing
Thavisak Souphaket, who interpreted at the Laotian refugee camp, Uboh
H. E. Peter Tripp, British Ambassador and his wife Rosemary, for their kindness and encouragement

Vietnam
*Bertram A. N. Collins, Representative, UNICEF, Hanoi, for his efforts, alas fruitless, to obtain a visa for me

Malaysia
Rajagopolan Sampatkumar, Regional Representative, UNHCR, Kuala Lumpur
Dr Tran ... (one of the boat people) who interpreted and told me what was going on inside Vietnam

Singapore
S. Y. Kwok, Administration Assistant, UNHCR

Hong Kong
Christopher Carpenter, Representative, UNHCR
The Revd Richard Tsang, Director, Home for Fishermen's and Workmen's Children
Miss Wendy, who interpreted

Japan
Mr Ishino, Director General, Children's and Families' Bureau, Ministry of Health and Welfare, Tokyo
Yukio Shimohira, Children's and Families' Bureau, for his invaluable help and kindness in Tokyo, Nagasaki and Hiroshima
Mr Kato, Director, Division of Child Allowance, Ministry of Health and Welfare

Dr Kondo, Assistant Director, Planning, Ministry of Health and Welfare
Mr Furuya, Research Institute on Child Welfare, Tokyo
Tatsuwo Sato, Director of Life and Welfare, Nagasaki
Shigeyuki Uyeda, Head of Children's and Day Nursery Section, Nagasaki
Taketo Taguchi, Assistant Head, Children's and Day Nursery Section
Mr Hayashi, Nagasaki Police Headquarters
Masato Araki, Vice-Director, International Cultural Hall, Nagasaki
Rumiko Shimozuma, whose interpreting, during two painful interviews, was most sensitive and skilful
Masakatsu Kubohara, Head of Child Welfare Section, Hiroshima
Mr Kohra, Hiroshima Peace Culture Foundation, Hiroshima, who interpreted
Hiroshi Takeda, Head of Children's Section, Public Welfare Department, Osaka
Hidetoshi Manabe, Assistant Head of Children's Section, Public Welfare Department, Osaka

Korea
Lee Dae Kun, Director, Korean Child Welfare Association, Pusan
Ray Dawson, Sponsorship Secretary, SCF, Pusan
Colonel Robert E. Lees, Commanding, US Army Garrison, Pusan
Shin Chul Yong, Administrator, Canadian SCF (Cansave)
Yi Hong Pae, who interpreted

Senegal
Alan Butler, Chargé d'Affaires, British Embassy
Otto Hagenbuchle, Chief of Mission, UNHCR, Dacca
René Kalberer, Assistant Chief of Mission, UNHCR
Malak El-Chichini, Programme Officer, UNHCR
Cupidon Sy, Administrateur des Programmes, Association Internationale pour la Communication et l'Action Sociale
Almamy Barry, Représentant des Refugiés
N'Grussaly Baba N'Draye, Promotion Humaine

Guinea Bissau
Senhor Domingos Brito dos Santos, Secretariat of the National Council of the PAIGC

Dr Boal, Deputy Director, Commissariat of Health
Senhora Teadora Gomez, Director, Commissariat of Freedom-Fighters

Gabon
Michel Dupoizat, Chargé de Mission, UNHCR, Libreville
H. E. Hervé Moutsinga, Minister of Social Affairs
H. E. Christopher Macrae, British Ambassador

Nigeria
David Jack, Director, Social Development Division, Ministry of Social Development, Youth and Sport
Dr Barbara Meister, Terre des Hommes

Brazzaville, Congo
Guy Darnal, the friendly stranger who, braving the curfew, took me to his home and put me up for the night.

Botswana
Gary Perkins, Representative, UNHCR, Gaborone
Paddy MacCallin, UNHCR
Charles Tibone, Permanent Secretary, President's Office
Julian N'Gunu, Ministry of Social Service
Dingilizwe Mguni, Botswana Christian Council for Refugees

Zambia
Cécil Kpénou, Representative, UNHCR, Lusaka
Roman Urasa, Deputy Representative, UNHCR
Finn Reske-Nielsen, UNHCR
Joshua N'Komo, President, Zimbabwean African Peoples' Union (ZAPU)

Tanzania
Chefeke Dessalegn, Representative, UNHCR, Dar-es-Salaam
Kwame Afriyie, UNHCR

Burundi
Dag Andreassen, Delegate, UNHCR, Bujumbura

Kenya
K. Matsumoto, Representative, UNHCR, Nairobi
Willem Veenstra, Programme Officer, UNHCR

D. Bautista, UNHCR
Aida Gindy, Regional Director, UNICEF
Virginia Hazzard, Programme Officer, UNICEF
Mrs M. J. Menya, Chief Executive Officer, Child Welfare Society of Kenya
Audrey Owina, Executive Officer, Child Welfare Society of Kenya
Stanley Kinga, Secretary-General, Joint Refugee Service of Kenya
Phoebe Manthi, Social Worker
David Kikaya, Friends' International Centre, Nairobi
Leslie Charles, Educational Adviser, Igunga School, Kisumu
Mr Ngare, Primary School, Kawangware
Tesager Habteslassie Asrat, who interpreted during my talks with Ethiopians and Eritreans

Newspapers in a number of countries were good enough to publish an appeal from me to their readers for information and anecdotes. Lack of space forbids me from mentioning by name the many people in all parts of the world who so kindly responded. The material received from each one, though I may not have used it in the book, had its place in helping me to understand the extent of children's suffering in times of conflict and how, in many cases, people helped them.

And finally my sincere thanks go to my secretary, Paulette Monchet, without whose expert and indefatigable help I could never have survived this marathon of research and writing.

Peter Townsend

Bibliography

Books

Adamovich, Ales, and Granin, Daniil, *The Blockade Book* (extracts published in *Sputnik*, 1978)

Appelfeld, Aharon, *In the Wilderness*, Al'shav Publishing House, Jerusalem 1965

Balss, Dzimtenes, *Daugavas Vanagi*, Latvian State Publishing House, Riga 1963

Barbary, James, *The Boer War*, Victor Gollancz, London 1971

Begin, Menachem, *The Revolt*, W. H. Allen, London 1951

Berg, Mary, *Warsaw Ghetto*, L. B. Fischer Publishing Corp., New York 1945

Brent, Peter, *The Mongol Empire*, Weidenfeld & Nicolson, London 1976

Brown, Dee, *Bury My Heart at Wounded Knee*, Barrie & Jenkins, London 1971

Burchett, W. G., *Democracy with a Tommy Gun*, Wadley & Ginn, London 1946

Burgess, Alan, *The Small Woman*, Evans, London 1957

Chick, N. A. (edited by David Hutchinson) *Annals of the Indian Rebellion 1857–8*, Ch. Knight & Co., London 1974

Coblentz, Stanton A., *From Arrow to Atom Bomb*, Peter Owen, London 1956

Comay, Joan, *Introducing Israel*, Methuen, London 1973

Courvoisier, Raymond, *Ceux qui ne devaient pas mourir*, Robert Laffont-Opéra Mundi, Paris 1978

Danan, Alexis, *La Guerre aux enfants*, published in *Cahiers de l'Enfance*, Paris 1956–8

Davidson, Basil, *In the Eye of the Storm*, Longman, London 1972

Doxiadis, K., *Devastation in Greece*, Imperial War Museum, London

Duffy, Christopher, *The Army of Frederick the Great*, David & Charles, Newton Abbot 1974

Edvardsen, Anna, *Det får intehändenigen* (Finnish War Children 1939–45), Stockholm 1977

Encyclopedia Britannica, 1967

Eprile, Cecil, *War and Peace in the Sudan 1955–1972*, David & Charles, Newton Abbot 1974

Erlanger, Philippe, St Bartholomew's Night, Weidenfeld & Nicolson, London 1962

Ertekun, Necati Munir, *Inter-Communal Talks and the Cyprus Problem*, Nicosia 1977

Freud, Anna, and Burlingham, Dorothy, *War and Children*, Westport, Connecticut 1943

Godechot, Jacques, *The Talking of the Bastille*, Faber & Faber, London 1970

Grant, Michael, *Herod the Great*, Weidenfeld & Nicolson, London 1971

Griffiths, Ruth (permission of Dr B. H. Burne), *Nervous Children* (private case notes), 1942

Griswold, Wesley S., *The Boston Tea Party*, Abacus Press, Tunbridge Wells 1972

Hachiya, Michiko, *Hiroshima Diary*, Victor Gollancz, London 1955

Hagop-Krikor, *Les Arméniens connus et inconnus*, La Pensée Universelle, Paris 1975

Hanbowski, Jerzy, *Le Monde se souviendra de ces enfants*, Editions Ruch, Poland 1972

Henry, Clarissa, and Hillel, Marc, *Children of the S.S.*, Hutchinson, London 1976

Hersey, John, *Hiroshima*, Penguin Books, London 1946

Hibbert, Christopher, *The Great Mutiny, India 1857*, Allen Lane, London 1974

Irving, David, *The Destruction of Dresden*, William Kimber, London 1963

Journal des Combattants, Paris 1958

Kardoff, Ursula von, *Diary of a Nightmare*, Rupert Hart-Davis, London 1965

Kleffens, E. N. van, *The Rape of the Netherlands*, Hodder & Stoughton, London 1940

Kruszynski, Michael, *The State of Health of Poles Evacuated from Russia to Persia, 1942*, Huddersfield 1976

Lapierre, Dominique, and Collins, Larry, *O Jerusalem*, Weidenfeld & Nicolson, London 1972

Lyons, Alec, Consultant Psychiatrist, Alexandra Gardens Day Hospital, Belfast, Pamphlets reprinted in *Community Health* (1973), *International Journal of Offender Therapy and Comparative Criminology* (1975), *The Northern Teacher* (1974)
McCreary, Alf, *Survivors*, Century Books, Belfast 1976
Marinić, Tatjana, *May It Never Happen Again*, Zagreb 1954
Matthews, Kenneth, *Memories of a Mountain War, Greece 1944–9*, Longman, London 1972
Murray-Brown, Jeremy, *Kenyatta*, Allen & Unwin, London 1972
Mydans, Carl and Shelly, *The Violent Peace*, Athenaeum, New York 1968
Nagai, Tashaki, *We of Nagasaki*, Victor Gollancz, London 1951
Orwell, George, *Homage to Catalonia*, Secker & Warburg, London 1938
Osada, Arata, *Children of the A-Bomb*, Uchida Rokakuho Publishing House, Tokyo 1959
Palestinian Liberation Organization, Foreign Information Department, Beirut, *Tal-al-Zaatar*
Palestinian Red Crescent, Central Committee, *Role of the Palestinian Red Crescent at Tal-al-Zaatar*, Beirut 1977
Pincus, Chasya, *Come from the Four Winds*, Herzl Press, New York 1971
Rahman, Mizanur, *Bangladesh*, University Press of America, Washington 1978
Richter, Lina, *Family Life in Germany under the Blockade*, London 1919
Runciman, Steven, *The Fall of Constantinople*, Cambridge University Press, 1965
Runciman, Steven, *A History of the Crusades*, Penguin Books, London 1971
Salzman, L. F., *English Life in the Middle Ages*, Oxford University Press, 1926
Shadrake, Alan, *The Yellow Pimpernels*, Robert Hale, London 1974
Snow, Edgar, *Red Star Over China*, Victor Gollancz, London 1968
Szabo, Thomas, *Boy on the Rooftop*, Heinemann, London 1958
Thomas, Hugh, *The Spanish Civil War*, Hamish Hamilton, London 1977
Tibbets, Paul W., *The Tibbets Story*, Stein & Day, New York 1978
Willern, J. P., *Médecin au Vietnam*, Editions France-Empire, Paris 1978
Women's International Democratic Federation (publishers), *La Bombe et le berceau*, Berlin

Young, Brigadier Peter, *Dictionary of Battles 1816–1976*, New English Library, London 1977

Newspapers

United Kingdom	*Daily Telegraph*
	New Statesman
	Observer
	The Times
	Sunday Times
	Belfast Newsletter
	Irish News and Belfast Morning News
	Irish Times
France	*La Monde*
	Le Figaro
	La Croix
	Paris-Match
	L'Humanité
	Le Nouveau Journal
	Libération
Belgium	*Le Soir*
Holland	*De Telegraaf*
West Germany	*Die Zeit*
Italy	*Il Tempo*
Spain	*El Pais*
Switzerland	*La Tribune de Genève*
Lebanon	*L'Orient-Le Jour*
Africa	*Jeune Afrique*
	Rhodesia Herald
Pakistan	*Pakistan Times*
India	*Indian Express*
Hong Kong	*South China Morning Post*
Japan	*Japan Times*

Publications issued by:
United Nations' International Children's Fund (UNICEF)
United Nations' High Commissioner for Refugees (UNHCR)

International Union for Child Welfare (IUCW)

Amnesty International
Burmese Muslims' Association – *Plight of the Muslims in Burma*
Caritas
Christian Aid
Collège Notre Dame de Jamhour, Beirut – *Nous du Collège*
Concern
Dangavas Vanagi (Latvian Welfare Association, London)
Hiroshima-Nagasaki Publishing Committee
Holt International Children's Services, Inc.
International Commission of Jurists
Jewish Agency, *Youth Aliyah Bulletin*, Jerusalem
Morocco, Ministry of Information
Oman, Sultanate of, Ministry of Information and Culture
Oxfam
Save the Children Fund
Society of Friends
SOS Children's Villages
Terre des Hommes
United States Committee for Refugees
War on Want
Zimbabwe-Rhodesia, Ministry of Information

HQ784 .W3T66X

a8030500220087 7c

WITHDRAWN
From Bertrand Library

11/19/80

DATE DUE

NOV 2 8 1993		
NOV 0 5 2002		
APR 1 2 2003		
MAR 1 4 2005		
GAYLORD		PRINTED IN U.S.A